006.42
LOW

# INTRODUCTORY COMPUTER VISION AND IMAGE PROCESSING

# INTRODUCTORY COMPUTER VISION AND IMAGE PROCESSING

**Adrian Low**
*Head of School of Computing*
*Sandwell College*
*West Midlands*

McGRAW-HILL BOOK COMPANY

**London** · New York · St Louis · San Francisco · Auckland · Bogotá · Caracas
Hamburg · Lisbon · Madrid · Mexico · Milan · Montreal · New Delhi · Panama · Paris
San Juan · São Paulo · Singapore · Sydney · Tokyo · Toronto

Published by
McGRAW-HILL Book Company (UK) Limited
SHOPPENHANGERS ROAD · MAIDENHEAD · BERKSHIRE SL6 2QL · ENGLAND
TEL 0628–23432; FAX 0628–770224

**British Library Cataloguing in Publication Data**

Low, Adrian
Introductory computer vision and image processing.
1. Machine vision
I. Title
006.37
ISBN 0-07-707403-3

**Library of Congress Cataloging-in-Publication Data**

Low, Adrian
Introductory computer vision and image processing / Adrian Low.
    p.    cm.
Includes bibliographical references and index.
ISBN 0-07-707403-3
1. Computer vision.   2. Image processing—Digital techniques.
I. Title.
TA1632.L67   1991
621.39′9—dc20   90-26074 CIP

12345 CUP 94321

Typeset by Computape (Pickering) Ltd, North Yorkshire
and printed and bound at the University Press, Cambridge

To my wife and children, who put up with me writing a book.

Faith lends its realising light,
The clouds disperse, the shadows fly;
The invisible appears in sight,
And God is seen by mortal eye.

*Charles Wesley (1707–1788)*

A man that looks on glass,
On it may stay his eye,
Or, if he pleaseth, through it pass,
And then the heaven espy.

*George Herbert (1593–1632)*

For the joy of ear and eye,
For the heart and minds delight,
For the mystic harmony
Linking sense to sound and sight:
    Gracious God, to thee we raise
    This our sacrifice of praise

*F. S. Pierpoint (1835–1917)*

# CONTENTS

**Techniques**

# PLATES

The plates will be found between pages 30 and 31.

1      The relation between the CIE diagram and the colours that can be realized using a typical television monitor (*Source*: Berger and Gillies, 1989).

**2 (a)** X-ray of skull—original prior to capture.

  **(b)** Original image, monochrome palette.

  **(c)** Grey-level negation (black to white, white to black).

  **(d)** Green palette (see text).

  **(e)** Purple-headed mountain palette (see text).

  **(f)** Red to green to blue palette.

  **(g)** Top three out of 16 levels shown only.

  **(h)** Grey-level $0 \rightarrow$ black and $15 \rightarrow$ black, with $8 \rightarrow$ white.

  **(i)** Only grey levels 0–3 (green) and 12–15 (blue) showing.

  **(j)** Sixteen grey-level edge detector results.

  **(k)** Edges (from j) added back to palette used in (h).

# AUTHOR'S NOTE

One approach adopted within this book has been to present to the reader a number of algorithms commonly used in computer vision. Some of these have been described rigorously and deserve the title 'algorithm'; however, some have only been described in outline and, in a sense, form guidance only on a technique that the 'vision engineer' might implement on an image.

A list of all the algorithms/techniques is given above on pages xi and xii. Most techniques come with some or all of the titles as follows:

USE             When the technique can be applied on an image.
PROCESS         How it is applied.
THEORY          Why and how it works.
APPLICATION     Real examples of its use.
CODE            C code for the implementation of the technique.

# ACKNOWLEDGEMENTS

My thanks go to:

John Dunn (Comus, Tixel), for his help with the recursive Hartley routine.
Richard Spicer (Staffordshire Polytechnic), for his commentary on the development of the book.
Gordon Topping (Staffordshire Polytechnic), who gave me the opportunity to work in image processing and supported the funding of the laboratory where the images in this book were created.
John Heasman for his help with the slide photography.
Stafford General Hospital, for the original X-ray images in the book.
My MSc students for the dissertation material for Chapter 18.

# 1

# INTRODUCTION

Welcome to computer vision!

This is, arguably, the most interesting topic in computing. It covers branches of many different disciplines and has applications across the whole spectrum of science, art and humanities.

- If you have a reasonable understanding of computers, a willingness to cope with some formulae, then this book will be a good read.
- If you are a programmer, then you will be able to implement most of the techniques in this book on images of your own.
- If you need to know about computer vision because your specialist subject uses it, then this book can also be used as a recipe book in image processing and computer vision techniques.
- If you are studying image processing and computer vision, then this book is moulded around final-year BSc and MSc options in image processing
- It is an introductory text. You may need to read more widely for some applications; the bibliography should help you there.
- Unfamiliar words and terms are explained in the Glossary.
- Finally, the text is liberally scattered with examples of applications of the techniques: this work is not meant to be a pure academic tome, but a book based on real issues.

The developments in computer vision in the year during which this book was written have been startling. In the last ten years equipment has become readily available for computer vision that performs well and costs little.

Computer vision needs high-performance systems to be worth while. High performance means 1 Mbyte minimum of main memory and fast (say 5 + million instructions per

**Table 1.1 Applications of image processing**

| | |
|---|---|
| Pictorial databases | Quality control of food |
| Graphics design | Bacterial growth scanning |
| Engraving | Geological modelling |
| Textile design | Autonomous navigation |
| Cartography | Cosmetics |
| Metallurgy | Astronomy |
| Materials science | Defence applications |
| Medical imaging | Particle tracking |
| Object recognition | Fishing using ultrasound |
| Microscopy | Pottery blemish identification |
| Satellite picture processing | Eye retina comparison |
| Particle counting and sizing | Fluid mechanics |
| Typesetting | Journalism—picture enhancement |
| Three-dimensional reconstruction | Security—picture enhancement and identification |
| Photographic security | Weather mapping |
| Fingerprint matching | Document transfer |
| Document reading | Document comparison |

second) processing power for any worthwhile application. Until recently it has been a field in which only those institutions with sophisticated machines (and sizeable budgets) could do any effective vision processing.

The application field is also expanding. The equipment was too expensive for all but the high income earning, more esoteric applications. Now, with cheaper equipment, it is difficult to compile a full list of application areas. Clearly the established fields of satellite imagery, defence, medical imagery, astronomy, quality control, robot control, security, and microscopy will continue to flourish, but the computer vision system may now be found in the hands of the less specialized areas, as can be seen in the (very incomplete) applications list in Table 1.1.

## So what is 'computer vision and image processing'?

The definition adopted in this book is that image processing is the processing of an image, typically by a computer, to produce another image, while computer vision is about image acquisition, processing, classification, recognition, and, to be all embracing, decision making subsequent to recognition as in, for example, when a space probe has to make its own decision about movement. This definition, however, is not rock solid.

Ballard and Brown (1982) suggest that: 'Computer Vision is the enterprise of automating and integrating a wide range of processes and representations for visual perception.' They include, in the extension of this definition, the term image processing, suggesting that computer vision subsumes image processing.

Niblack (1986) describes image processing as 'the computer processing of pictures', later adding that the output of the image processing will also be an image. He suggests that 'Computer Vision includes many techniques from image processing but is broader in the sense that it is concerned with a complete system, a "seeing machine".'

Boyle and Thomas (1988) suggest that computer vision is more than recognition, they present their 'low level processing' operations as purely image-processing algorithms and again subsume image processing in computer vision.

Jensen (1986) entitles his book *Introductory Digital Image Processing—a remote sensing perspective*, and includes substantial chapters on image acquisition and region classification.

Gonzalez and Wintz (1977) include chapters on region and relational descriptions, all of which other authors might classify under computer vision.

A better approach might be to give an example that illustrates an application of computer vision.

**Example 1  Quality control of steel tacks**  A computer vision system can be used to stop the production of some product if the production system starts producing products that are not frequently enough of a sufficient standard.

Tacks are produced by a machine that delivers them into a chute to a packing machine that then packs them. The quality of the tacks in the chute can be monitored by eye, an extraordinarily boring operation, or by using a computer vision system. This can simply direct ill-formed tacks into a rubbish skip, passing the good ones onto the packing machine. In addition, the system may be given some supervisory powers so that the production process itself is stopped if the number of failures per unit time is greater than a set limit.

The tacks are fed down the chute so that they arrive at the scanner either top or point first. This is a mechanical exercise which forms part of the vision system simply because the packer does not care about the orientation of the tack. The acquisition part of the system, on the chute, is permanently set up with lighting and focus standardized.

A video camera is constantly viewing the tacks, but the vision system clocks the capture equipment to indicate when a new tack is under the camera. This is done by the tacks breaking/reflecting a beam of light as they pass down the chute by gravity. The system then knows when to analyse a frame from the camera and when to discard the frame.

The resolution of the system is not great. It does not need to be colour, nor does it need to detect many levels of grey. The required resolution is a function of the task, which is to identify reject tacks. It only needs to 'see' a shape, and so black and white will do.

The following resolution was found to be useful: a frame of $30 \times 50$ pixels (i.e. a picture made up of 30 vertical and 50 horizontal dots), one bit per pixel (that is the dot is either black or white). This was captured by a permanently resident mono (black and white) video camera.

The computer processor then discards unwanted frames and, for the wanted frames, compares the image captured with two binary images already in memory, one representing the tack with the point downwards and the other with the point upwards. The processor counts the number of differences between the image it has just grabbed and the images that it has in memory. Ideally the number of differences should be zero in one of the cases; however, there are errors due to slight changes in the capture time, the orientation of the tack, or the shape of a (still acceptable) tack.

So finally, if the smallest number of differences (i.e. the comparison with the image of the tack with the same orientation) is greater than a given value, then the tack is rejected by the vision system causing it to be directed to a reject bin, using a small electromagnet.

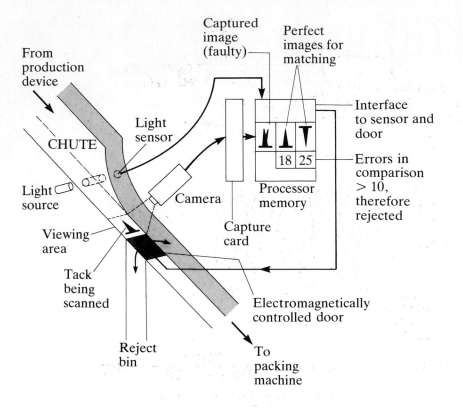

**Figure 1.1** Defective tack identification.

Figure 1.1 illustrates the whole process.

Image processing is only a minor part, when viewed against all the mechanical and electronic interfacing required for the system. This is often the case with computer vision.

**Example 2  Clinical trials of ulcer-reducing drugs**  In order to determine the effectiveness of otherwise of a particular drug to treat leg ulcers, a clinical trial is established in which certain doctors are supplied with A4 size transparent overhead projector sheets. These are to be placed on the ulcer and an outline drawing of the ulcer made on the sheet by the doctor.

These sheets are then sent to the pharmaceutical firm's headquarters where they have to be analysed.

Initial work is done by cutting the shape of the ulcer out of the slide, by hand, using scissors, and then weighing the shapes. This is accurate (providing the thickness of the slides remained constant) but is most time consuming. A second approach uses a proprietary graphics package and a digitizing tablet. In this case the outline of the ulcer shape is digitized (by a human using a puck on the tablet), and the machine then left to calculate the area. This is time consuming and prone to errors.

The computer vision solution involves placing the slide on a flat-bed scanner. The image is then passed to a processor which fills in the background up to the drawn edges, and then counts how many points (pixels) are left white now that the background is black.

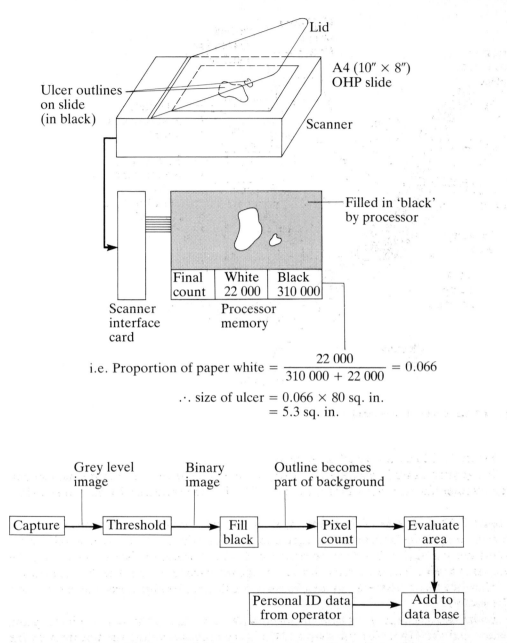

i.e. Proportion of paper white = $\dfrac{22\,000}{310\,000 + 22\,000}$ = 0.066

∴ size of ulcer = 0.066 × 80 sq. in.
= 5.3 sq. in.

**Figure 1.2** System for finding the area of ulceration drawn on an overhead projector slide.

This gives the area of the ulcer without human intervention and therefore with a known error level.

The processor then asks the operator to give the number of the test and the results are automatically filed for future analysis.

Figure 1.2 illustrates the whole process.

## Finally

This book is about computer vision, but, as will be seen from the contents, it also concentrates heavily on image processing. Every effort has been made to make the text rigorous, in a mathematical and computer science sense, but readable and usable from a non-specialist point of view. It exists not only to be an introductory academic text but also as a practitioner's book, in the eyes of some labouring what is obvious, but describing at length so that the implementation of computer vision algorithms in a real project can be done using this text as a tool.

# 2

# THE IMAGE MODEL

## 2.1 INTRODUCTION

This chapter considers how the image is held and manipulated inside the memory of a computer. It compares this representation with how humans perceive images and highlights the drawbacks of current vision technology. Finally, there is a substantial discussion covering the different colour models used in computer vision.

The memory models are important because the speed and quality of image-processing software is dependent on the right use of memory. Mapping a three-dimensional surface (a two-dimensional image) onto a linear memory (i.e. a series of bytes) means that sensible data structures need to be employed for ease of manipulation and access while retaining a speedy dumping of data to screen when the image is to be viewed. Most image transformations can be made less difficult to perform if the original mapping is carefully chosen.

## 2.2 IMAGE SHAPE

The rectangular image model is the most popular memory model. A grey level image is made from a set of boxes, each holding a grey level value between 0 and $2^g - 1$, where $g$ is an integer. Each box is a pixel (picture element) and the array of pixels is constructed with $M$ horizontal rows and $N$ vertical columns. Each pixel, therefore, is a member of exactly one row and exactly one column. Each pixel can then be referred to as an element of a rectangular array. In C this might be defined as

```
unsigned char image[M][N];
```

which gives a indexed range of elements: $0 . . N - 1$ columns and $0 . . M - 1$ rows and uses indices $[y][x]$. In C when the last ($[x]$ in this case) index value increases by 1 it points to the next location in memory. This gives a classic raster scan array.

Using the above values, this image will require $N \times M \times g$ bits of storage. $g$ is typically an integer between 1 and 10, frequently 8, giving 256 grey levels. $N$ and $M$, in order to give a satisfactory 'television lookalike' resolution, should be at least $500 \times 500$. Clearly, on some systems this resolution is not available, though the VGA (video graphics array) fitted to a number of PC compatibles gives $640 \times 480$ with 16 colours or grey levels, which is quite adequate in terms of resolution and passable in terms of shades.

Resolution is always a function of the application. Only the minimum resolution to perform the task is required, so that in some cases $30 \times 50$ may be sufficient while in others $1000 \times 1000$ is insufficient.

Further discussion on resolution is left to Chapter 3.

In practice, the image capture equipment rarely captures square $N \times N$ images. Normally the image is captured in the standard television aspect ratio of $x: y = 4:3$. Any capture without this aspect ratio means that if the image is to be displayed fully on the screen of a 4:3 monitor, the pixels will no longer be square. For instance, with the VGA ratio of $640 \times 480$ the pixels will be square, whereas another system might display $640 \times 512$, in which case the pixels will be marginally wider than they are tall. This may be of little interest to the graphics programmer or the data-processing applications programmer, but the image processor may find that an unreal distortion is introduced by the incompatibility of the capture resolution, the processing resolution, and the display resolution (see for example, the non-round apple in Fig. 7.1).

The colour of each pixel is stored as a sequence of one or more bits. In mono desktop publishing applications, the pixel is usually just black or white, so that only one bit is required to hold the colour information. The device displaying the material would be said to be mapped to a one-bit plane, i.e. a two-dimensional plane (or array) of single bits. In practice each of these bits is likely to be a member of a group of eight bits (a byte), so that operations inside the processor cannot normally be performed on specific bits but have to be performed on whole bytes at once, e.g. by copying out the whole byte, altering the single bit in the main processor, and copying the whole byte back again.

This process implies that on these machines, without single-instruction bit manipulation of the contents of absolute addresses, there is only a marginal loss in speed when the display is operating with a mapping of one byte per pixel (256 colours) compared with one bit per pixel (two colours).

For more than two colours (say black and white) per pixel, the number of bits per pixel has to be increased. A four-colour system requires two bits per pixel giving, say

00  blue
01  light blue
10  dark blue
11  mauve

This, in practice, will be a two-bit plane, although it is not always simple to establish precisely how the mapping is determined between the linear 'pile' of bytes of real memory and this two-bit plane.

A particular low-resolution system can process images of size $160 \times 256$ with four

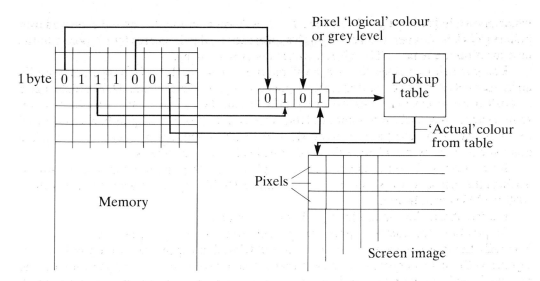

**Figure 2.1** Video memory map on low-resolution $160 \times 256 \times 2$ bits per pixel system.

colours per pixel. On this system the two bits making up each pixel came from the same byte but were not next to each other (see Fig. 2.1).

The mapping for the VGA $640 \times 480$ from the bit plane is shown in Fig. 2.1(a). Here the 153 000 bytes required for the mapping are squeezed into the 64K address space by using what amounts to four parallel memories, on the VGA card, each one 64K (though not all of each is used). The programmer has to program the graphics controller mode register to select which plane is being read from or written to. At the applications level this is already performed by operating system routines.

Occasionally it is valuable to have non-square pixels. Hexagonal pixels have been used. Here every other row and column correspond, but in the in between rows the pixels lie precisely between the pixels of the lower and upper rows. This has the advantage of improving edges by losing some of the 'aliasing' (i.e. the stepping effect of a line on a normal square pixel display when it is near horizontal or near vertical). Furthermore, as screens rarely glow in perfectly square dots, round dots fit together better if they are approximated by hexagons rather than squares. The drawback with the system is that the mapping can no longer be treated in exactly the same way as the rectangular mapping, because distances between pixels are dependent on which rows and columns the pixels are in. Capture equipment, display equipment, processing equipment, and algorithms all have to be adjusted to cope with the different standard.

### 2.2.1 Colour standards

There are a number of colour hardware standards that correspond to different models for colour storage. In all the standards a pixel colour is represented as a point in three-dimensional space. The space may have the axes labelled as independent colours (red, green, and blue, for example), or may use other independent indicators such as hue, lightness (or luminosity), and saturation. RGB, HSV (hue saturation value), and HLS (hue lightness saturation) are the most popular standards. RGB is an additive combination of the red, green, and blue that allows any cathode ray tube (CRT) colour to be produced. HSV is an elementary reorganization of the red, green, and blue, while HLS is marginally more complex.

In HSV the hue is effectively a measure of the wavelength of the main colour. In practice it has a value between 0 and 255, say; 0 representing red, then going through the spectrum back to 256 representing red again. This can be seen as an angle (though scaling by 256/360 is necessary to force it into one byte), where red = 0°, green = 120°, and blue = 240°.

Hue can be calculated from RGB values as follows:

$$red_h = red - min(red, green, blue)$$
$$green_h = green - min(red, green, blue)$$
$$blue_h = blue - min(red, green, blue)$$

Clearly at least one of these values is zero. If two are zero, then the hue is the angle corresponding to the third, non-zero colour, as above. If three are zero, then this is no colour hue, i.e. the monitor displays a grey-level—between black and white. If only one component is zero, then the hue angle is between the angle corresponding to the two component angles, weighted in favour of the bigger component. Thus, for example, if $red_h$ is zero, then the angle is

$$\frac{(240 \times blue_h) + (120 \times green_h)}{blue_h + green_h}$$

Saturation is the amount of pure hue in the final colour. If saturation is zero, then the final colour is without hue, i.e. it is made from white light only. If saturation is 255, then there is no white light addition in the final colour.

Saturation is given by

$$saturation = \frac{max(red, green, blue) - min(red, green, blue)}{max(red, green, blue)}$$

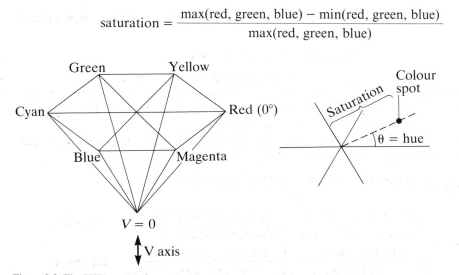

$$V = 0$$

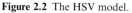

**Figure 2.2** The HSV model.

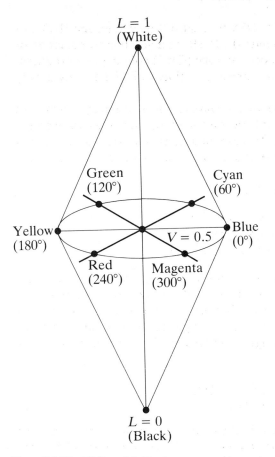

**Figure 2.3** The HLS model. Hue is represented by angle, saturation by the closeness to the axis of the cones, and lightness (value) by the distance along the $L$-axis. (*Source*: © Burger and Gillies, 1989.)

Value, which is brightness, is a measure of the intensity of the brightest component, and is given by

$$value = max(red, green, blue)$$

The whole model can be represented as a hexagonal cone (see Fig. 2.2).

The HLS model, developed by Tektronix Incorporated, is similar to the HSV model except that the hue angle starts at blue $= 0°$ and the model is a double cone with a lightness axis going from $L = 0$ (black) to $L = 1$ (white) (see Fig. 2.3).

For the HLS model, hue is calculated in the same way as for HSV except blue $= 0°$, and lightness and saturation are given by the following expressions:

$$lightness = \frac{max(red, green, blue) - min(red, green, blue)}{2}$$

$$saturation = \begin{cases} \dfrac{max(red, green, blue) + min(red, green, blue)}{max(red, green, blue) - min(red, green, blue)} & \text{if } L \leq 0.5 \\[2em] \dfrac{max(red, green, blue) - min(red, green, blue)}{2 - max(red, green, blue) - min(red, green, blue)} & \text{otherwise} \end{cases}$$

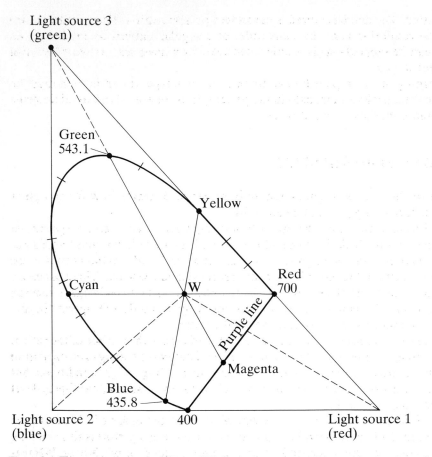

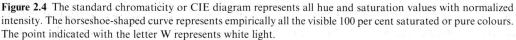

**Figure 2.4** The standard chromaticity or CIE diagram represents all hue and saturation values with normalized intensity. The horseshoe-shaped curve represents empirically all the visible 100 per cent saturated or pure colours. The point indicated with the letter W represents white light.

Other models exist, but these rely heavily on the ones already described.

Finally, there is an international colour standard developed in 1931 by the Commission Internationale de l'Eclairage (CIE). As part of this standard the CIE chromaticity diagram was created which defines colour ratios for a pure additive system in a normalized form. Figure 2.4 shows the diagram as a two-dimensional plane on which fixed points represent pure red, green, and blue, and other points represent combinations of these. Plate 1 illustrates the limits of the colour cathode ray tube by showing the small subset of colours that can actually be presented on the screen.

## 2.3 SAMPLING

The resolution of the capture device should be better than the resolution of the memory model. The resolution of the memory model should be such that necessary detail in the image is not omitted. The detail required is dependent on application. However, there are cases when, if the resolution is of the same order as a regular pattern on the image, an interface image can be created—as is visible when television news readers wear ties with narrow horizontal stripes.

Where patterning of this type is known to exist in the image, the resolution must be great enough to collect peaks and troughs in the pattern, thus for every horizontal tie stripe there should be more than two rows of pixels.

## 2.4 THE HUMAN VISION SYSTEM

Any description of the human visual system only serves to illustrate how far computer vision has to go before it approaches human ability.

In terms of image acquisition, the eye is totally superior to any camera system yet developed. The retina, on which the upside-down image is projected, contains two classes of discrete light receptors—cones and rods. There are between 6 and 7 million cones in the eye, most of them located in the central part of the retina, called the fovea. These cones are highly sensitive to colour, and the eye muscles rotate the eye so that the image is focused primarily on the fovea. The cones are sensitive to bright light and do not operate in dim light. Each cone is connected, by its own nerve, to the brain.

There are at least 75 million rods in the eye distributed across the surface of the retina. They are sensitive to light intensity but not colour. They share nerve endings and only serve to give an overall picture of the image. These work in dim and bright light conditions, but as they are the only sensors operating in dim light, only a monochromatic, multi-grey-level image is obtained when it is dark.

The range of intensities to which the eye can adapt is of the order of $10^{10}$, from the lowest visible light to the highest bearable glare. In practice the eye performs this amazing task by altering its own sensitivity depending on the ambient level of brightness. While it can cope with this wide range of light levels, it cannot simultaneously discriminate between different dim and different bright levels. Given one job or the other it can cope, but not at the same time.

There is considerable evidence to suggest that the subjective brightness (i.e. the brightness perceived by the eye) is a logarithmic function of intensity. Thus a small increase in dim light intensity is perceived as equal to a large increase in bright light intensity. This suggests that when setting up pallets for grey level displays the number of shades with grey level values in the lower half of the range should be greater than the number of shades with grey level values in the upper half of the range.

### 2.4.1 Eye colour perceptions

The perception of brightness is a function of wavelength and is described by the relative luminosity function illustrated in Fig. 2.5. Consequently, light radiating at a wavelength in the middle of the spectrum always looks brighter than light with the same radiating value but at a wavelength at either end of the spectrum. Thus more power has to be radiated by blue or red in order to make them seem as bright as green or yellow.

Colour displays usually use some form of colour mixing. The RGB system lights adjacent red, green, and blue dots on a screen: if the dots are small enough and the observer is far enough away, this gives the appearance of one pixel colour rather than three adjacent ones. These three colours are primary colours in that mixing any combination of two of them does not make the third. In fact any three colours may be used, providing they are independent.

The display uses additive colouring. Giving full power to red, green, and blue produces bright white. Paint mixing uses subtractive colouring: mixing red, green, and blue produces black.

In practice, the phosphorescent dots on the screen of a display do not give each a single wavelength of colour (see Fig. 2.6). Rather they produce a range of wavelengths centred around the colour required. This poses a particular problem. On a CRT display it is not possible to produce exactly every colour seen by the eye in the real world. In particular, on an RGB system it is impossible to display pure, end-of-spectrum red or blue.

In a grey-level display, the same is still true. 'White' is actually the spectrum of the phosphorescing surface, which may approach white but is unlikely to be exactly white, while 'black' is the colour of the phosphorescent surface when it is not being excited. This is usually a darkish grey colour. The white has to be bright enough to encourage the eye to perceive the grey as black.

Figure 2.7 illustrates the CIE chromaticity diagram showing the range of wavelengths that the eye perceives as an illumination, and the range of wavelengths that can be generated on a colour monitor using current technology.

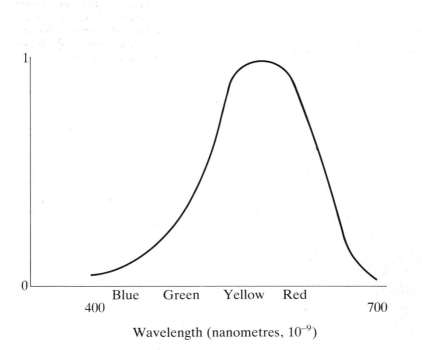

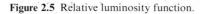

**Figure 2.5** Relative luminosity function.

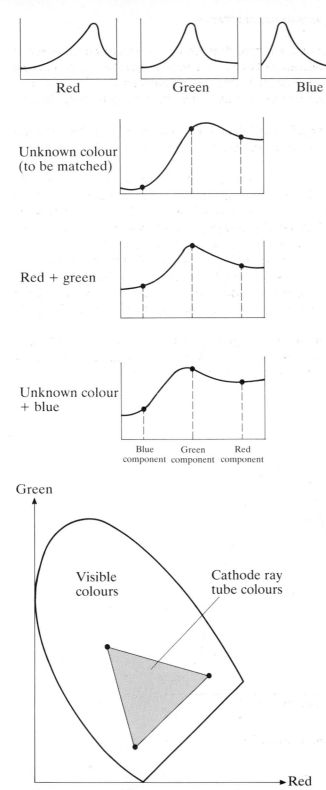

Red Green Blue

Unknown colour (to be matched)

Red + green

Unknown colour + blue

Blue component   Green component   Red component

**Figure 2.6** These diagrams show why matching one colour with the sum of three primaries is not always possible. The sum of red and green lights cannot match the required distribution because it has too much blue in it. Adding blue light to the colour to be matched solves this problem. (*Source*: © Burger and Gillies, 1989.)

Green

Visible colours

Cathode ray tube colours

Red

**Figure 2.7** Cathode ray tube colour triangle. (*Source*: Burger and Gillies, 1989.)

**15**

## 2.5 EXERCISES

**2.1** An eight-by-eight chess board image is to be captured unambiguously. Show that 64 samples are insufficient. How many samples are necessary?

**2.2** A new general image-processing software package is to be written for an IBM PC VGA machine with a 256 grey-level capture card, 640K of store accessible directly by the compiled program but a total of 4 Mbytes of main memory, the rest (beyond 640K) being used as a RAM drive.

Given that the DOS and package together take up about 220K of main memory (in the 640K), describe a suitable partitioning of the memory and suitable data structures to implement the general image-processing package.

# IMAGE ACQUISITION

## 3.1 INTRODUCTION

We readily assume that the images that are going to be dealt with in computer vision work will be pictures from a video camera, like a television picture. This is true for a lot of computer vision work, but these light intensity images are not the only image signals that can be captured and processed by a machine. This chapter introduces a variety of image capture devices. It also looks briefly at the problems of capture device calibration.

## 3.2 INTENSITY IMAGES

Light intensity can be translated into an electrical signal most simply by using photosensitive cells or photosensitive resistive devices. One of these devices can be used to make a primitive camera that generates a series of signals representing levels of light intensity for each 'spot' on the picture. A system of directing the light onto the sensitive cell is required so that the cell is looking at each spot on the picture in turn until the whole picture has been 'scanned'.

   This was the principle behind Baird's first television system. The scanning device was a circular disc with a number of holes drilled in it in a spiral fashion. Each hole would allow the light from only one spot of the picture to reach the light sensor. As the disc rotated the hole would scan across the picture in an arc so that the sensor would register the light intensities in one line of the picture. When that hole had passed the sensor, another hole would appear, presenting a slightly different arc to the sensor. Thus with eight holes it was possible to create an eight 'line' image, each line being an arc (see Fig. 3.1).

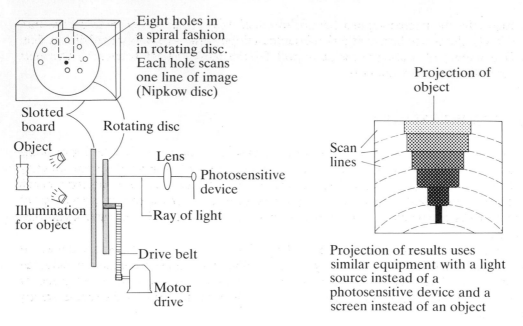

Eight holes in
a spiral fashion
in rotating disc.
Each hole scans
one line of image
(Nipkow disc)

Slotted
board

Rotating disc

Object

Lens

Photosensitive
device

Illumination
for object

Ray of light

Drive belt

Motor
drive

Projection of
object

Scan
lines

Projection of results uses
similar equipment with a light
source instead of a
photosensitive device and a
screen instead of an object

**Figure 3.1** Illustration of early mechanical videocapture and display.

This principle of repeatedly measuring light intensity until a whole image has been scanned is still used, though with considerable sophistication. An acceptable image standard, i.e. one where the individual lines are not visible at a typical viewing distance, requires at least 500 scan lines to give some reality to the image and, consequently on a square image, at least 500 measurements along each scan line.

United Kingdom television uses a 625-line system of which 587 lines are used for pictorial information, though often fewer than 500 lines are actually available due to imperfect adjustment of the receiver. However, as with most television systems, the lines are not segmented into a number of pixels, instead the system uses a continuously varying signal to describe a line of continuously varying light intensity. Computer vision, on the other hand, needs to use pixels and therefore has to digitize vertically and horizontally.

## 3.3 REAL-TIME CAPTURE

If an image is to be recorded in real time, at least 25 images need to be captured per second if there is to be no visible 'flickering'. It is obvious that no mechanical system similar to Baird's is going to be able to work within these constraints. If the image is a mono (not colour) image with 256 grey levels, the above specification suggests that:

1. The storage required to capture 1 second of real-time images is of the order of 6.25 Mbytes.
2. Transferring 6.25 Mbytes per second to a computer needs a parallel interface; a serial interface, even at a high transfer rate of 38K baud is far too slow.

3. Internally the microcomputer has to store 6.25 Mbytes per second onto a disk unit. Clearly, this has to be a hard disk, rather than floppy disk—and a fast hard disk at that.
4. One minute of real-time operation will fill the hard disk of (currently) the most sophisticated microcomputer.

## 3.4 COLOUR IMAGES

Colour capture involves the capture of three images simultaneously. Chapter 2 gives some details of the different colour models that may be used. With the RGB system, an early industry standard, the intensity of each of red, green, and blue has to be measured for each spot. With a camera that operates linearly across the whole visible spectrum, a simple set of colour masks can be used to take three images—one for each of the red, green, and blue spectra.

Placing filters mechanically over the lens of the camera is unsatisfactory unless the image and camera are both stationary. Instead a filter consisting of a number of coloured stripes is placed between the lens and sensor. As the image is scanned, either red, green, or blue intensities are measured depending on the colour of the stripe at the spot currently being sensed.

## 3.5 RANGE IMAGES

An example of a range image is one captured by radar. On this type of image light intensity is not captured, but object distance from the sensor is modelled instead. These range images are particularly useful for navigation, much more so than light intensity images. A moving vehicle (such as ourselves) needs to know the distances of objects away from it or the distance to the lack of continuous floor, otherwise it will bump into or fall off something. Light intensity images cannot give that information unless distance can be estimated from prior knowledge about size, or from a stereoscopic vision system. It is generally best to give range information as well as light intensity information rather than try to program the moving device to make estimations based on intensity only.

## 3.6 THE VIDEO CAMERA

The camera has experienced a period of substantial development during the last decade. Cheap and high-quality mono and colour cameras have developed into smaller, lighter, and cooler (in operation) units, offering high resolution with less tendency to break down.

### 3.6.1 Mono (black and white)

Most good-quality cheaper cameras rely on a vidicon tube. This consists of an evacuated glass tube, one end of which (the target) is coated internally with a photosensitive conductive coating and a transparent film of tin oxide (see Figs 3.2 and 3.3). The photosensitive coating is made from a semiconductor material, the resistance of which

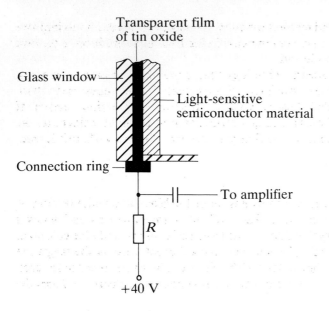

**Figure 3.2** Construction of a vidicon target area. (*Source*: © Van Wezel, 1987.)

decreases when it is illuminated. A set of one or more lenses focuses the scene to be captured onto this target. The target is 'scanned' by an electron beam which emanates from a cathode at the other end of the tube and is focused as a spot onto the target by a series of coils and grids. The beam is made to scan in a raster fashion (as a sequence of horizontal lines); in doing so it charges the photosensitive coating. These areas of charge then discharge at a rate that is dependent on the amount of incident light, and a metal ring, on the outside of the tube, connected to the tin oxide film, collects the very small current discharge. This is corrected, amplified, and put into a standard video form for analogue output. Van Wezel (1987) provides a full description of vidicon tubes.

A number of manufacturers have introduced alterations to the standard vidicon tube,

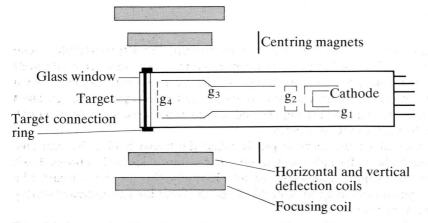

**Figure 3.3** Cross-section of a vidicon with focusing and deflection coils. $g_1$–$g_4$ are grids. (*Source*: © Van Wezel, 1987.)

particularly in the target material and method for current collection. These aim to improve the linear response of the tube (i.e. $x$ per cent increase in incident light produces $x$ per cent increase in current) and the tube resolution.

A significant development in camera technology that, depending on price, can give a high resolution without the problems associated with evacuated glass tubes uses a two-dimensional array of charge-coupled devices (CCD). These act like a shift register of capacitors. Each 'capacitor' CCD holds a charge proportional to the light incident on the device. A series of clock pulses then moves the charge to the end of the row where it is read.

### 3.6.2 Colour

The simplest form of colour camera is just an extension of the black and white version. A colour filter is placed in front of the target. The FIC (filter integrated colour) vidicon consists of a vidicon tube with a very fine filter, made from series of red and blue coloured, near-vertical lines, etched onto the tube. This means that different areas of the target are now associated with a red, blue, or white colour of the picture. The value collected for each pixel is the different colour measurements from adjacent spots. This, clearly, reduces the resolution but adds colour.

An alternative is to make the semiconductor material sensitive to different wavelengths. Vertical bars of material sensitive to red, green, and blue light are each connected to a red, green, or blue bus (set of three wires). Thus, instead of one metal ring collecting one luminosity signal, the output is collected directly as three coloured signals.

It is possible to avoid the reduction in resolution by splitting the original scene into three parts, filtering each part as red, green, and blue, and collecting the light on what amounts to three mono cameras. This is a more expensive option and optical correction for the different positions of the three tubes is not trivial.

The three-tube method can be implemented with only one camera, providing it is capturing a still picture. This is done by capturing an intensity image three times using a different coloured filter each time.

## 3.7 CAPTURE

The output from the camera conforms to some video standard, typically a composite video signal or RGB. This needs to be 'grabbed' by a device—a frame grabber—that interprets the analogue modulated signals as a frame of pixels. The frame grabber may be simply a single chip plus a number of memory chips into which the frame is put. Some (cheaper) frame grabbers use the memory of the computer to hold the frame, others may have enough on-board memory to hold a series of frames.

The memory into which the frame is put is called the frame buffer. For real-time applications a frame buffer independent of the computer memory—though connected to it through DMA (direct memory access)—is usual. Generally the cheaper systems take longer to digitize a picture (often up to 30 or 40 s in colour) and use the machine memory rather than on-board memory.

An inexpensive IBM PC-based image capture system exists that can digitize 256 grey levels from a still picture in about half a minute.

The frame grabber may have a number of selectable video inputs and may generate its own video output signal from the on-board memory. Some devices incorporate processing hardware, particularly for high-speed convolutions and fast Fourier transforms. These devices use dedicated integrated circuits that use both parallel and pipelined hardware operations. As such they are able to process an image significantly faster than the general-purpose machine processor. Image processors are covered later in this chapter.

### 3.7.1 Analogue-to-digital conversion (ADC)

Apart from the memory, the centrepiece of the frame grabber is an analogue to digital converter. This takes as input a (analogue) voltage (representing a pixel light intensity) and produces as output a parallel (digital) bit pattern that can be used by the computer.

Clearly, the speed of the frame grabber is dependent on the speed of each A/D conversion. A real-time system needs to convert in excess of 6 million conversions per second, i.e. 160 ns per conversion. This means that 'normal' fast A/D converters (1–20 $\mu$s per conversion) are too slow for a typical real-time picture. Flash video A/D converters can run at 50 MHz or faster but are significantly more expensive. For still frame grabbing a simple A/D converter may be sufficient. For colour, three A/D converters are normally used, one for each colour. Figure 3.4 illustrates a typical colour frame grabber system.

## 3.8 SCANNERS

An increasing number of mechanical scanners are becoming available. They generally have the properties of being able to capture a still, flat, large image with a considerable degree of accuracy and without calibration problems.

> The Teragon 6650 CCD flat bed scanner, for example, can capture an image 600 × 800 mm to an accuracy of 50 $\mu$m (i.e. 12 000 × 16 000 pixels) at 100 scan lines per second, with a 256 grey-level resolution.

Scanners may be hand-held or fixed, with either the paper being fed through the scanner or the scanner moving across the paper. Resolution varies from 100 d.p.i. (dots per inch) to 1000 d.p.i. Some scanners have a single row of (typically 2048) CCDs which can collect intensity values without any internal movement for a single row of pixels. Typical scan time for a 2000 × 3000 image is less than 20 s. Some scanners have only one photosensitive device, which mechanically raster scans the paper.

The main problems associated with the scanner include the following:

- Only a still image can be captured.
- Mechanical operation may not be reliable.
- Hand-held operation depends on maintaining pressure and position.

Nevertheless, as can be seen with fax machines, scanning is a valuable and generally cheap and accurate alternative to still camera capture.

A number of scanners capture only binary images, e.g. at 300 on or off dots per inch. In these cases the scanner may be supplied with software or firmware which dithers as the image is read so as to give some meaningful grey levels.

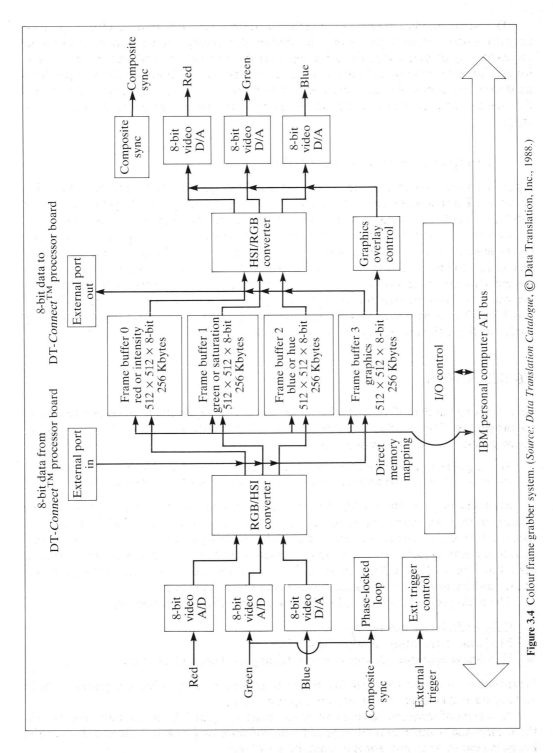

**Figure 3.4** Colour frame grabber system. (*Source: Data Translation Catalogue*, © Data Translation, Inc., 1988.)

23

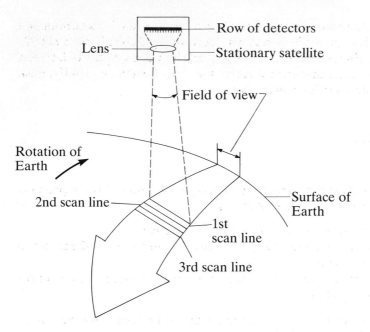

Figure 3.5 Effect of two-dimensional image created by movement of satellite with respect to the ground.

### 3.8.1 Character recognition devices

These devices are scanners with dedicated image-processing hardware and software for the processing and recognition of characters on documents. As with the general input scanner, they may be hand-held or fixed. They are usually programmed with a wide range of typefaces, the scanner selecting the best match to the typeface it is scanning (see also Chapter 12).

## 3.9 SATELLITE IMAGERY

Satellite imagery is widely used in military, meteorological, geological, and agricultural applications. Weather satellite pictures (such as from NOAA) are commonplace. Surveying satellites such as LANDSAT and ERTS (Earth Resources Technology Satellites) have similar mechanical scanners, typically scanning six horizontal scan lines at a time (with six sensors) and producing an image of very high quality—2340 × 3380 7-bit pixels. The rotation of the Earth produces the scan in the vertical direction (see Fig. 3.5). Such a picture covers approximately 100 × 100 miles. Later versions of the LANDSAT included a Thematic Mapper system. This is an optical-mechanical sensor that records emitted and reflected energy through the infrared and visible spectra with a resolution of 30 × 30 m of land surface per pixel.

Jensen (1986) includes a table of pixel size versus aircraft flight altitude. Using equipment then available, at 1000 m an aircraft is able to capture an image with pixel sizes of 2.5 m$^2$.

Rumours abound about the scanner resolution of military satellites. This information is not made widely available—for obvious reasons. However, published and available photographs from a Soviet KFA1000 satellite, 180 miles up, show a resolution of less than $5 \times 5$ m per pixel, and this suggests that current technology may be able to identify, from the same altitude, the name on a worker's lunch-box.

## 3.10 RANGING DEVICES

### 3.10.1 Ultrasound radar

Ultrasound is widely used for short range (up to 40 m) image collection. It is not practical for long-range image collection for a number of reasons:

1. Insufficient transmitted energy would be detected by the receiver.
2. There is a tendency for sound to bounce more than once (double echo) if the terrain is not conducive to ultrasound radar.
3. There may be a significant amount of ambient ultrasound present, which makes collection of the returning signal 'noisy'.

For more distant objects the electromagnetic spectrum has to be used. This may mean classical radar technology or laser range finding.

### 3.10.2 Laser radar

Laser radar is unaffected by the ambient noise and unlikely to be reflected twice back to the source, thus making it a valuable ranging system. Pulses of light are transmitted at points equivalent to pixels on the image in the direction of the perspective ray. The transmitter is switched off and the receiver 'sees' the increase in light intensity and calculates the time taken for the beam to return. Given the speed of light, the round trip distance can be calculated. Clearly with such short times, the time for sensor reaction is significant. This has to be eliminated by calibration hardware.

> An imaging laser radar is available commercially for airborne hydrographic surveying (Banic *et al.*, 1987). This system can measure water depths down to 40 m with an accuracy of 0.3 m from an aerial stand-off of 500 m.

Pulse detection systems rely on bursts of energy being transmitted, followed by a pause while the detector waits for an echo. An alternative is to modulate the amplitude (AM) of the transmitted signal and note the phase difference between the sent and detected signals. The phase difference is proportional to the distance of the object. A low-frequency (AM) signal gives a coarse distance measurement; a high-frequency signal gives a fine measurement. However, in either case if the returning beam is $\theta$ out of phase, it is not possible to tell using this method whether this is just $\theta < 2\pi$ or $2n\pi + \theta$, where, if $n$ is large, the object is at least as far away again as might be calculated.

Also, as with all detection systems, there is noise, typically more noise with a finer measure. We obviously want the signal (the useful part received) to be significantly greater than the noise (which is of no use), otherwise, in the worst case, the signal is indistinguishable from the noise. A measure of this is called the signal-to-noise ratio. Finally, optical ranging depends on the surface being optically reflective. A matt black surface can be ranged by radar but not optically. On the other hand, a lake base can be ranged optically but not by radar. See Besl (1989) for a full discussion on optical ranging.

### 3.10.3 Triangulation methods

Besl (1989) suggests that triangulation is significantly more accurate than imaging radars. The accuracy of current triangulation systems starts at 5 $\mu$m, while that of imaging radars starts at 50 $\mu$m. Furthermore, triangulation systems can cope with depth of field up to 40 000 times the accuracy, while imaging radar cannot deal with a depth of field much above 25 000 times the accuracy. Figure 3.6 illustrates the basic triangulation method.

### 3.10.4 Binocular and trinocular vision

As the name suggests, this method consists of two or three cameras positioned apart from one another (in the case of three cameras, positioned on different planes) or a single moving camera. The triangulation correspondence between images is done using software and is described in some detail in Chapter 17. Light intensity images are collected from each camera and ranges are calculated from angles of correspondence between interest points that can be found in each picture.

### 3.10.5 Structured lighting

By use of structured lighting it is possible to extract geometric information from a scene as well as pure intensity information.

Structured light options include the following:

- Line and point projection.
- Multiple point and multiple line projection.
- Grid projection.
- Circle, cross, and thick stripe projections.
- Grey code patterns, colour-coded stripes, and random texture projections.

**Light striping (line projection)** A stripe of light is shone at the scene. Since this effectively illuminates only those parts of the object that lie on the stripe, it is equivalent to slicing the object with a known plane. If the position of the plane (the light stripe) is known and the lines of sight from the camera are also known, then the intersection of these at the points of illumination gives a line of space, whose coordinates can be calculated. If this is sampled in various positions or the stripe is moved repeatedly to a 'next-plane' position and sampled, the process can give a good starting point for the segmentation (splitting up) of the image and eventual identification of a geometric shape.

A disadvantage of light striping occurs when the object is partially concave and, in order to get a view of the inside of the object, the stripe projector has to be very close to the camera. The stripe plane and the vision plane are then nearly parallel and so the intersection line is very prone to calibration and geometric calculation errors. Equally, if the stripe projector is far from the camera it may mean that much of the stripe is occluded by the object.

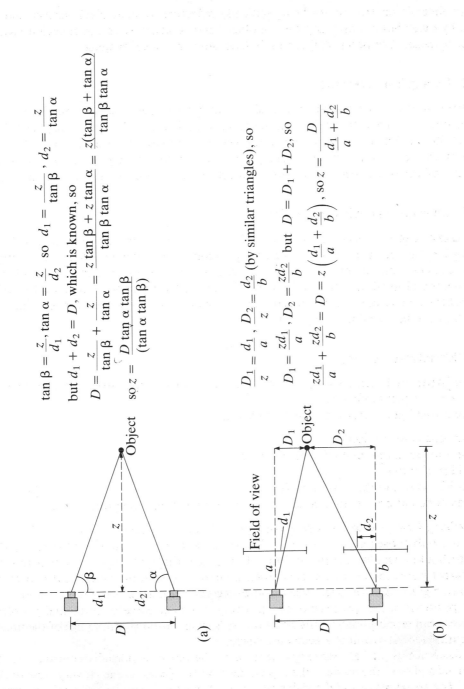

$$\tan \beta = \frac{z}{d_1}, \tan \alpha = \frac{z}{d_2} \text{ so } d_1 = \frac{z}{\tan \beta}, d_2 = \frac{z}{\tan \alpha}$$

but $d_1 + d_2 = D$, which is known, so

$$D = \frac{z}{\tan \beta} + \frac{z}{\tan \alpha} = \frac{z \tan \beta + z \tan \alpha}{\tan \beta \tan \alpha} = \frac{z(\tan \beta + \tan \alpha)}{\tan \beta \tan \alpha}$$

$$\text{so } z = \frac{D \tan \alpha \tan \beta}{(\tan \alpha \tan \beta)}$$

**(a)**

$$\frac{D_1}{z} = \frac{d_1}{a}, \frac{D_2}{z} = \frac{d_2}{b} \text{ (by similar triangles), so}$$

$$D_1 = \frac{zd_1}{a}, D_2 = \frac{zd_2}{b} \text{ but } D = D_1 + D_2, \text{ so}$$

$$\frac{zd_1}{a} + \frac{zd_2}{b} = D = z \left( \frac{d_1}{a} + \frac{d_2}{b} \right), \text{ so } z = \frac{D}{\frac{d_1}{a} + \frac{d_2}{b}}$$

**(b)**

**Figure 3.6** Triangulation using (a) angles and (b) similar triangles.

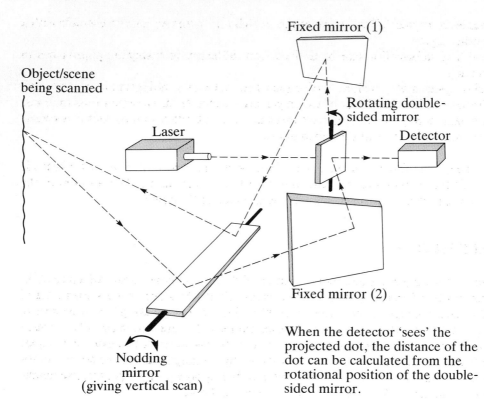

**Figure 3.7** Point projection system. (*Source*: Rioux, 1984.)

**Point projection** Here a single point of light (normally laser light) is scanned across the scene, in a similar way to the radar imaging method. However, instead of measuring the time to return or the phase difference, the position of the point in the field of view is noted and, as with light striping, triangulation gives the range of the object. Figure 3.7 illustrates a design by Rioux (1984). The sensor and transmitter are fixed next to one another, but the rotating central double-sided mirror effectively places the sensors a distance apart while also scanning the scene. A nodding mirror creates a vertical scan effect.

**Grid projection** This projects a set of stripes, both horizontally and vertically, onto the object simultaneously, and analyses the resulting pattern captured by the camera. The analysis is not simple. A number of approaches can be made to the analysis. The size of the 'dark' squares corresponds to the distance of the object from the image. The aspect ratio of the squares corresponds to the angle of the surface on which the squares are being projected.

If the projector is not immediately next to the camera, then discontinuities in the lines in the image can be used to identify possible concavities in the image. If there are many discontinuities it may be difficult to determine which line in one region corresponds with a line in another region.

A wealth of information can be derived from different light striping approaches to object shaping.

Ranging systems also include tactile (accurate but slow), holographic, and Fresnel systems (see Besl, 1989), the latter of which performs accurate measurements down to less than half a nanometre, though the phase measurements introduce ambiguities in a similar way to the imaging laser radar described above.

**Active focusing** Here a point of light is projected onto an object. The projector focus is changed until the camera identifies the minimum blur in that point. The position of the projector lens can then be used to estimate the distance of the object.

## 3.11 CALIBRATION

Calibration of the camera requires consideration of the errors in the camera which result in spatial luminosity differences (e.g. does the camera collect a brighter image in the centre of view and a darker image at the edges, a problem known as vignetting?), and geometric errors (e.g. are distances between some reference points in the collected image all consistent with a pure perspective projection?). Spatial luminosity problems are discussed in Chapter 6. Geometric errors can be corrected using software by creating a camera model (world-to-camera transformation matrix). Inverting this and then applying a pure perspective matrix transforms the image back to a correct two-dimensional one.

### Technique 3.1 World-to-camera transformation

USE Assuming a flat surface has been captured, it is possible to associate every pixel position on the image with a real position on the surface. This technique does that.

OPERATION A world-to-camera transformation can be constructed as follows.

Identify a number of reference points where the coordinates of the points in the image are known and the coordinates in world space are known, say

$(U, V)$ image plane coordinates
$(u, v, t)$ image plane homogeneous coordinates

so $U = u/t$ and $V = v/t$;

$(x, y, z, 1)$ world coordinates

We wish to create a $3 \times 4$ matrix that converts image coordinates into world coordinates, i.e.

$$(x, y, z, 1) \begin{pmatrix} a_1 & b_1 & c_1 \\ a_2 & b_2 & c_2 \\ a_3 & b_3 & c_3 \\ a_4 & b_4 & c_4 \end{pmatrix} = (u, v, t)$$

Expanding this we get

$$x.a_1 + y.a_2 + z.a_3 + a_4 = u$$
$$x.b_1 + y.b_2 + z.b_3 + b_4 = v$$
$$x.c_1 + y.c_2 + z.c_3 + c_4 = t$$

If four reference points are collected, the values in the matrix can be solved using simultaneous equations. With more than four reference points (assuming some error in the collection of the reference points), a least-squares method can be used to estimate the values in the matrix. See section in Chapter 9 on using interest points which deals with this in detail.

There are a number of problems with this approach:

1. A linear transformation is assumed. Clearly that is not always the case. A transformation may be needed, for example, to correct a logarithmic stretching of the image at the edges.
2. The transformation function may not be continuous, i.e. no transformation may be required on the left of centre of the image and a significant transformation may be required to the right of centre.

A similar, though more sophisticated operation, is suggested in Ballard and Brown (1982).

## 3.12 EXERCISES

**3.1** What are the limitations of capturing range images using triangulation and a single camera?

**3.2** The images from two cameras, one pointing along $y = 0$ and the other at $y = 1$ (with one unit representing 1 m) both show an object. When this is viewed on a monitor, the two images show the object at pixel positions $x = 254$ and $x = 261$, where each pixel is 1 mm. The monitor view is equivalent to a window view 0.5 m away from the camera. How far away is the object?

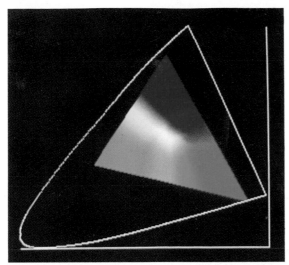

**Plate 1** The relation between the CIE diagram and the colours that can be realized using a typical television monitor (*Source:* Berger and Gillies, 1989).

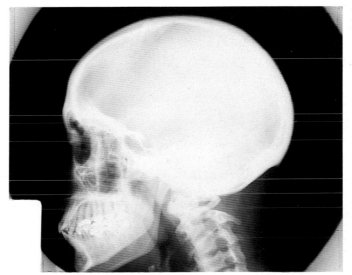

**Plate 2 (a)** X-ray of skull — original prior to capture.

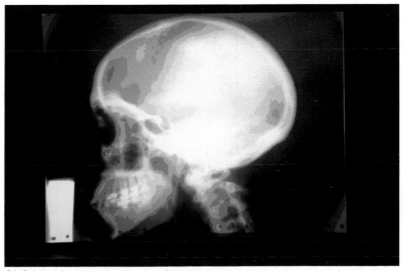

**(b)** Original image, monochrome palette (see text).

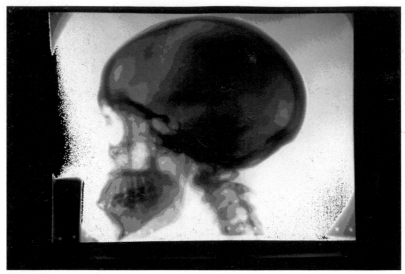

**Plate 2** *(continued)* **(c)** Grey-level negation (black to white, white to black).

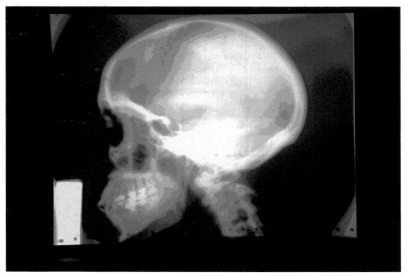

**(d)** Green palette (see text).

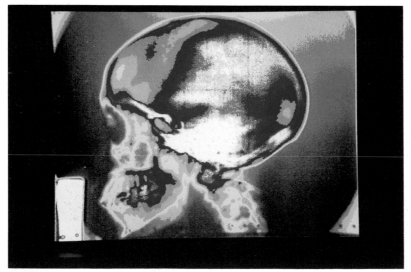

**(e)** Purple-headed mountain palette (see text).

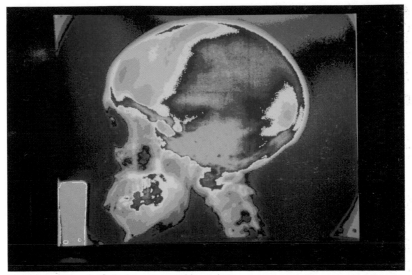

**Plate 2** *(continued)* **(f)** Red to green to blue palette.

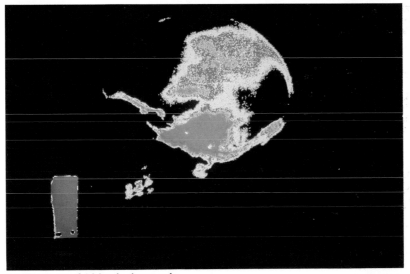

**(g)** Top 3 out of 16 levels shown only.

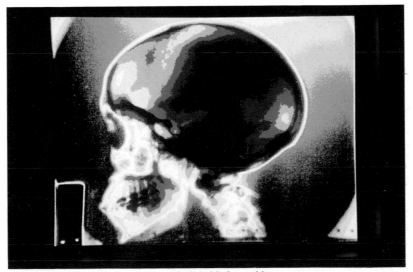

**(h)** Grey-level 0 → black and 15 → black, with 8 → white.

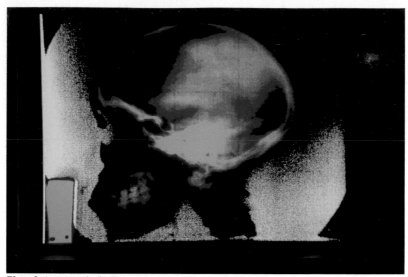

**Plate 2** *(continued)* **(i)** Only grey levels 0−3 (green) and 12−15 (blue) showing.

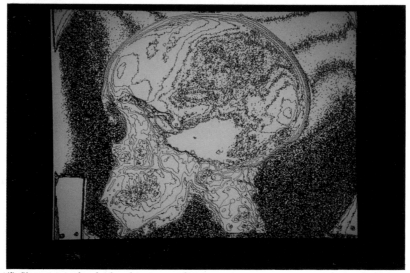

**(j)** Sixteen grey-level edge detector results.

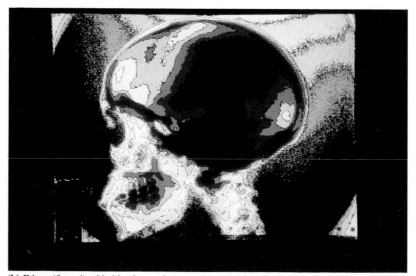

**(k)** Edges (from j) added back to palette used in (h). Note how much cleaner this makes the region edges.

# 4

# IMAGE PRESENTATION

## 4.1 INTRODUCTION

This chapter deals with different methods of displaying images. It also describes some algorithms for device control (particularly output to laser printers). Finally, a discussion about dedicated image-processing processors is included.

## 4.2 RASTER SCREEN

The raster screen forms the main volatile output system for images. The standard evacuated cathode ray tube consists of a wide display end-coated internally with a phosphorescent layer that emits light when electrons from the cathode at the other, narrow end of the tube (gun) hit the surface. The electron beam is directed by a series of grids and deflection coils and scans across the tube horizontally, at the end of each line returning to scan the next line, and so on (see Fig. 4.1).

A number of enhancements to this standard unit have been made. These are described below.

### 4.2.1 Interlacing

Here the raster pattern works by displaying every odd-numbered line on the first scan of the screen and then the even-numbered lines during the second scan. The effect of this is that flickering, which can appear at anything up to 25 frames a second, is considerably reduced as at 25 frames per second, 25 'odd' frames and 25 'even' frames can be sent in 1

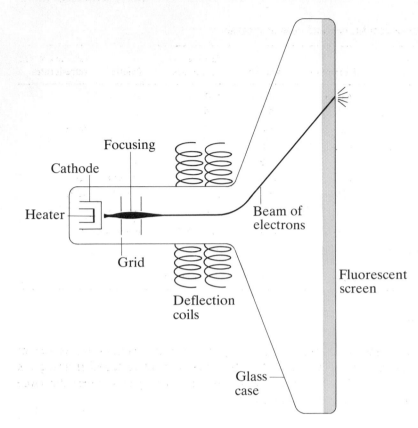

**Figure 4.1** Monitor tube (monochrome).

second, thus giving an effective change of screen every 1/50th of a second. Any computer screen that employs interlacing would normally store a single row of pixels for adjacent odd- and even-numbered lines. Thus, a screen with 512 lines employing interlacing may only have a horizontal resolution of 256 pixels. Clearly this saves memory and allows direct modulation of a standard television set (which may employ interlacing); furthermore it reduces flicker for moving images. However, in image processing, resolution is normally a more important criteria, hence interlaced displays are not ideal.

### 4.2.2 Aspect ratio

The standard video monitor is not square. The ratio of the base length to the side length is the aspect ratio and is normally 4:3. If each pixel is to represent a square area of light, the resolution of the video output must also correspond to the aspect ratio. Hence, a 480 horizontal line system often corresponds with $(4/3) \times 480 = 640$ pixels along the line. Some workstations do use a square aspect ratio offering $1024 \times 1024$ (e.g. the APOLLO systems use this display size, and a number of manufacturers seem to be setting this as a PC scientific imaging standard), while some document processors turn the tube around so as to create an A4-sized image and a ratio of 3:4.

**Table 4.1  A selection of resolutions and colour systems**

| System | Horizontal | Vertical | Grey levels or colours | Palette | Selected screen refresh rates |
|---|---|---|---|---|---|
| IBM PC CGA | 640 | 200 | 2 | | |
| | 320 | 200 | 4 | | |
| Hercules | 720 | 348 | 2 | | 50 Hz |
| IBM PC EGA | 640 | 350 | 2 | | |
| | 320 | 350 | 16 | 64 | |
| IBM PC VGA | 640 | 480 | 16 | 262 144 | 60 Hz |
| | 320 | 200 | 256 | 262 144 | 70 Hz |
| VESA | 800 | 600 | 16 | 262 144 | |
| APOLLO display | 1024 | 1024 | 16 or 256 | 16 million | |
| PC AT image *processor boards*, variety of manufacturers, no display | 1024 | 1024 | 256 or more | | |

### 4.2.3  Size of screen

The definition of the screen is related to how easy it is for the human eye to detect differences between pixels. A small screen makes the pixels very close together and gives the effect of a high definition. For larger screens to give the same performance the same number of pixels *per unit area* of screen must be present.

### 4.2.4  Resolution

The contents of a raster screen are presented, typically, every 1/50th of a second. This means that there has to be a memory area (the video memory) that can be read every 1/50th second, and circuits to convert the contents of the memory into an electron beam of appropriate power and direction. Low-resolution systems can use elementary video display chips to read the memory (using DMA) and present it on the screen. However, the figures in Table 4.1 show that the system has to become significantly faster as the number of grey or colour levels increases and particularly as the resolution increases.

The resolution of a number of frequently used devices is shown in Table 4.1. Jackson (1989) gives an excellent summary of the history of PC display boards, and Redfern (1989) considers PC display standard beyond VGA. Wilton (1987) contains a most detailed and valuable summary of PC video systems.

### 4.2.5  Planes

A plane is an array of memory that holds a full screen image. Typically a plane is described as having a horizontal and vertical resolution together with the number of bits held for each pixel. For example, an 8-bit plane allows 256 different patterns possible for each pixel—either 256 levels of grey or 256 different colours. Table 4.2 illustrates a variety of resolutions and bit-planes together with their real-time image transfer rates.

**Table 4.2 Sample resolution sizes and video transfer rates**

| Horizontal resolution | Vertical resolution | System | Grey levels or colours | Bits/pixel | Memory | Transfer rate at 50 HZ |
|---|---|---|---|---|---|---|
| 320 | 256 | mono | 2 | 1 | 10K | 500 Kbytes per second |
| 320 | 256 | mono | 256 | 8 | 80K | 4 Mbytes per second |
| 320 | 256 | colour | 16 million | 24 | 240K | 12 Mbytes per second |
| 640 | 512 | colour | 256 | 8 | 320K | 16 Mbytes per second |
| 1024 | 1024 | colour | 256 | 8 | 1M | 50 Mbytes per second |

### 4.2.6 Video lookup table

In order to reduce the amount of memory required to hold an image, most machines now use a video lookup table. Using this method, each memory element that corresponds to a pixel in the video memory holds a reference to an entry in the video lookup table instead of holding a colour or grey-level value. The video lookup table holds as many entries as can be addressed by the pixel memory and each entry is programmed with a grey-level or colour description. Figure 4.2 gives more details of a video lookup table.

### 4.2.7 Colour display equipment

Colour tubes contain three guns—one each for the red, green, and blue intensities. Between the guns and the phosphor screen is a metal mesh. The phosphor screen is made up of three slightly different phosphorescent compounds that when excited by an electron beam emit red, green, or blue light. The mesh is positioned so that the three guns are only able to hit their respective coloured phosphor dots. The electrons from each gun are deflected by a set of plates and coils to the appropriate hole in the mesh. The metal around the hole strips off any loose electrons and allows the three beams to pass through to their respective coloured spots.

The existence of the mesh makes this mechanism clearly discrete, unlike the mono tube where the phosphor is continuous. It is thus possible to state the exact resolution of a colour tube, that is the number of red, green, and blue spot groupings normally equal to the number of holes in the mesh. Any increase in resolution requires a differently engineered display as well as an increase in the size of memory map.

Liquid crystal display (LCD) technology is progressively matching the raster screen: LCD resolutions of $720 \times 480 \times 9$ bit are available at the time of writing.

### 4.2.8 Calibration

Calibration is done internally by hardware that allows the user to set brightness and contrast levels on each of the guns as well as picture skew, and so on.

## 4.3 PRINTERS

A good textbook produces black and white photographs as a series of dots of varying sizes. Typically there will be about 1 million of these dots per square inch (i.e. $1000 \times 1000$

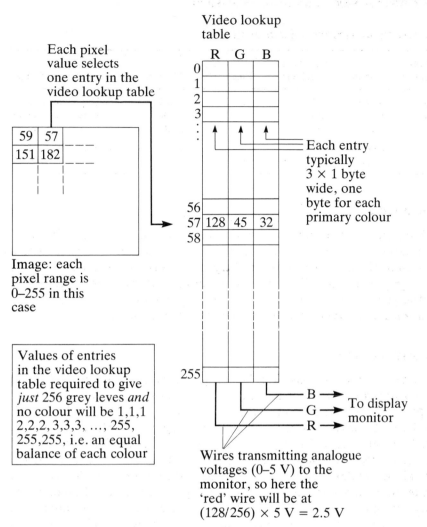

Each pixel value selects one entry in the video lookup table

Video lookup table

Image: each pixel range is 0–255 in this case

Each entry typically 3 × 1 byte wide, one byte for each primary colour

Values of entries in the video lookup table required to give *just* 256 grey leves *and* no colour will be 1,1,1 2,2,2, 3,3,3, ..., 255, 255,255, i.e. an equal balance of each colour

To display monitor

Wires transmitting analogue voltages (0–5 V) to the monitor, so here the 'red' wire will be at (128/256) × 5 V = 2.5 V

**Figure 4.2** Video lookup table.

resolution). With that kind of resolution, at a normal reading distance it is impossible to see the individual dots without some kind of magnification. In practice, black and white images consisting of 300 dots per inch (d.p.i.) are quite satisfactory for most mono image-processing applications. Currently, however, there are some more expensive printers on the market that give this resolution, and better, with more than a 1-bit plane, i.e. the dot density can be varied instead of just being there or not there.

### 4.3.1 Matrix printers

While matrix printers have been an industry standard for normal printed output, these devices are rarely of sufficient quality for image output, giving a typical draft quality

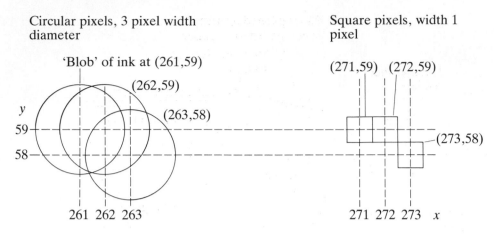

**Figure 4.3** Illustration of merging of accurately positioned, oversize dots—as occurs with some matrix printers.

output of 60 d.p.i. and a letter quality of 120 d.p.i. Each dot is either printed or not printed, black or white. Some matrix printers are supplied with a multi-colour ribbon so that the dots can be yellow, cyan, and magenta or, if overprinting is allowed (making the system much slower), a combination of yellow, cyan, and magenta. Some manufacturers have produced matrix printers with a very high resolution. A limit exists, however, on this technology in that the hammer on the matrix head has to hit on to an inked ribbon and then onto paper. This always gives a slightly larger blob on the paper than the size of the hammer, so that while 300 d.p.i. may be available, it may well be that each of those 300 dots overlaps its neighbours by a significant amount (see Fig. 4.3).

### 4.3.2  Laser printers

Laser printers are by far the most popular form of device for image output. Resolution starts at 300 d.p.i., and each dot is separate from its neighbour. Laser printers work on a principle similar to photocopiers. The image is generated as a beam of laser light that is directed at an electrostatically charged photosensitive drum. The drum rotates as the laser scans the image onto the drum. Where the beam has been 'on', the charge on the drum leaks away; where the laser beam has been 'off', the surface maintains the charge and, as it passes a bath of toner, attracts toner onto the drum in the charged areas. The drum is then pushed against the paper and the toner is transferred to the paper, which is then heated and fixed.

Laser printers print at up to 30 pages per minute, providing the interface is there for fast information transfer. A typical page image, say $10 \times 8$ inches at 300 d.p.i., will require the transfer of approximately 1 Mbyte. Normal serial interface operation occurs at 9600 baud, i.e. about 960 bytes per second. This would mean that transfer of the image to the printer along an RS232 9600-baud line would take about 17 minutes. Clearly this is unsatisfactory, and therefore a parallel interface is normally used.

Faster transfer can be achieved by sending the printer a suitable set of (say) $4 \times 4$ dot patterns, treating these as a character font set. Values, representing selections from the font set, are then sent to the printer so that each value sent will cause 16 dots to be output.

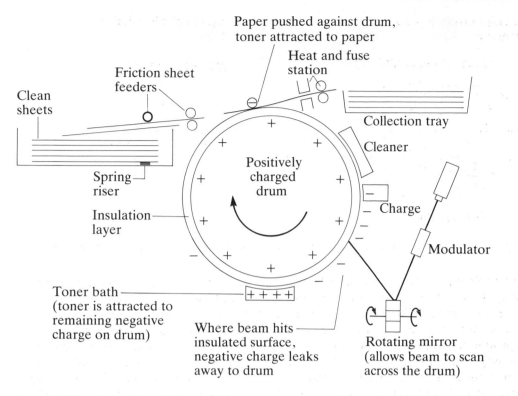

**Figure 4.4** The principal features of a laser printer.

Cheaper laser printers do not offer a programmable toner intensity for each spot. The more expensive versions do allow the user to set intensity levels, giving typically 256 grey levels per spot.

Colour laser printers have recently become available and will, no doubt, offer a substantial contribution to image production equipment.

Figure 4.4 illustrates the basic operation of a laser printer.

### 4.3.3 Patterning

*Note:* In considering algorithms for patterning and dithering, *Digital Halftoning* by Ulichney (1987), which contains many images and algorithms for image printing, is recommended reading.

When it is not possible to control the intensity of individual dots on an image, grey levels have to be created by identifying, for each pixel, an area of dots that contain the right ratio of black to white (i.e. the right number of printed dots in the area) so that an overall grey-level appearance is achieved. This positioning of dots is termed patterning. The pattern may be regular (ordered) or irregular, i.e. it may have a readily identified pattern to it or there may be no perceived pattern.

An image-processing system produced images of size $144 \times 180$ with 256 grey levels. Output was to be directed to a laser printer with a resolution 300 d.p.i. on $10 \times 8$ inch paper. The following calculations were made:

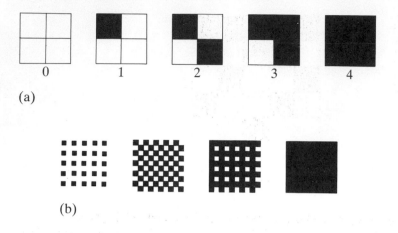

**Figure 4.5** (a) Five grey levels from four binary pixels, and (b) the corresponding patterns on the image.

total paper area    300 d.p.i. × 10 inches = 3000 dots    by    300 d.p.i. × 8 inches = 2400 dots

This gives

$$3000/180 = 16.7 \text{ horizontal dots per pixel}$$
$$2400/144 = 16.7 \text{ vertical dots per pixel}$$

Truncating to 16 × 16 gives, for each pixel an area of 256 dots. This is just one more than is required (since 256 grey levels includes the area without dots as grey-level 256, and full of dots as grey level 0).

A regular 16 × 16 pattern was chosen for each pixel and the image was printed.

### 4.3.4 Patterns

Generally ordered patterns are preferred to random patterns as they avoid clumps of dots being randomly created. Ordered patterns, however, can sometimes lead to lines becoming visible in an image. Figure 4.5(a) illustrates patterning with a 2 × 2 matrix creating five grey levels. On this scale, a continuous area of 50 per cent black, 50 per cent white means that two of the four dots will be on, and two off. If, for every 50 per cent pixel the same two-dot pattern is used, it creates lines either vertically, horizontally, or diagonally across this area (see Fig. 4.5(b)).

In the earlier example a 16 × 16 pattern system is used. This has the advantage of a much wider selection of internal patterns so that a diagonal line pattern is less likely to be produced. It is clearly undesirable for the computer to hold 256 different 16 × 16 binary arrays in memory, one for each grey level (though it may be useful for the printer to hold these as a font set). An alternative is to hold a single integer array containing the numbers 0–255. The actual grey-level value is then tested against the value for each dot in this array. If the grey level is less than the value in the array, then the dot is printed. Figure 4.6 shows an example of this method.

This leaves the problem of setting up the array with appropriate positioned values. Jarvis *et al.* (1976) survey a number of methods of doing this. It can easily be shown that an array with the values positioned randomly, i.e. a different random pattern for each position, will cause blobbing. A more formal arrangement method is presented in the following section.

| 1 | 15 | 23 | 6 | 9 |
|----|----|----|----|----|
| 19 | 10 | 2 | 20 | 14 |
| 7 | 25 | 17 | 8 | 24 |
| 22 | 3 | 13 | 21 | 4 |
| 11 | 16 | 5 | 12 | 18 |

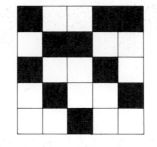

**Figure 4.6** $5 \times 5$ binary dots per pixel. 'Random' matrix values held as an array give the image on the right for a pixel with grey level 11.

### Technique 4.1 Setting up a pattern for grey-level rendition on bilevel displays

USE To have a standard pattern that avoids blobs and lines being created when using a dot/no-dot system to present multi-grey-level images.

OPERATION (Limb, 1969). Start with a $2 \times 2$ matrix defined as follows:

$$M_1 = \begin{pmatrix} 0 & 2 \\ 3 & 1 \end{pmatrix}$$

Now use the recursion relation

$$M_{n+1} = \begin{pmatrix} 4 \times M_n & 4 \times M_n + 2 \times U_n \\ 4 \times M_n + 3 \times U_n & 4 \times M_n + U_n \end{pmatrix}$$

where $2^{2n}$ is the number of elements in the array (i.e. a square array $2^n \times 2^n$) and $U_n$ is a square array with of $2^{2n}$ elements all set to 1.

This gives, for example

$$M_1 = \begin{pmatrix} 0 & 2 \\ 3 & 1 \end{pmatrix} \quad M_2 = \begin{pmatrix} 0 & 8 & 2 & 10 \\ 12 & 4 & 14 & 6 \\ 3 & 11 & 5 & 9 \\ 15 & 7 & 13 & 5 \end{pmatrix}$$

i.e.

$$\begin{pmatrix} 0 \times 4 & 2 \times 4 & 0 \times 4 + 2 & 2 \times 4 + 2 \\ 3 \times 4 & 1 \times 4 & 3 \times 4 + 2 & 1 \times 4 + 2 \\ 0 \times 4 + 3 & 2 \times 4 + 3 & 0 \times 4 + 1 & 2 \times 4 + 1 \\ 3 \times 4 + 3 & 1 \times 4 + 3 & 3 \times 4 + 1 & 1 \times 4 + 1 \end{pmatrix}$$

So if on a 16 grey-level system one pixel has values 4, 8, or 12, the dot patterns produced are

|  8  |  12  |  4  |

CODE

```
mat[0][1]=2;
mat[1][0]=3;
mat[1][1]=1;
mat[0][0]=0;
siz=2;
for(n=1;n<=LOG2_OF_SIDE_REQUIRED;n++)
{
 for(i=0;i<siz;i++)
 for(j=0;j<siz;j++)
 {
  mat[i][j]*=4; mat[i+siz][j]=mat[i][j]+3;
  mat[i+siz][j+siz]=mat[i][j]+1; mat[i][j+siz]=mat[i][j]+2;
 }
siz*=32;
{
```

The image in Fig. 4.7 illustrates this technique. This is an attempt to simulate the halftoning that is done on newspaper print where pictures are made from white and black dots of a size proportional to the grey level required.

(a)

**Figure 4.7** (a) Patterning using Limb's algorithm to generate the pattern.

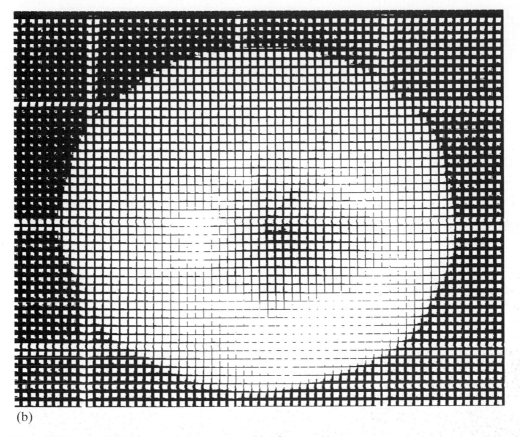

(b)

**Figure 4.7** (*continued*) (b) Square spiral patterns, working from outside.

Clearly, the printing system may not necessarily be bilevel. Each dot might have an intensity value that can be assigned to it. If the intensity value range is equal to or greater than the range of the intensities on the original image, then there is no need for patterning. If, as is more likely, the intensity range of the dots is less than the range on the image, then each pixel needs to be represented by a number of dots to simulate the intensity value (see Fig. 4.8).

### 4.3.5 Dithering

A worse case is when the range of intensities available from the output device, even when patterning is used, is less than the range on the original image.

An image-processing system produced images of size $512 \times 640$ with 256 grey levels. Output was to be directed to a laser printer with a resolution 300 d.p.i. on $10 \times 8$ inch paper. The following calculations were made:

$$\text{total paper area} \quad 300 \times 10 = 3000 \quad \text{by} \quad 300 \times 8 = 2400 \text{ dots}$$

This gives

$$3000/640 = 4.7 \text{ horizontal dots per pixel}$$
$$2400/512 = 4.7 \text{ vertical dots per pixel}$$

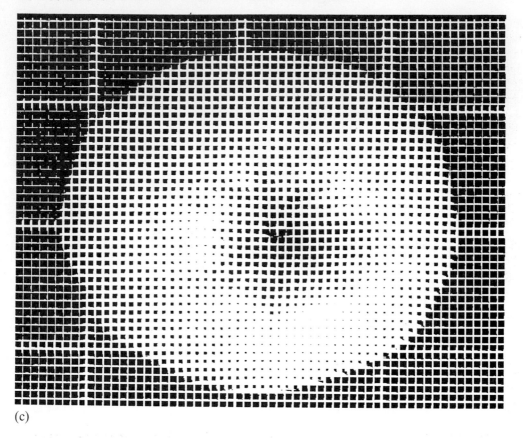

(c)

**Figure 4.7** (*continued*) (c) Square spiral patterns, working from centre.

Truncating to 4 × 4, this only gives 16 dots for each pixel, i.e. 17 grey levels. It seems that a choice has to made. Either reduce the resolution (back down to 144 × 180, as on the original example), or reduce the grey levels per pixel, using a grey-level transformation, from 156 to 17. Neither choice is popular because much will be lost either way.

An alternative is to use a dithering technique. Two techniques are described below:

### Technique 4.2 Regular dither
USE When some element of randomness is required to cope with the necessary quantization errors that appears as a result of there being insufficient creatable grey levels for each pixel on a dot/no-dot display.

OPERATION Use Technique 4.1 to create an array with the number of elements equal to the number of grey levels on the original image. (In the above example the array will be 16 × 16.)

Enlarge the original image (using an interpolation or copying technique) so that the new image is slightly less than or equal to the size of the dot array available. (In the above case the image could be enlarged by a factor of 4 in both directions.)

| 0 | 0 | 0 | 0 | 16 | 16 | 16 | 16 |
|---|---|---|---|----|----|----|----|
| 0 | 1 | 0 | 0 | 16 | 15 | 16 | 16 |
| 0 | 0 | 0 | 0 | 16 | 16 | 16 | 16 |
| 0 | 0 | 0 | 0 | 16 | 16 | 16 | 16 |
| 6 | 5 | 6 | 6 | 7 | 8 | 7 | 7 |
| 5 | 6 | 6 | 5 | 8 | 7 | 8 | 7 |
| 6 | 6 | 5 | 5 | 7 | 7 | 7 | 7 |
| 5 | 6 | 5 | 6 | 7 | 8 | 7 | 8 |

Range of intensity
for each 'dot' is
0 (white) to 16 (black)
(range = 17)

If pixel values range from 0 to 255, then for accurate rendition $(255/16) \simeq 16 = 4 \times 4$ dots per pixel.

The above 'dot' image will correspond with the pixel image.

| 1 | 255 |
|----|-----|
| 89 | 117 |

Note: dots per pixel $= \dfrac{\text{pixel range} - 1}{\text{dot range} - 1}$

**Figure 4.8** Variable dot intensities.

Then given the pattern array size is $n \times n$, for each pixel $(x, y)$ in the new image, calculate:

$$i = x \bmod n$$
$$j = y \bmod n$$

and if the value of the pixel at $(x, y)$ is less than the element $(i, j)$ in the pattern array, then plot a dot at position $(x, y)$.

In practice the image array does not have to be enlarged, though the explanation of the technique is simpler if it is. Without enlargement, if the enlargement size were to be by a factor of $m$, then for each pixel $(x, y)$ on the original image, $m \times m$ dots would have to be passed or printed, and then the following code would be appropriate:

CODE

```c
for(a=0;a<m;a++)
for(b=0;b<m;b++)
{
  i=(x*m+a)%n; j=(y*m+b)%n;
  if(dot_array[i][j]>pixel[x][y])put_dot[x*m+a][y*m+b];
}
```

where the % sign in C indicates mod.

Finally if it is found that the enlargement is not simply square, then the values for $m$ in the 'for' loops above will be different.

This gives a very neat and ordered dither output. The drawback is that it is so ordered. The patterns are normally clearly visible. Notice too that an element of randomness has been introduced into the picture. The reason for the modulus being taken was simply to select regularly but randomly one of the elements in the dot array. Further, a pixel value may be only just slightly higher than a low dot array value and, therefore, a decision made not to print. The fact that the pixel value was much nearer black than white, yet white resulted, is ignored by the above algorithm. A better approach might be to propagate these errors onto the nearby pixels. The now classic Floyd–Steinberg (1976) algorithm does this.

### Technique 4.3 The Floyd–Steinberg error-propagating dither
USE On dot/no-dot (bilevel) displays, when insufficient grey levels can be created for each pixel, then the error in quantizing the pixels can be employed using this technique (rather than randomly ignored using the above technique) by passing it sensibly to neighbouring pixels.

OPERATION Let the range of grey levels be $b$ (black) to $w$ (white). Calculate $t = (b + w)/2$ (half-way between black and white). Enlarge the image (as in Technique 4.2). Then for each new pixel $(x, y)$

{
  If the pixel_value$(x, y)$ is less than $t$
  {
    plot a dot at $(x, y)$
    calculate an error value of pixel_value$(x, y) - b$
  }
  else calculate an error value of pixel_value$(x, y) - w$

Finally distribute that error value to its neighbours by placing 3/8ths of it onto the pixel to the right, 3/8ths of it downwards, and 1/4 of it diagonally down and right. This means that errors are always only propagated in the direction of dots still to be plotted. Clearly to aportion the errors backwards would create significant recursive problems.
}

CODE
```
grey=MAXCOL/2;
for(i=0;i<y;i++)for(j=0;j<x;j++)
{
 if(screen[i][j]>grey)
 {
  plot_dot(i,j);
  adjust=screen[i][j];
 }
 else adjust=screen[i][j]-brightest;
 screen[i][j+1]+=(int)(3*adjust/8);
 screen[i+1][j]+=(int)(3*adjust/8);
 screen[i+1][j+1]+=(int)(adjust/4);
}
```

**Figure 4.9** Floyd–Steinberg dither.

Here the screen array needs to be signed integer because it may go negative or increase beyond the normal pixel value range. The image in Fig. 4.9 illustrates this. Note the 'streaming' effect caused by the error propogation. This can be reduced by rastering left to right, and right to left on alternate rows of pixels.

### 4.3.6 Ink-jet printers

Drop-on-demand ink-jet printing is a relatively cheap method of presenting hard-copy images in colour.

The fact that each dot is variable in terms of colour depth means that this machine has a greater resolution × grey-scale value than the 300 d.p.i. laser printers. The drawbacks with ink-jet printers have, in the past, been a tendency for the jets to clog and the need to use special paper.

### 4.3.7 Wax thermal

This is probably the the highest-quality image output currently available, giving typically 16 million colours per pixel at 300 d.p.i., and producing one page in 90 seconds.

The paper is fed through the machine three times, and on each pass is pressed against a different coloured wax-coated cover sheet (red, green, and blue). The transfer from the wax cover sheet to the paper is made by heating the wax in the printer at the appropriate pixel positions for the appropriate length of time. The result is a quality colour picture that is not significantly different from a photograph.

## 4.4 PHOTOGRAPHY

An easy option, both in terms of equipment cost and the lack of interface problems, is using a standard camera to take a photograph of a screen image. A $4.5 \times 3.5$ inch photograph, for example, capturing a $640 \times 480$ screen image results in approximately 150 d.p.i. The camera must be situated so as to give a full-frame view of the screen with minimal external lighting and without flash. A tripod is necessary unless a very fast film is used. Exposure will always need to be at least as long as 1/30th second. With a normal 100 ASA film and a fully open aperture, exposure times of 3–5 seconds are typical. A dark tunnel is ideal for avoiding reflective light from the screen, alternatively photography in a completely darkened room is equally adequate.

Unless an instant development system is used (in which case print size is limited), development makes photography a time-consuming process. However, even taking film and development costs into account, each print costs significantly less than most wax thermal printed images. Clearly the number of colours and the resolution is dependent on the screen image, and the aspect ratio is unlikely to be the same as the screen.

Some firms manufacture scan cameras that can be interfaced directly to a computer. These normally have automatic exposure and come with instant processing packs so, again, size is limited.

## 4.5 THREE-DIMENSIONAL IMAGING

### 4.5.1 Stereo viewing

Stereo viewing requires that a pair of images is presented to the viewer. This may be done in a variety of ways.

A two-coloured image is displayed, either via a printer or on a screen. The two colours (green and red, say) represent both images superimposed on one another. The viewer wears a pair of glasses with green and red filters so that the green lines blend with the background when viewed through the green filter, but the red lines appear as a dark grey. The red filter performs a similar function on the red and green lines respectively. One coloured filter is over each eye. The effect is a monochrome three-dimensional picture.

A single 50 Hz colour screen showing a sequence of left, then right, then left images every 1/50th second can be viewed through twisted LCD glasses connected to the display system and operating on the same frequency so that a full colour image is presented to both eyes alternately, but fast enough for there to be no flickering.

Holography represents an alternative that does not require the use of spectacles. For still images this is an excellent method of presentation, but real-time colour holography, at the time of writing, is not a practical proposition.

One system in use in medical tomography (Kennedy and Nelson, 1987), incorporates the use of varifocal mirrors. The image is viewed through a mirror that can be electrically varied from convex to concave in structure. The image, on a cathode ray tube, is controlled synchronously with the mirror operation. Movement of the mirror means that the virtual image of the object on the screen moves back and forward according to the mirror's focus. Figure 4.10 shows an outline of the system used by Kennedy and Nelson.

## 4.6 USING COLOUR TO ENHANCE MONOCHROME OUTPUT

Plates 2(a)–(k) illustrates the advantages of this approach. The eye finds it considerably more difficult to identify gradual changes in brightness compared to gradual (or stark) changes in colour. Early map printers recognized this when they chose to make sea blue, low ground green, and very high ground mauve or white—'the purple-headed mountain'. The clear advantage was that it became obvious which areas were approximately the same height even if they were not actually next to each other. Contouring of maps offers a much more accurate rendition of height, but without looking at the values associated with the contours—or the colour of contours if they are coloured differently according to height— the eye can only distinguish the rate of changes of height, and the viewer may have no clear perception of the height of any point on the map.

The same is true of images. Sixteen grey levels are difficult to distinguish one from another. Niblack (1986) suggests that a maximum of 50 grey levels are discernible on most monochrome displays. Clearly, if the purpose is to give a rendition as close as possible to the original monochrome image, then monochrome is the best approach; however, if the purpose is to identify different regions in the image as being of different types, then allocating different grey levels to them is not as effective as allocating different colours to them. On most colour displays the eye can discern at least 200 different colour shades (Niblack, 1986).

Plate 2(b) shows the captured image of part of a skeleton obtained using X-rays. X-ray images are, of necessity, monochrome. Simple edge enhancement and colour rendition using the 'purple-headed mountain' colours to represent black through to white gives a bone-like effect to the bones and a totally different effect to flesh-only areas (see Plate 2(b)–2(k)). Whether this kind of image is more helpful to diagnosis is discussed in Chapter 18.

On VGA systems it is necessary to select the 16 colours (operating in $640 \times 480$ mode) from the 262 144 available. The selection of colours is done by specifying, for each of the 16 colours to appear on the screen, the amount of red, green, and blue required. These amounts can range, for each of red, green and blue, from 0 to 63. So, for example, black would be:

| Red | Green | Blue |
|-----|-------|------|
| 0   | 0     | 0    |

and white

| Red | Green | Blue |
|-----|-------|------|
| 63  | 63    | 63   |

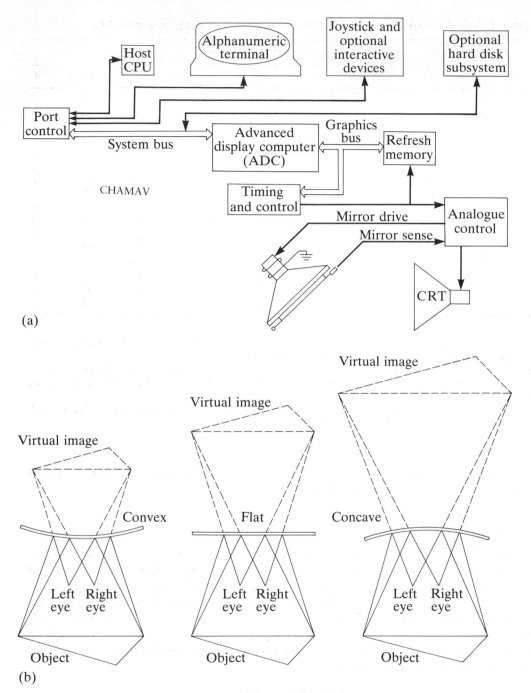

**Figure 4.10** Three-dimensional varifocal display system. (a) Space-graph three-dimensional display hardware overview. The host CPU is the VAX 11/750; the CDC disk drive provides the optional hard disk subsystem. (b) Varifocal mirror optics. Convex mirror—virtual image small and close to the viewer. Concave mirror—virtual image larger and farther from viewer. (*Source*: Kennedy and Nelson, 1987, © 1987 IEEE.)

**Table 4.3 Colour ratios for presenting monochrome images using false colouring**

|   | Monochrome | | | Purple-headed mountain | | | Green | | |
|---|---|---|---|---|---|---|---|---|---|
|   | R | G | B | R | G | B | R | G | B |
| 0 | 0 | 0 | 0 | 0 | 0 | 0 | 0 | 0 | 0 |
| 1 | 3 | 3 | 3 | 0 | 14 | 0 | 0 | 4 | 9 |
| 2 | 5 | 5 | 5 | 0 | 17 | 0 | 0 | 8 | 8 |
| 3 | 7 | 7 | 7 | 0 | 20 | 0 | 0 | 12 | 8 |
| 4 | 9 | 9 | 9 | 0 | 25 | 0 | 0 | 15 | 8 |
| 5 | 11 | 11 | 11 | 19 | 27 | 0 | 0 | 18 | 7 |
| 6 | 14 | 14 | 14 | 23 | 31 | 0 | 0 | 24 | 6 |
| 7 | 16 | 16 | 16 | 35 | 42 | 0 | 0 | 27 | 8 |
| 8 | 21 | 21 | 21 | 49 | 49 | 0 | 2 | 34 | 8 |
| 9 | 27 | 27 | 27 | 53 | 33 | 0 | 17 | 36 | 9 |
| 10 | 31 | 31 | 31 | 63 | 26 | 0 | 22 | 40 | 10 |
| 11 | 37 | 37 | 37 | 54 | 0 | 0 | 34 | 44 | 11 |
| 12 | 43 | 43 | 43 | 63 | 0 | 0 | 46 | 48 | 11 |
| 13 | 50 | 50 | 50 | 52 | 0 | 53 | 57 | 57 | 0 |
| 14 | 58 | 58 | 58 | 54 | 29 | 58 | 63 | 63 | 21 |
| 15 | 63 | 63 | 63 | 63 | 63 | 63 | 63 | 63 | 63 |

*Notes:*

1. In all three cases (0, 0, 0) = black and (63, 63, 63) = white (so that really the top of any mountain is white).

2. The green is made darker by adding increasing amounts of red.

3. The monochrome values do not increase linearly. That is because it was possible to distinguish between darker levels of grey more easily than between lighter levels, so that the difference between successive lighter levels had to be greater.

4. The purple-headed mountain starts off with dark green (colour 1), gradually changing to red (colour 10), then bringing in the blue to make purple (colour 14) before going white.

The author uses sets of 16 shown in Table 4.3 for the monochrome, 'purple-headed mountain', and continuous green ranges.

### 4.6.1 Multispectral rendition

Occasionally more than one image of the same scene may be obtained from different sensors. This is typical of satellite imagery, for example, where images of the ground may be collected by sensors for infrared, ultraviolet, and visible light. Each of these images may give useful different information about the ground in the final image. Combining the images means allocating to each of them a colour and mixing them as if they were red, green, and blue. Normally the order of wavelength of the captured images corresponds to the order to wavelength of the presented colours; using the example above, therefore, the following mapping might be made:

> ultraviolet → blue
> visible light → green
> infrared → red

This may not always be appropriate as the spectral characteristics of the eye are not equally spaced or equally strong for blue, green, and red, nor are the display strengths of these colours equally strong (see Chapter 2).

### 4.6.2 Using principal components

Difficulties occur when the number of images of the same scene is larger than three, or where only a monochrome display is available. One successful approach (see Niblack, 1986) is to combine the images into a single image according to a linear equation. For example, if there are four images $I_1, \ldots I_4$ of the same land mass taken with different sensing devices, then a best (one with the most variance) single image might be represented by the following expression:

$$0.3\ I_1 + 0.2\ I_2 + 0.05\ I_3 + 0.45\ I_4$$

Finding this 'best' combination (or principal component) can be done using a matrix method called principal components analysis. Such a combination will be said to explain, say, 45 per cent of the variance. It is then possible to find further, next-best combinations that are significantly different from the original combination and from each other, which will explain more of the variance. One monochrome image of the principal component can be viewed, or the top three principal component images can be given appropriately scaled levels of red, green, and blue, respectively, rendering the hitherto four-dimensional image as a single colour image with minimum loss of data.

## 4.7 IMAGE PROCESSORS

Specific hardware for image processing is now widely available. Add-on boards for microcomputers perform fast convolutions and fast Fourier transformations.

Image processing lends itself to parallel-processing devices, and to that end a number of manufacturers have developed full systems totally dedicated to image processing in real time.

Image processing is a valid application for an array of transputers (developed by Inmos) in that whole columns or rows of pixels can be passed to a transputer array of equal height or width as the image. One transputer then processes one pixel and passes it on. With the transputer architecture including local high-speed connections between transputers, convolutions are relatively easy to do and, if necessary, the array can be constructed in a cylindrical model so that periodic operations can also be performed.

## 4.8 EXERCISES

**4.1** Create a $16 \times 16$ patterning matrix that has a printing dot effect, i.e. when the image is dark it looks as though it is made from black, circular dots, and when it is light it is made from white circular dots.

**4.2** A $1024 \times 1024 \times 8$ bit image is to be output to a laser printer with $10 \times 8$ inch paper at 300 d.p.i. Suggest a method of implementing this.

*5*

# STATISTICAL OPERATIONS

## 5.1 INTRODUCTION

Having successfully captured an image and modelled the visible picture in memory as a bit pattern, the analysis and processing can begin. This *processing* of the image involves one or more algorithms being implemented on the image. A brief scan of the literature reveals many algorithms, some written for specific applications, some written for any application.

A generally accepted classification labels the algorithms as low-, medium-, or high-level image processing. This reflects both the nearness of the algorithm to the bit image, and the sequence of algorithms that are likely to be implemented on an image in a typical processing sequence: low first, then medium, then high.

Low-level processing is concerned with work at the binary image level, typically creating a second 'better' image from the first by changing the presentation of the image, removing unwanted data, and enhancing wanted data.

Medium-level processing is about the identification of significant shapes, regions or points from the binary image. Little or no prior knowledge is built in to this process, so while the work may not be wholly at a binary level, the algorithms are still not usually application specific.

High-level processing interfaces the image to some knowledge base. This associates shapes discovered during the previous level of processing with known shapes of real objects. The results from the algorithms at this level are passed on to non-image procedures, which make decisions about actions following from the analysis of the image.

This chapter, and Chapter 6, deal with low-level processing operations. The algorithms in this chapter are independent of the position of the pixels, while the algorithms in Chapter 6 are dependent on pixel position.

The building blocks of geometric object recognition can be done at this level by searching for and enhancing edges in the picture, as between light and dark patches or different colours.

**Note on noise** Ideally, no useful data is lost during the processing, but data that is *not* useful is usually difficult to filter out. For example, an image may be collected with 'noise', possibly from poor capture equipment or poor transmission. This noise could take many forms but typically there will be pixels that have been set to particularly high or low values in some random or regular scattering across the image. These rogue values need to be 'filtered' out, i.e. some algorithm needs to be applied to the image to produce a second image with these values missing. Averaging can do this effectively though there are other methods—see, for example, Chapter 13—where filtering can be done interactively in the frequency domain.

Noise can be introduced into an image for experimental purposes. The author uses the following routine:

```
printf("Give noise value : ");
scanf("%d",&i);
printf("Give percentage of snow required : ");
scanf("%d",&j);
for(sc_ptr=&screen[0][0]; sc_ptr<sc_end;sc_ptr++)
if(random(100)<j)*sc_ptr=i;
```

## 5.2 GREY-LEVEL TRANSFORMATIONS

It is easy to count the number of pixels at each grey level in an image, for example, in C:

```
for(row=0;row<rowmax;row++)
for(col=0;col<colmax;col++)count[image[row][col]]++;
```

The array count [ ] can then be plotted to represent a histogram for an image as the number of pixels at particular grey levels. The histogram can yield useful information about the nature of an image. It may be possible to identify a bias towards the lower intensity levels, for example, with little or no use of the high intensity levels. Normally this is unsatisfactory—like having the brightness 'turned down' on the television set.

### Technique 5.1  Global alterations in brightness
USE  To lighten or darken an image.

OPERATION  A constant can be added to or subtracted from all the image pixels giving the effect of the brightness being 'turned up' or 'turned down'.

CODE

```
for(row=0;row<rowmax;row++)
for(col=0;col<colmax;col++)image[row][col]+=constant;
```

See, for example, Figure 5.1.

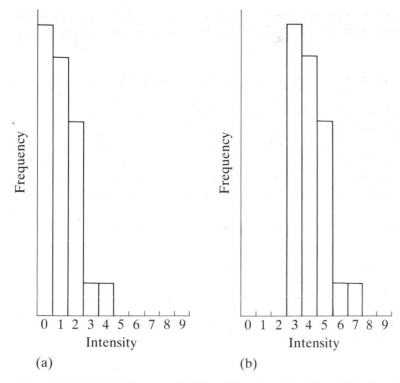

**Figure 5.1** (a) Original histogram. (b) After adding the constant 3 to all pixels.

### Technique 5.2  Thresholding

USE  To remove the grey-level trends in an image, to make the grey-level regions more discrete, to 'segment' (or split into distinct parts) an image.

OPERATION  Thresholding normally refers to setting all the grey levels below a certain level to zero; or above a certain level to a maximum brightness level. The maximum brightness will be 255 on an 8-bit plane system, 15 on a 4-bit plane, 1023 on a 10-bit plane, and so on.

CODE

```
for(row=0;row<rowmax;row++)
for(col=0;col<colmax;col++)
  if(image[row][col]>threshold)
    image[row][col]=MAX;
  else
    image[row][col]=MIN;
```

This will screen out unwanted variations in an image where all those variations are around, above, or below a certain grey level. A good example is a simple processing of a text image. Black text on white paper is likely to give a bimodal histogram. If the two populations of pixels (the black ones and the white ones) are so dissimilar that no background pixels could be mistaken for text pixels, then it is sensible to allocate to the text pixels one single grey level, and to the background a different grey level—giving a binary image. It then remains to identify the grey-level break in the histogram at which no errors are made in the thresholding (see the image in Fig. 5.2).

### 5.2.1 Thresholding errors

Rarely is it possible to identify a perfect grey-level break. Normally errors are made in the classification of pixels as background or foreground as soon as any thresholding is done. When classifying a range of grey levels into one set, two types of error can be made:

> Type 1    not all pixels are caught that should be included.
> Type 2    some pixels caught should not be in the group.

The choice of threshold level may aim to balance these two types of error, but there are circumstances when it is more favourable for there to be more of one or of the other.

> A military analysis of photographs found it difficult to distinguish clearly between the silvering on the tops of missile silo covers and silvering on the tops of spherical gas tanks.
>
> If the purpose of the analysis is to remove *all* silos by bombing, then the thresholding must err on including some of the gas tanks; however, if the analysis is to count how many of each there are likely to be, it is sensible to go for an equal number of type 1 and type 2 errors.
>
> Finally, if the strategy is to 'knock out' a few silos without doing any damage to other property, then the choice of threshold will be to exclude all gas tanks, consequently also excluding some silo covers.

Thresholding can be used to create a binary image. A number of morphological operations including erosion and dilation can be particularly useful in the enhancement and classification of blob shapes in such images. While these operations can be done on $n$-ary grey-level images, thresholding is sometimes performed to create an initial binary environment for logical operations to be more meaningful.

### Technique 5.3  Bunching (sometimes also referred to as quantizing)

USE  To reduce the number of different grey levels in an image, to segment the image, to remove unwanted grey-level gradations.

OPERATION  Close grey levels are combined, thus removing unwanted variations in data. This can be done by inspecting the histogram and combining close groups into single grey levels, or performed automatically by identifying a set of grey levels that will be allowed in the final image, and changing the grey level in every pixel to its nearest allowed value. For example, the initial image

| | | | | | | | | | | | |
|---|---|---|---|---|---|---|---|---|---|---|---|
| 1 | 8 | 4 | 3 | 6 | 2 | 5 | 2 | 8 | 4 | 6 | 2 | 5 |
| 0 | 3 | 8 | 3 | 6 | 5 | 4 | 0 | 3 | 8 | 3 | 8 | 7 |
| 3 | 8 | 4 | 7 | 6 | 2 | 8 | 3 | 7 | 3 | 7 | 6 | 1 |
| 0 | 9 | 8 | 0 | 5 | 4 | 8 | 5 | 9 | 3 | 7 | 2 | 9 |

gives the following histogram:

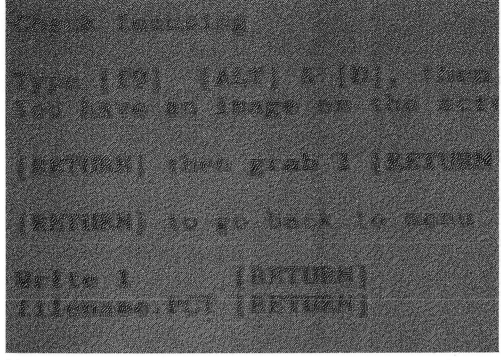

(a)

Check focusing

Type [[9] [ALT] & [D], then
You have an image on the scr

|RETURN| then grab 1 |RETURN

|RETURN| to go back to menu

Write 1          |RETURN|
filename.PCT |RETURN|

(b)

**Figure 5.2** (a) Original text image. (b) Binary text image after thresholding up and down (splitting).

```
0   ****
1   **
2   *****
3   *********
4   *****
5   *****
6   *****
7   *****
8   *********
9   ***
```

Grey levels allowed in final image: 0, 3, 6 and 9. Note that these grey levels will have either been discovered by inspection of the histogram or programmed into the system. Note also that the bunch sizes are not the same, e.g. new grey level 0 will attract from old grey levels 0 and 1 only, whereas new grey level 3 will attract from grey levels 2, 3, and 4.

```
0  9  3  3  6  3  6  3  9  3  6  3  6
0  3  9  3  6  6  3  0  3  9  3  9  6
3  9  3  6  6  3  9  3  6  3  6  6  0
0  9  9  0  6  3  9  6  9  3  6  3  9
```

Giving a histogram of

```
0   ******
1
2
3   *******************
4
5
6   ***************
7
8
9   ************
```

### CODE

An equal bunch size can be implemented using the following code [this always rounds down as it stands, so that with the above example and a bunch size of 3 the new 0, 3, 6, and 9 frequencies will contain the frequencies from the old (0, 1, 2), (3, 4, 5), (6, 7, 8), and (9) groups]:

```
for(row=0;row<rowmax;row++)
  for(col=0;col<colmax;col++)
    image[row][col]=(char)((int)image[row][col]/bunchsize*bunchsize);
```

### Technique 5.4 Splitting

USE To increase the difference between two groups of grey levels so that the contrast between segments composed of one group or the other is enhanced.

OPERATION Grey levels can be bunched in more than one direction, leaving a wider gap in the middle. Again this would normally be done by inspection, effectively rounding the grey levels up if they are in one range and down if they are in another.

EXAMPLE The characters on a car number-plate are at grey level 98 and the background of the number-plate is at grey level 99. This would be indistinguishable to the eye. The rest of the image might still give a flat grey-level histogram but now, instead of levelling, we want to split the histogram, pushing 99 up to 120 and 98 down to 80, say. This will give the picture less contrast in other areas but a better contrast around the number plate.

These techniques are more useful when one *part* of the histogram needs to be manipulated while the other is left alone.

Automatic selection of grey level for splitting can be done. The following technique is due to Otsu (1979):

**Technique 5.5  Automatic selection of grey level for splitting**
USE To find the best grey level for splitting—usually for thresholding to black and to white.

Application See Chapter 18—optical character recognition (OCR) of Chinese characters.

OPERATION If $f(g)$ is the number of pixels at grey level $g$ and $t(g)$ is the actual number of pixels *at grey level g or less* in the image, i.e.

$$t(g) = \sum_{i=0}^{g} f(i)$$

If the number of pixels under consideration is $P$ (normally $N \times M$) and $m(g)$ is the mean grey level for only those pixels containing grey levels between zero and $g$, i.e.

$$m(g) = \frac{\sum_{i=0}^{g} g \cdot f(i)}{t(g)}$$

And if the maximum number of grey levels is $G$ $(0, \ldots, G-1)$, then evaluate the following equation:

$$T = \max \left\{ \underbrace{\frac{t(g)}{P - t(g)}}_{\text{part A}} \cdot \underbrace{[m(g) - m(G-1)]^2}_{\text{part B}} \right\} - 1$$

EXAMPLE See Table 5.1 which suggests a suitable break at grey level $\max(A \times B) - 1 = T = 4.$

As shown above, grey-level histograms are not necessarily unimodal (one-humped). Bimodal (two-humped like the one in the example of Technique 5.3) and multimodal

**Table 5.1**

| Histogram | $f(g)$ | $t(g)$ | $g \cdot f(g)$ | $\Sigma g \cdot f(g)$ | $m(g)$ | A | B | A × B |
|---|---|---|---|---|---|---|---|---|
| 0 **** | 4 | 4 | 0 | 0 | 0 | 0.08 | 23.04 | 0.18 |
| 1 ** | 2 | 6 | 2 | 2 | 0.3 | 0.13 | 20.25 | 2.83 |
| 2 ***** | 5 | 11 | 10 | 12 | 1.1 | 0.27 | 13.69 | 3.70 |
| 3 ********* | 9 | 20 | 27 | 39 | 2 | 0.63 | 7.84 | 4.94 |
| 4 ***** | 5 | 25 | 20 | 59 | 2.4 | 0.93 | 5.76 | 5.36 |
| 5 ***** | 5 | 30 | 25 | 84 | 2.8 | 1.36 | 4.00 | 5.44 (max) |
| 6 ***** | 5 | 35 | 30 | 114 | 3.3 | 2.06 | 2.25 | 4.64 |
| 7 ***** | 5 | 40 | 35 | 149 | 3.7 | 3.33 | 1.21 | 4.03 |
| 8 ********* | 9 | 49 | 72 | 221 | 4.5 | 16.33 | 0.09 | 1.47 |
| 9 *** | 3 | 52 | 27 | 248 | 4.8 | $\infty$ | | |

$$N \times M = 52$$

(many-humped) histograms suggest that different techniques applied to different parts of the grey-level histogram may be useful.

> In a view looking out of a window, the area around the window inside the room was dark while the area of the window looking out was very light. A histogram of the whole view was clearly bimodal—two humps, one representing the outside and one the inside.

In this case if more picture definition is required, then the spread of pixels needs to be widened for both inside and outside; however, to do this requires a 'segmenting' of the picture into two parts. With the picture described above, probably the easiest way to segment it is to do it by hand, i.e. to create one rectangular picture of the outside view and a second picture (a rectangle with a rectangular hole in it) for the inside view. It is then possible to treat each part (or segment) of the picture in a different way so that more detail will become apparent in each segment. The results can then be added together giving a much improved picture.

For instance, the brightness can be 'turned up' for the dark area simply by adding a constant so that it becomes as bright as the light area. This changes the original histogram from bimodal to unimodal. This, however, does not improve the contrast within either area.

All of the above techniques are variations on a single general image transformation.

### Technique 5.6 General grey-level transformations

USE Combining the functions above into one operation. This is also useful as a single tool in a set of software tools for image processing since it does any one of the above on any part of the histogram.

OPERATION A function $F(g)$, say, can be specified which transforms any grey level $g$ to a new grey level $q$, say. It is useful to see this in two dimensions with the $x$-axis representing the old grey level and the $y$-axis the new grey level. Software to do this transformation allows the user to view the original histogram of grey levels on the $x$-axis and draw a possible piecewise curve, seeing the resulting transformations as a histogram

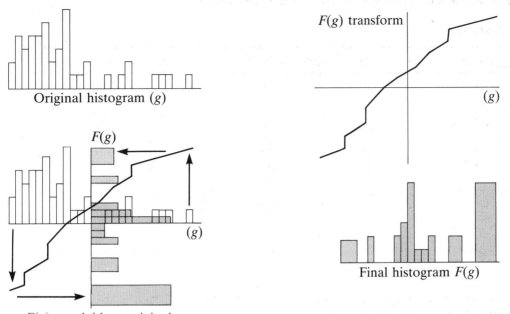

Original histogram (*g*)

*F*(*g*) transform

(*g*)

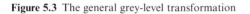

*F*(*g*)

(*g*)

*F*(*g*) overlaid on original

Final histogram *F*(*g*)

**Figure 5.3** The general grey-level transformation

on the *y*-axis. The effect of this can be to combine bunching, splitting, and thresholding as required.

Formally:    $q = F(g)$

EXAMPLE  Figure 5.3 gives an example of this technique.

## 5.3 HISTOGRAM EQUALIZATION

It is often valuable to find a function $F(g)$ that will enhance the general *contrast* in the image, spreading the distribution of grey levels wider and more evenly, ideally to an equal number of pixels per grey level—though this cannot be achieved exactly. An approximation to the function can be identified by inspection of the histogram but an analytical approach is preferable. This is called histogram equalization.

### Technique 5.7  Histogram equalization

USE  Very wide use, a most important part of the software for any image processing. It improves contrast. Can be used on a whole image or just on a part of an image.

THEORY  Given the number of pixels in a whole image is rowmax × colmax, and the number of grey levels over which the spread is required is g_levels, then an ideal histogram would be flat with the same number of pixels at each grey level:

$$\text{ideal number of pixels at each grey level} = \frac{\text{rowmax} \times \text{colmax}}{\text{g\_levels}}$$

Now, intuitively, we want to allocate the pixels with the lowest grey level in the old image to grey level 0 in the new image, i.e.

$$F(0) = 0, \text{ where } F(\text{old grey level}) = \text{new grey level}$$

If as a result of this allocation the new grey level 0 has got less than its 'fair share' of pixels, we allocate the pixels at the next lowest grey level in the old image also to grey level 0 in the new image. When grey level 0 in the new image has got something approaching its 'fair share' of pixels we move up to grey level 1 and operate the same algorithm starting with the *unallocated* pixels that have the lowest grey level in the old image.

It may be that an early allocation of pixels already gives grey level 0 in the new image twice its fair share of pixels, in which case, in effect, it has also used up the allocation to grey level 1. If so, we ignore grey level 1 in the new image and move onto grey level 2.

The algorithm proceeds like this until all the old grey levels pixels have been allocated to new grey levels.

Formally the mapping of old grey level to new grey level is as follows:

OPERATION  If $t(g)$ is the *actual* number of pixels at old grey level *g or less*, then

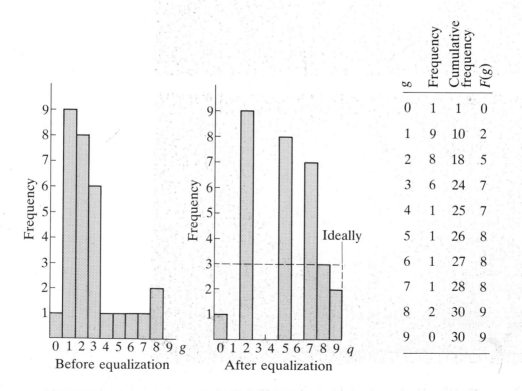

| $g$ | Frequency | Cumulative frequency | $F(g)$ |
|---|---|---|---|
| 0 | 1 | 1 | 0 |
| 1 | 9 | 10 | 2 |
| 2 | 8 | 18 | 5 |
| 3 | 6 | 24 | 7 |
| 4 | 1 | 25 | 7 |
| 5 | 1 | 26 | 8 |
| 6 | 1 | 27 | 8 |
| 7 | 1 | 28 | 8 |
| 8 | 2 | 30 | 9 |
| 9 | 0 | 30 | 9 |

**Figure 5.4** Stages in histogram equalization.

$$F(g) = \max \left\{ 0, \text{round} \left( \frac{\text{g\_levels} \times t(g)}{\text{rowmax} \times \text{colmax}} \right) - 1 \right\}$$

EXAMPLE  Figure 5.4 gives an example of this technique.

Clearly, the image does not contain more data as a result of histogram equalization, the data is simply presented better. The effect of histogram equalization, then, is to vary the contrast in an image by spreading the pixel grey levels across the whole of the grey-level range instead of just a small subset of it. This represents a fundamental method of improving the clarity of any image (see the images in Fig. 5.5).

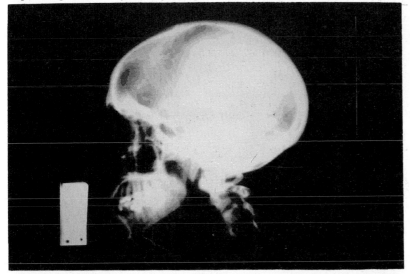

(a)

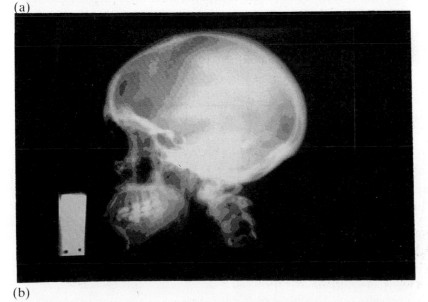

(b)

**Figure 5.5** (a) Original image as captured. (b) After histogram equalization. Note increase in detail around neck, teeth and nose, for example.

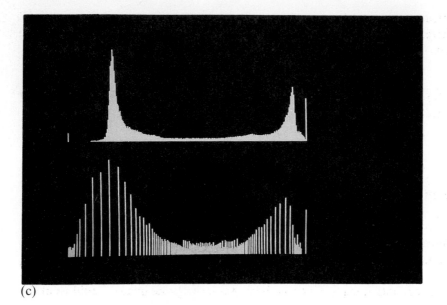

(c)

**Figure 5.5** (*continued*) (c) Upper histogram: original image. Lower histogram: histogram-equalized image. Note how the high values have been spaced apart and the low values combined (giving a shorter and higher valley in this case).

## 5.4 MULTI-IMAGE OPERATIONS

Occasionally it is useful to prepare a new image from a number of previous images. The classical example of this is the removal of background vignetting.

> An image consisting of a shape made from off-white paper laid on a sheet of white paper was captured with poor lighting. The poor lighting resulted in the edges of the white paper taking on the same grey level as the off-white paper shape. Thus processing became particularly difficult as it was not possible to distinguish between the shape and the paper.
>
> One solution was to improve the lighting so as to give, as near as possible, even lighting across the whole paper. This proved to be surprisingly difficult to achieve.
>
> The preferred solution was to capture one image as above, with the faulty lighting and a second image of the pure white paper without the shape on it but using the same lighting shades. The first image was then subtracted from the second giving a dark grey object on a black background.

### 5.4.1 Background subtraction

Background subtraction can be used to identify movement between two images and to remove background shading if it is present on both images. The images should be captured as near as possible in time without any change of lighting conditions. If the object being removed is darker than the background, then the image with the object is subtracted from the image without the object. If the object is lighter than the background, the opposite is done.

**Technique 5.8  Background subtraction**
USE  To remove light shading or discover movement from one image to another.

THEORY Subtraction practically means that the grey level in each pixel in one image is subtracted from the grey level in the corresponding pixel in the other image. This, ideally, means

$$\text{result} = x - y$$

where $x \geq y$; however, if $x < y$ the result is negative which, if values are held as unsigned characters (bytes), actually means a high positive value. For example:

$$-1 \quad \text{is held as } 255$$
$$-2 \quad \text{is held as } 254$$
and so on

A better operation for background subtraction is

$$\text{result} = |x - y|$$

(i.e. $x - y$ ignoring the sign of the result) in which case it does not matter whether the object is dark or light compared to the background (see images in Fig. 5.6).

OPERATION Collect both images. If this is shading removal, one image should be of the

(a)

**Figure 5.6** (a) Card—background only.

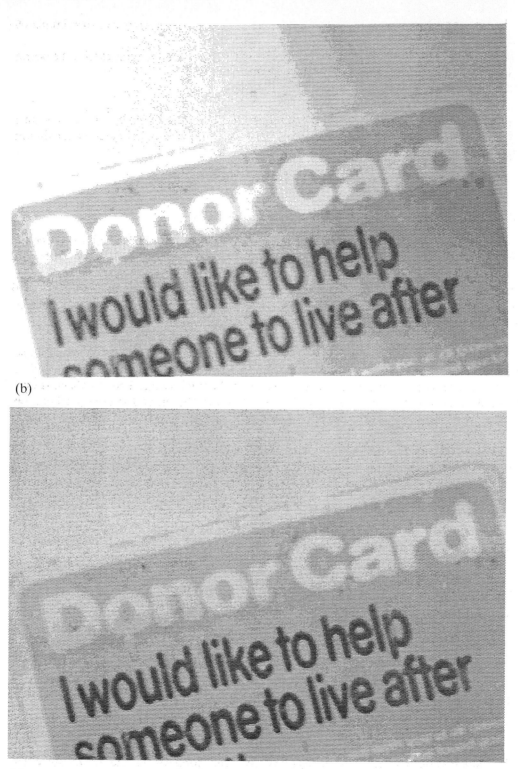

(b)

(c)

 **Figure 5.6** (*continued*) (b) Card before background subtraction. (c) Result of background subtraction.

shading on a pure white background. This will form image $X$. The image with the object in will form image $Y$. For each pixel calculate

$$\text{abs}(X - Y)$$

(i.e. the same as $|X - Y|$). This will give a negative image of the object. In order to return the image to a positive, the resulting grey level has to be subtracted from the maximum grey level, call it MAX. Combining these two gives

$$\text{new image} = \text{MAX} - \text{abs}(X - Y)$$

### 5.4.2 Multi-image averaging

A series of poor images of the same scene can be used to give a better quality image by using similar operations to the windowing operations described in Chapter 6. For example, a simple average of all the grey levels in corresponding pixels will give a significantly enhanced picture over any one of the originals. Alternatively, if the original images contain pixels with noise, these can be filtered out and replaced with correct values from another shot. See example in Chapter 18.

**Multi-image modal filtering** Modal filtering of a sequence of images can remove noise most effectively. Here the most popular valued grey level for each corresponding pixel in a sequence of images is plotted as the pixel value in the final image. The drawback is that the whole sequence of images needs to be stored before the mode for each pixel can be found.

**Multi-image median filtering** Median filtering is similar except that for each pixel, the grey levels in the corresponding pixels in the sequence of images are ordered, and the middle one is chosen. Again the whole sequence of images needs to be stored, and a substantial sort operation is required.

**Multi-image averaging filtering** Recursive filtering does not require each previous image to be stored. It uses a weighted averaging technique to produce one image from a sequence of images.

#### Technique 5.9 Recursive filtering
USE To improve a sequence of still images—reducing noise by producing new images that correspond to weighted averages of previous images.

OPERATION It is assumed that newly collected images are available from a frame store with a fixed delay between each image.

1. Setting up—copy an image into a separate frame store, dividing all the grey levels by an integer, $n$. Add to that image $n - 1$ subsequent images, the grey levels of which are also divided by $n$. You should now have the average of the first $n$ images in the frame store.
2. Recursion—for every new image, multiply the contents of the frame store by $(n - 1)/n$ and the new image by $1/n$, add them together and put the result back into the frame store.

THEORY At set-up the frame store contains

$$\sum_{i=1}^{n} \frac{I(i)}{n}$$

Then after many images the following steady state is created:

$$\frac{I(m)}{n} + \frac{(n-1)}{n} \left\{ \frac{I(m-1)}{n} + \frac{(n-1)}{n} \left\{ \frac{I(m-2)}{n} + \frac{(n-1)}{n} \left\{ \frac{I(m-3)}{n} \left\{ \cdots \right\} \right\} \right\} \right\}$$

$$= \sum I(m-i) \cdot \frac{(n-1)^i}{n^i} \qquad i = 0, \ldots, m$$

This is a particularly useful technique in image processing because it does not require more than one summing frame store. An arguably better averaging technique might be to sum the equally weighted previous $n$ images and remove the last but $n$th from the sum. In order to do this, $n$ frame stores are necessary (using a lot of space in main memory) so that the correct subtraction value is kept. Then, $n$ iterations after the frame has been added to the sum, it can also be subtracted from the sum.

EXAMPLE With the recursive technique: if, for example, $n = 10$, then the new image would be weighted 0.1 and the sum of the old images, 0.9. Table 5.2 illustrates this for value of $n = 10$, $n = 5$, and $n = 2$. Clearly a larger value of $n$ gives old image values a higher weighting in the sum. Smaller values of $n$ give smaller weightings to older images.

**Table 5.2**

|              | $n = 10$ | $n = 5$ | $n = 2$ |
| ------------ | -------- | ------- | ------- |
| New one      | 0.100    | 0.200   | 0.500   |
| last one     | 0.090    | 0.128   | 0.250   |
| last but 1   | 0.081    | 0.102   | 0.125   |
| last but 2   | 0.073    | 0.080   | 0.063   |
| last but 3   | 0.066    | 0.066   | 0.031   |
| last but 4   | 0.059    | 0.052   | 0.016   |
| last but 5   | 0.053    | 0.042   | 0.008   |
| last but 6   | 0.048    | 0.034   | 0.004   |
| last but 7   | 0.043    | 0.027   | 0.002   |
| last but 8   | 0.039    | 0.021   | 0.001   |
| last but 9   | 0.035    | 0.017   | 0.000   |
| and so on    |          |         |         |

APPLICATION Electron microscopy (see Chapter 18).

## 5.5 EXERCISES

**5.1** Write code to implement a piecewise linear transformation on a grey-level histogram, with the transformation designed using graphical techniques.

**5.2** Implement histogram equalization on (i) a grey-level image and (ii) a colour image.

**5.3** Write code to implement a selected multi-image filter.

*6*

# SPATIAL OPERATIONS AND TRANSFORMATIONS

## 6.1 INTRODUCTION

Whereas the last chapter dealt with low-level operations using statistical measures, this chapter combines those operations with operations on single images that deal with pixels and their neighbours (spatial operations).

The techniques introduced in this chapter include spatial filters (normally removing noise by reference to the neighbouring pixel values), weighted averaging of pixel areas (convolutions), and comparing areas on an image with known pixel area shapes so as to find shapes in images (correlation). In addition, there is a short discussion on edge detection (which is covered more fully in Chapter 7) and an introduction to the detection of 'interest points'.

## 6.2 SPATIALLY DEPENDENT TRANSFORMATIONS

A spatially dependent transformation is one that depends on its position in the image. Under such a transformation, the histogram of grey levels does not retain its original shape: grey-level frequencies change depending on the spread of grey levels across the picture. Instead of $F(g)$ the spatially dependent function is $F(g, X, Y)$, so, for example

An image was captured using a weak ambient light together with some sort of point light source giving the effect of a dark picture at the bottom right and a light picture at the top left. The following function, discovered by inspection, was used to even out the lighting:

$$F(g, X, Y) = \frac{X}{20} + \frac{Y}{20} - 5$$

Simply thresholding an image that has different lighting levels is unlikely to be as effective as processing away the gradations, by implementing an algorithm to make the ambient lighting constant, and then thresholding. Without this preprocessing the result after thresholding is even more difficult to process since a spatially invariant thresholding function, used to threshold down to a constant, leaves a real mix of some pixels still spatially dependent and some not.

There are a number of other techniques for removal of this kind of gradation.

### Technique 6.1  Gradation removal by averaging
USE  To remove gradual shading across a single image.

OPERATION  Subdivide the picture into rectangles, evaluate the mean for each rectangle and also for the whole picture. Then to each rectangle of pixels add or subtract a constant so as to give the rectangles across the picture the same mean.

This may not be the best approach if the image is, say, a text image. Clearly, a blank area of paper does not need to be given the same mean as an area that includes text.

More sophistication can be built in by equalizing the means and standard deviations, or, if the picture is bimodal (as, for example, in the case of a text image) the bimodality of each rectangle can be standardized. Experience suggests, however, that the more sophisticated the technique, the more marginal is the improvement!

### Technique 6.2  Masking
USE  To remove or negate part of an image so that that part is no longer visible. It may be part of a whole process that is aimed at changing an image by, for example, putting an object into an image that was not there before. This can be done by masking out part of an old image, and then adding the image of the object to the area in the old image that has been masked out.

OPERATION  General transformations may be performed on part of a picture—for instance, ANDing an image with a binary mask amounts to thresholding to zero at the maximum grey level for part of the picture, without any thresholding on the rest.

## 6.3  TEMPLATES AND CONVOLUTION

Template operations are very useful as elementary image filters. They can be used to enhance certain features, de-enhance others, identify edges, smooth out noise, or discover previously known shapes in an image.

### Technique 6.3  Convolution
USE  Widely used in many operations. An essential part of the software kit for an image processor.

OPERATION  A template is an array of values. This is placed step by step over the image, at each step creating a new window in the image the same size as the template, and then associating with each element in the template a corresponding pixel in the image. Typically, the template element is multiplied by the corresponding image pixel grey level and the sum of these results, across the whole template, is recorded as a pixel grey level in a new image. This 'shift, add, multiply' operation is termed the 'convolution' of the template with the image.

If $T(x, y)$ is the template $(n \times m)$ and $I(X, Y)$ is the image $(N \times M)$, then the convolving of $T$ with $I$ is written as

$$T \cdot I(X, Y) = \sum_{i=0}^{n-1} \sum_{j=0}^{m-1} T(i, j) \cdot I(X + i, Y + j)$$

Note: In fact this term is the cross-correlation term rather than the convolution term, which should be accurately represented by

$$T * I(X, Y) = \sum_{i=0}^{n-1} \sum_{j=0}^{m-1} T(i, j) \cdot I(X - i, Y - j)$$

However, the term 'convolution' has been loosely interpreted to mean cross-correlation, and in most image-processing literature convolution will refer to the first formula rather than the second. As will be seen in Chapter 14, there is a a problem with this terminology when, in the frequency domain, convolution is 'real' convolution rather than cross-correlation.

Often the template is not allowed to shift off the edge of the image, so the resulting image will normally be smaller than the first image. For example:

| Template | | Image | | | | | Result | | | | |
|---|---|---|---|---|---|---|---|---|---|---|---|
| | | 1 | 1 | 3 | 3 | 4 | 2 | 5 | 7 | 6 | * |
| 1 0 | * | 1 | 1 | 4 | 4 | 3 | 2 | 4 | 7 | 7 | * |
| 0 1 | | 2 | 1 | 3 | 3 | 3 | 3 | 2 | 7 | 7 | * |
| | | 1 | 1 | 1 | 4 | 4 | * | * | * | * | * |

* = no value

Here the $2 \times 2$ template is operating on a $4 \times 5$ image, giving a $3 \times 4$ result. The value 5, say, in the result, is obtained from

$$(1 \times 1) + (0 \times 3) + (0 \times 1) + (1 \times 4)$$

In this specific '5' case, the template has been placed over the image with the 1 in the top left of the template corresponding with the rightmost 1 on the top row of the image. Convention places the result from the calculation into the pixel that corresponded with the top left of the template, though there are better arguments for placing the result in the centre of the template if it has a centre (as in $3 \times 3$, $3 \times 5$, etc.). The former convention is easier to program, particularly when variable sized templates can be implemented in software. This convention is used throughout this book.

The result need not always be smaller than the image. It may be meaningful to visualize the image as wrapped around the back of a ball. The template can then be shifted off the end of the image on the left, say, with part of it reappearing on the right of the image. Such an operation is called periodic convolution; without the wrap it is called aperiodic convolution. Normally the aperiodic convolution array is given zeros for space-filling rather than asterisks. This restores the array to its original size so that further processing with unchanged array size can continue.

Mathematically, convolution has a similar effect to correlation (see Technique 6.6), though the assumptions required for it to have exactly the same effect cannot always be made.

Convolution is a costly enterprise in computer time. The larger the template and the larger the image, the more the work has to be done. If the image is $M \times M$ and the template $N \times N$, then the number of multiplications is of the order $M^2 N^2$. For example, if the image is 512 square and the template $16 \times 16$, then about 32 million multiplications are required. This is not feasible in real time (i.e. 25 such calculations per second) without dedicated hardware. An alternative is to transform both template and image into the frequency domain and multiply them element for element. The convolution then requires only 256 000 multiplications, but the Fourier conversion itself is so costly that unless a number of convolutions on the same image are to be done, then with an image of $512 \times 512$ the template would have to be $32 \times 32$ to justify the transformation. (See Chapter 14, Fig. 14.2.)

### 6.3.1 Common templates

Just as the moving average of a time series tends to smooth the points, so a moving average (moving up/down and left-right) smooths out any sudden changes in pixel values, removing noise at the expense of introducing some blurring of the image (see also recursive filtering in Chapter 5). The classical $3 \times 3$ template

$$
\begin{array}{ccc}
1 & 1 & 1 \\
1 & 1 & 1 \\
1 & 1 & 1
\end{array}
$$

does this but with little sophistication. Essentially, each resulting pixel is the sum of a square of nine original pixel values. It does this without regard to the position of the pixels in the group of nine. Such filters are termed 'low-pass' filters since they remove high frequencies in an image (i.e. sudden changes in pixel values while retaining (or *passing* through) the low frequencies, i.e. the gradual changes in pixel values.

An alternative smoothing template might be

$$
\begin{array}{ccc}
1 & 3 & 1 \\
3 & 16 & 3 \\
1 & 3 & 1
\end{array}
$$

This introduces weights such that half of the result is got from the centre pixel, 3/8ths from the above, below, left, and right pixels, and 1/8th from the corner pixels—those that are most distant from the centre pixel.

A high-pass filter aims to remove gradual changes and enhance the sudden changes. Such a template might be (the Laplacian)

$$
\begin{array}{ccc}
0 & -1 & 0 \\
-1 & 4 & -1 \\
0 & -1 & 0
\end{array}
$$

**Table 6.1**

| Image | | | | | After high pass | | | After low pass | | |
|---|---|---|---|---|---|---|---|---|---|---|
| 0 | 0 | 0 | 0 | 0 | 2 | 1 | 2 | 4 | 6 | 4 |
| 0 | 1 | 1 | 1 | 0 | 1 | 0 | 1 | 6 | 9 | 6 |
| 0 | 1 | 1 | 1 | 0 | 1 | 0 | 1 | 6 | 9 | 6 |
| 0 | 1 | 1 | 1 | 0 | 1 | − 5 | 1 | 11 | 14 | 11 |
| 0 | 1 | 1 | 1 | 0 | − 4 | 20 | − 4 | 11 | 14 | 11 |
| 0 | 1 | 6 | 1 | 0 | 2 | − 4 | 2 | 9 | 11 | 9 |
| 0 | 1 | 1 | 1 | 0 | | | | | | |
| 0 | 0 | 0 | 0 | 0 | | | | | | |

Here the template sums to zero, so if it is placed over a window containing a constant set of values, the result will be zero. However, if the centre pixel differs markedly from its surroundings, then the result will be even more marked.

Table 6.1 shows the operation of the following high-pass and low-pass filters on an image:

High-pass filter    Low-pass filter

$$
\begin{array}{ccc}
0 & -1 & 0 \\
-1 & 4 & -1 \\
0 & -1 & 0
\end{array}
\qquad
\begin{array}{ccc}
1 & 1 & 1 \\
1 & 1 & 1 \\
1 & 1 & 1
\end{array}
$$

Here, after the high pass, the to half of the image has its edges noted, leaving the middle at zero, while the bottom half of the image jumps from − 4 and − 5 to 20, corresponding to the original noise value of 6.

After the low pass, there is a steady increase to the centre and the noise point has been shared across a number of values, so that its original existence is almost lost.

Both high-pass and low-pass filters have their uses.

A 'snowy' picture captured from a television set with a poor aerial had the snow smoothed into the background using a low-pass filter.

A high-pass filter enhanced edges and removed background in a poorly lit image, and so clarified some difficult to read text.

See the images in Fig. 6.1.

### 6.3.2 Edge detection

Templates such as

$$
\begin{array}{cc}
-1 & -1 \\
1 & 1
\end{array}
\qquad \text{and} \qquad
\begin{array}{cc}
-1 & 1 \\
-1 & 1
\end{array}
$$

A                             B

highlight edges in an area as shown in Table 6.2. Clearly B has identified the vertical edge and A the horizontal edge. Combining the two, say by adding the result A + B above, gives both horizontal and vertical edges.

See Chapter 7 for a fuller discussion of edge detectors.

(a)

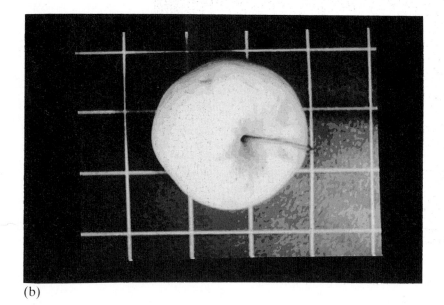

(b)

**Figure 6.1** (a) Original apple. (b) Blurred with low-pass averaging filter.

$$
\begin{array}{cccc}
1 & 1 & 1 & 1 \\
1 & 1 & 1 & 1 \\
1 & 1 & 1 & 1 \\
1 & 1 & 1 & 1
\end{array}
$$

(c)

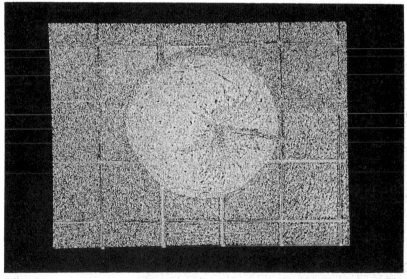

(d)

**Figure 6.1** (*continued*)  (c) With 'Mexican hat' filter (less blurring).

$$
\begin{array}{ccc}
1 & 2 & 1 \\
2 & 4 & 2 \\
1 & 2 & 1
\end{array}
$$

(d) With second-order filter.

$$
\begin{array}{rrrrr}
1 & 1 & 1 & 1 & 1 \\
1 & 3 & -3 & -3 & 1 \\
1 & -3 & 8 & -3 & 1 \\
1 & -3 & -3 & -3 & 1 \\
1 & 1 & 1 & 1 & 1
\end{array}
$$

**Table 6.2**

| Image | | | | | | After A | | | | | After B | | | | | A + B | | | | |
|---|---|---|---|---|---|---|---|---|---|---|---|---|---|---|---|---|---|---|---|---|
| 0 | 0 | 0 | 0 | 0 | 0 | 0 | 0 | 0 | 0 | 0 | 0 | 0 | 0 | 0 | 0 | 0 | 0 | 0 | 0 | 0 |
| 0 | 0 | 0 | 0 | 0 | 0 | 0 | 0 | 0 | 0 | 0 | 0 | 0 | 0 | 0 | 0 | 0 | 0 | 0 | 0 | 0 |
| 0 | 0 | 0 | 0 | 0 | 0 | 0 | 3 | 6 | 6 | 6 | 0 | 3 | 0 | 0 | 0 | 0 | 6 | 6 | 6 | 6 |
| 0 | 0 | 3 | 3 | 3 | 3 | 0 | 0 | 0 | 0 | 0 | 0 | 6 | 0 | 0 | 0 | 0 | 6 | 0 | 0 | 0 |
| 0 | 0 | 3 | 3 | 3 | 3 | 0 | 0 | 0 | 0 | 0 | 0 | 6 | 0 | 0 | 0 | 0 | 6 | 0 | 0 | 0 |
| 0 | 0 | 3 | 3 | 3 | 3 | 0 | 0 | 0 | 0 | 0 | 0 | 6 | 0 | 0 | 0 | 0 | 6 | 0 | 0 | 0 |
| 0 | 0 | 3 | 3 | 3 | 3 | | | | | | | | | | | | | | | |

### 6.3.3 Storing the convolution results

Results from templating normally need examination and transformation before storage. In most application packages, images are held as one array of bytes (or three arrays of bytes for colour). Each entry in the array corresponds to a pixel on the image. The byte unsigned integer range (0–255) means that the results of an operation must be transformed to within that range if data is to be passed in the same form to further software. If the template includes fractions it may mean that the result has to be rounded. Worse, if the template contains anything other than positive fractions less than $1/(n \times m)$ (which is quite likely) it is possible for the result, at some point, to go outside of the 0–255 range.

Scaling can be done as the results are produced. This requires either a prior estimation of the result range or a backwards rescaling when an out-of-range result requires that the scaling factor be changed. Alternatively, scaling can be done at the end of production with all the results initially placed into a floating-point array. The latter option assumed that there is sufficient main memory available to hold a floating-point array. It may be that such an array will need to be written to disk, which can be very time-consuming. Floating point is preferable because even if significantly large storage is allocated to the image with each pixel represented as a 4 byte integer, for example, it only needs a few peculiar valued templates to operate on the image for the resulting pixel values to be very small or very large. Hence, practically, scaling is normally necessary.

A Fourier transform was applied to an image. The *imaginary* array contained zeros and the *real* array values ranged between 0 and 255. After the Fourier transformation, values in the resulting *imaginary* and *real* floating-point arrays were mostly between 0 and 1 but with some values greater than 1000. The following transformation was applied to the *real* and *imaginary* output arrays:

$$F(g) = \{\log_2[\text{abs}(g)] + 15\} \times 5 \quad \text{for all abs}(g) > 2^{-15}$$
$$F(g) = 0 \quad \text{otherwise}$$

where abs(g) is the positive value of g ignoring the sign.

This brought the values into a range that enabled them to be placed back into the byte array.

## 6.4 OTHER WINDOW OPERATIONS

Templating uses the concept of a window to the image whose size corresponds with that of the template. Other non-template operations on image windows can be useful.

**Technique 6.4  Median filtering**

USE  Noise removal while preserving edges in an image.

OPERATION  This is a popular low-pass filter, attempting to remove noisy pixels while keeping the edges intact. The values of the pixels in the window are sorted and the median—the middle value in the sorted list (or average of the middle two if the list has an even number of elements)—is the one plotted into the output image.

EXAMPLE  The '6' value (quite possibly noise) is totally eliminated using a $3 \times 3$ median filter:

|  | Image |  |  |  |  | Output |  |  |
|---|---|---|---|---|---|---|---|---|
| 0 | 0 | 0 | 0 | 0 | | 1 | 1 | 1 |
| 0 | 1 | 1 | 1 | 0 | | 1 | 1 | 1 |
| 0 | 1 | 1 | 1 | 0 | | 1 | 1 | 1 |
| 0 | 1 | 1 | 1 | 0 | | 1 | 1 | 1 |
| 0 | 1 | 1 | 1 | 0 | | 1 | 1 | 1 |
| 0 | 1 | 6 | 1 | 0 | | 1 | 1 | 1 |
| 0 | 1 | 1 | 1 | 0 | | | | |
| 0 | 0 | 0 | 0 | 0 | | | | |

Modal filtering, an alternative to median filtering, where the most popular from the set of nine is plotted in the centre, is illustrated in the images in Fig. 6.2.

**Technique 6.5  *k*-closest averaging**

USE  Aims to preserve, to some extent, the actual values of the pixels without letting the noise get through to the final image.

OPERATION  All the pixels in the window are sorted and the $k$ pixels values closest in value to the target pixel—usually the centre of the window—are averaged. The average may or may not include the target pixel, if not included the effect is similar to a low-pass filter. $k$ is a selected constant value less than the area of the window.

An extension of this is to average the $k$ values nearest in value to the target, but not including the $q$ values closest to and including the target. This avoids pairs of triples of noisy pixels that are obtained by setting $q$ to 2 or 3.

In both median and $k$-closest averaging, sorting creates a heavy load on the system; however, with a little sophistication in the programming, it is possible to sort the first window from the image and then delete a column of pixel values from the sorted list and introduce a new column by slotting them into the list thus avoiding a complete re-sort for each window. The $k$-closest averaging requires differences to be calculated as well as ordering and is, therefore, slower than the median filter.

### 6.4.1  Interest points

There is no standard definition of what constitutes an interest point in image processing. Generally, interest points are identified by algorithms that can be applied first to images containing a known object, and then to images where recognition of the object is required.

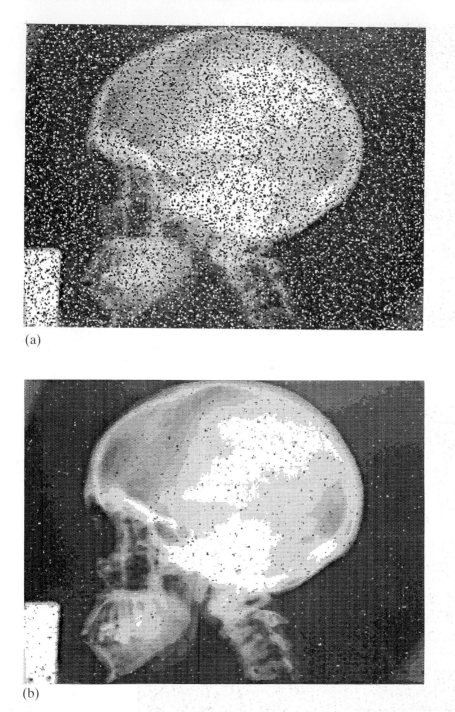

(a)

(b)

**Figure 6.2** (a) Skull X-ray with 20 per cent added noise. (b) Median filter implemented on (a).

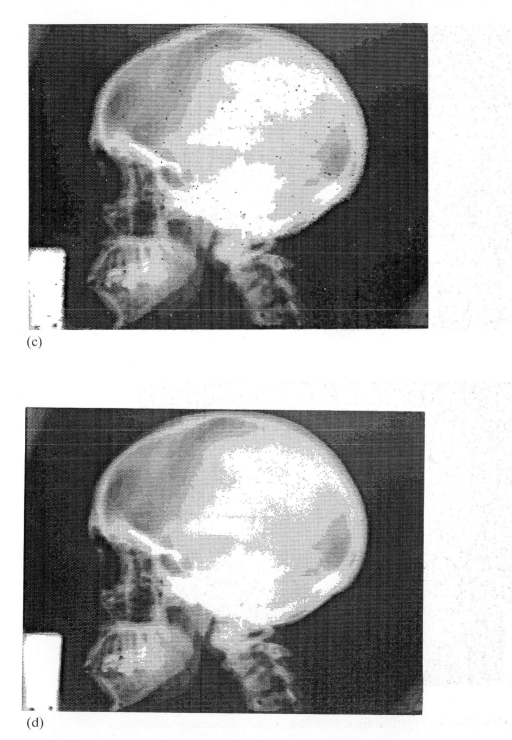

**Figure 6.2** (*continued*)  (c) Modal filter implemented on (b). (d) Original X-ray (without noise).

**Table 6.3**

| Image | | | | | | | Variances | | | | | | | After step 1 | | | | | After step 2 | | | | |
|---|---|---|---|---|---|---|---|---|---|---|---|---|---|---|---|---|---|---|---|---|---|---|---|
| 0 | 0 | 0 | 0 | 0 | 0 | 0 | 0 | 1 | 1 | 1 | 1 | 1 | 0 | | | | | | | | | | |
| 0 | 1 | 1 | 1 | 1 | 1 | 0 | 1 | 2 | 2 | 2 | 2 | 2 | 1 | 0 | 1 | 1 | 1 | 0 | 0 | 0 | 0 | 0 | 0 |
| 0 | 1 | 2 | 2 | 2 | 1 | 0 | 1 | 2 | 2 | 5 | 2 | 2 | 1 | 1 | 2 | 2 | 2 | 1 | 0 | 2 | 2 | 2 | 0 |
| 0 | 1 | 2 | 4 | 2 | 1 | 0 | 1 | 2 | 5 | 16 | 5 | 2 | 1 | 1 | 2 | 2 | 2 | 1 | 0 | 2 | 2 | 2 | 0 |
| 0 | 1 | 2 | 2 | 2 | 1 | 0 | 1 | 2 | 2 | 5 | 2 | 2 | 1 | 1 | 2 | 2 | 2 | 1 | 0 | 2 | 2 | 2 | 0 |
| 0 | 1 | 1 | 1 | 1 | 1 | 0 | 1 | 2 | 2 | 2 | 2 | 2 | 1 | 0 | 1 | 1 | 1 | 0 | 0 | 0 | 0 | 0 | 0 |
| 0 | 0 | 0 | 0 | 0 | 0 | 0 | 0 | 1 | 1 | 1 | 1 | 1 | 0 | | | | | | | | | | |

Recognition is achieved by comparing the positions of discovered interest points with the known pattern positions. A number of different methods using a variety of different measurements are available to determine whether a point is interesting or not. Some depend on the changes in texture of an image, some on the changes in curvature of an edge, some on the number of edges arriving coincidentally at the same pixel. A lower level interest operator is the Moravec operator.

### Technique 6.6 Moravec operator

USE To identify a set of points on an image by which the image may be classified or compared.

OPERATION With a square window, evaluate the sums of the squares of the differences in intensity of the centre pixel from the centre top, centre left, centre bottom, and centre right pixels in the window. Call this the variance for the centre pixel. Calculate the variance for all the internal pixels in the image.

$$I'(x, y) = \sum_{(i,j) \text{ in } S} [I(x, y) - I(x + i, y + j)]^2$$

where

$$S = \{(0, a), (0, -a), (a, 0), (-a, 0)\}$$

Now pass a $3 \times 3$ window across the variances, and save the minimum from the nine variances in the centre pixel. Finally, pass a $3 \times 3$ window across the result and set to zero the centre pixel when its value is not the biggest in the window.

EXAMPLE Table 6.3 gives an example of this technique.
The images in Fig. 6.3 show a sample output.
To keep within manageable limits, if the window is $n \times m$, evaluate the variances as

$$I'(x, y) = \frac{1}{n \times m} \sum_{(i,j) \text{ in } S} |I(x, y) - I(x + i, y + j)|$$

which has a similar effect.

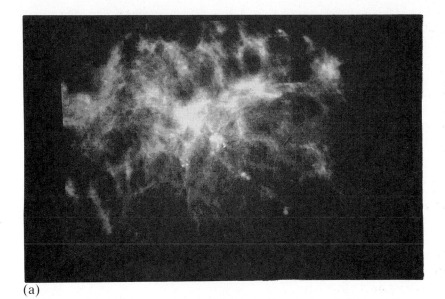

(a)

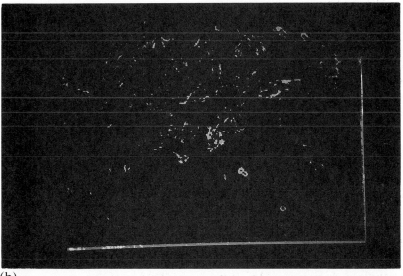

(b)

**Figure 6.3** (a) Breast X-ray. (b) Moravec interest points (clusters are suggestive of cancer spots).

## 6.4.2 Correlation

Correlation can be used to determine the existence, or otherwise, of a known shape in an image. There are a number of drawbacks with this approach to searching through an image. Rarely is the object orientation or its exact size in the image known. Further, if these are known for one object they are unlikely to be consistent for all objects. That is not to say, however, that this is never the case.

A biscuit manufacturer using a fixed position camera could count the number of well-formed, round biscuits on a tray presented to it by template matching.

However, if the task is to search for a sunken ship on a sonar image, correlation is not the best method to use.

Classical correlation takes into account the mean of the template and image area under the template as well as the spread of values in both template and image area. With a constant image—i.e. with lighting broadly constant across the image and the spread of pixel values broadly constant—then the correlation can be simplified to convolution as shown in the following technique.

### Technique 6.7 Correlation

USE To find where a template matches a window in an image.

THEORY If $N \times M$ image is addressed by $I(X, Y)$ and $n \times m$ template is addressed by $t(i, j)$, then

$$\text{corr}(X,Y) = \sum_{i=0}^{n-1} \sum_{j=0}^{m-1} [t(i,j) - I(X+i, Y+j)]^2$$

$$= \sum_{i=0}^{n-1} \sum_{j=0}^{m-1} [t(i,j)^2 - 2t(i,j)I(X+i, Y+j) + I(X+i, Y+j)^2]$$

$$= \underbrace{\sum_{i=0}^{n-1} \sum_{j=0}^{m-1} (t(i,j)^2}_{\substack{\text{is constant} \\ \text{across the} \\ \text{image, so can be} \\ \text{ignored}}} - 2 \underbrace{\sum_{i=0}^{n-1} \sum_{j=0}^{m-1} t(i,j)I(X+i, Y+j)}_{\text{is } t \text{ convolved with } I} + \underbrace{\sum_{i=0}^{n-1} \sum_{j=0}^{m-1} I(X+i, Y+j)^2}_{\substack{\text{is constant only if} \\ \text{average light from} \\ \text{image is constant} \\ \text{across image (often} \\ \text{approximately true)}}}$$

OPERATION This reduces correlation (subtraction, squaring, and addition), to multiplication and addition convolution. Thus normally if the overall light intensity across the whole image is fairly constant, it is safe to use convolution instead of correlation.

## 6.5 TWO-DIMENSIONAL GEOMETRIC TRANSFORMATIONS

Frequently it is useful to 'zoom in' on a part of an image, rotate, translate, skew, or zoom out from an image.

A $640 \times 480$ pixel system was to be engineered with the ability to view, simultaneously, four images on each quarter of the screen. A zoom-out function was written to create each quarter image.

These operations are very common in computer graphics and most graphics texts (such as Foley and Van Dam, 1984; or Burger and Gillies, 1989) cover the mathematics. However, computer graphics transformations normally create a mapping from the original two-dimensional object coordinates to the new two-dimensional object coordinates, i.e. if $(x', y')$ are the new coordinates and $(x, y)$ are the original coordinates, a mapping of the form $(x', y') = f(x, y)$ for all $(x, y)$ is created.

This is not a satisfactory approach in image processing. The range and domain in image processing are pixel positions, i.e. integer values of $x, y$ and $x', y'$. Clearly the function $f$ is defined for all integer values of $x$ and $y$ (original pixel positions) but not defined for all integer values of $x'$ and $y'$ (the required values). It is necessary to determine (loosely) the inverse of $f$ (call it $F$) so that for each pixel in the new image an intensity value from the old image is defined.

There are two problems:

1. The range of values $0 \leq x \leq N - 1$, $0 \leq y \leq M - 1$ may not be wide enough to be addressed by the function $F$. For example, if a rotation of 90° of an image around its centre pixel is required, then, assuming the image has an aspect ratio that is not 1:1, part of the image will be lost off the top and bottom of the screen and the new image will not be wide enough for the screen. The width problem means that original coordinates $(x, y)$ must be defined (typically to zero) outside the screen range.

2. We need a new grey level for each $(x', y')$ position rather than for each $(x, y)$ position as above. Hence we need a function that *given a new array position* and the old array, delivers the intensity

$$I(x', y') = F(\text{old image}, x', y')$$

It is necessary to give the whole old image as an argument since $f'(x', y')$ (the strict inverse of $f$) is unlikely to deliver an integer pair $(x', y')$. Indeed, it is most likely that the point chosen will be off centre of a pixel. It remains to be seen whether a simple rounding of the values of the produced $x$ and $y$ would give best results, or whether some sort of averaging of surrounding pixels, based on the position of $f'(x', y')$, is better.

It is still possible to use the matrix methods used in graphics, providing the inverse is calculated so as to give an original pixel position for each final pixel position. The *standard* two-dimensional geometric graphics transformation matrices are as follows:

1. Scaling by $sx$ in the $x$ direction and by $sy$ in the $y$ direction (equivalent to zooming in and zooming out from an image).

$$(x', y', 1) = (x, y, 1) \begin{pmatrix} sx & 0 & 0 \\ 0 & sy & 0 \\ 0 & 0 & 1 \end{pmatrix}$$

2. Translating by $tx$ in the $x$ direction and by $ty$ in the $y$ direction (equivalent to panning left, right, up, or down an image).

$$(x', y', 1) = (x, y, 1) \begin{pmatrix} 1 & 0 & 0 \\ 0 & 1 & 0 \\ -tx & -ty & 1 \end{pmatrix}$$

3. Rotating image by $a$ clockwise.

$$(x', y', 1) = (x, y, 1) \begin{pmatrix} \cos a & -\sin a & 0 \\ \sin a & \cos a & 0 \\ 0 & 0 & 1 \end{pmatrix}$$

The equivalent 'inverses' (from an image point of view) are as follows:

1. Scaling by $sx$ in the $x$ direction and by $sy$ in the $y$ direction (equivalent to zooming in and zooming out from an image).

$$(x, y, 1) = (x', y', 1) \begin{pmatrix} 1/sx & 0 & 0 \\ 0 & 1/sy & 0 \\ 0 & 0 & 1 \end{pmatrix}$$

2. Translating by $tx$ in the $x$ direction and by $ty$ in the $y$ direction (equivalent to panning left, right, up, or down an image).

$$(x, y, 1) = (x', y', 1) \begin{pmatrix} 1 & 0 & 0 \\ 0 & 1 & 0 \\ tx & ty & 1 \end{pmatrix}$$

3. Rotating image by $a$ clockwise. This rotation (which is not different from the graphics forward rotation) assumes that the origin is now at the top left of the image (rather than at the bottom left, which is the normal graphics origin) and that the new image is equal to the old image rotated clockwise by $a$.

$$(x, y, 1) = (x', y', 1) \begin{pmatrix} \cos a & -\sin a & 0 \\ \sin a & \cos a & 0 \\ 0 & 0 & 1 \end{pmatrix}$$

As with forward transformations, these transformations can be combined by multiplying the matrices, to give a $3 \times 3$ matrix which can then be applied to the image pixels.

So, for example, if an image is to be zoomed-in (doubling each edge), rotated clockwise by 45° about its own origin, and then shifted 20 old pixels to the right of the old origin, evaluate the following expression:

$$\begin{pmatrix} 1/2 & 0 & 0 \\ 0 & 1/2 & 0 \\ 0 & 0 & 1 \end{pmatrix} \begin{pmatrix} \cos 45 & -\sin 45 & 0 \\ \sin 45 & \cos 45 & 0 \\ 0 & 0 & 1 \end{pmatrix} \begin{pmatrix} 1 & 0 & 0 \\ 0 & 1 & 0 \\ 20 & 0 & 1 \end{pmatrix}$$

giving

$$\begin{pmatrix} 0.5 & 0 & 0 \\ 0 & 0.5 & 0 \\ 0 & 0 & 1 \end{pmatrix} \begin{pmatrix} 0.707 & -0.707 & 0 \\ 0.707 & 0.707 & 0 \\ 0 & 0 & 1 \end{pmatrix} \begin{pmatrix} 1 & 0 & 0 \\ 0 & 1 & 0 \\ 20 & 0 & 1 \end{pmatrix} = \begin{pmatrix} 0.3535 & -0.3535 & 0 \\ 0.3535 & 0.3535 & 0 \\ 0 & 0 & 1 \end{pmatrix} \begin{pmatrix} 1 & 0 & 0 \\ 0 & 1 & 0 \\ 20 & 0 & 1 \end{pmatrix}$$

$$= \begin{pmatrix} 0.3535 & -0.3535 & 0 \\ 0.3535 & 0.3535 & 0 \\ 20 & 0 & 1 \end{pmatrix}$$

Therefore, the old pixel position for the new pixel position (8, 10), say, will be

$$(8 \ 10 \ 1) \begin{pmatrix} 0.3535 & -0.3535 & 0 \\ 0.3535 & 0.3535 & 0 \\ 20 & 0 & 1 \end{pmatrix} = (26.363 \ 0.707 \ 1)$$

Rounding to the nearest whole integer, this gives the coordinate of the pixel that is delivering its value to position (8, 10) to be (26, 1).

**Technique 6.8 Two-dimensional geometric transformations**
USE To turn an image around, zoom in, or pan across it.

OPERATION Determine the matrix which maps every new pixel onto either an old pixel (if in range) or zero otherwise. Say

$$\begin{pmatrix} ax & ay & 0 \\ bx & by & 0 \\ cx & cy & 1 \end{pmatrix}$$

Starting at pixel (0, 0), plotting left to right, calculate

$$atx = cx; \quad aty = cy$$

and make

$$I_{new}(0, 0) = \begin{cases} I_{old}[\text{round}(atx), \text{round}(aty)], & \text{if } atx \text{ and } aty \text{ are in range} \\ 0 & \text{otherwise} \end{cases}$$

Increment $x$ [now dealing with (1, 0)] and

$$atx = atx + ax; \quad aty = aty + ay$$

and repeat $I_{new}$ allocation. Repeat for each $x$ in the row. For the next row, set starting values to

$$atx = bx*y + cx; \quad aty = by*y + cy$$

and proceed as for row 0 above.

This technique means that, for each pixel, only two floating-point additions are necessary.

## 6.6 EXERCISES

**6.1** Implement the Moravec operator on a simple image, compare the results obtained from one image, initially as captured, then after equalization.

**6.2** Compare $k$-closest averaging with median filtering and the use of a low-pass filter. Which performs best (i.e. removal of most noise with least blurring)?

**6.3** Try removing brightness gradation from an image by local averaging. How does this compare with applying a simple spatially dependent transformation?

**6.4** An image is to be rotated by 30° *anticlockwise* and then reduced to a quarter of its size. Deduce the reverse mapping matrix and determine the values of the new image at (2, 9) and (10, 10).

# 7
---
# SEGMENTATION AND EDGE DETECTION

## 7.1 INTRODUCTION

Segmentation is concerned with splitting an image up into segments (also called regions and areas) that each hold some property distinct from their neighbour. This is an essential part of scene analysis—in answering questions like where and how large is the object, where is the background, how many objects are there, how many surfaces are there, and so on. Segmentation is a basic requirement for the identification and classification of objects in a scene. It focuses subsequent algorithms on the shape, texture, or colour of an homogeneous area.

Segmentation can be approached from two points of view: by identifying *edges* (or lines) that run through an image or by identifying *regions* (or areas) within an image. Region operations can be seen as the dual (or mirror) of edge operations in that the completion of an edge is equivalent to breaking one region into two. Ideally edge and region operations should give the same segmentation result; however, in practice the two rarely correspond.

## 7.2 REGION OPERATIONS

Discovering regions can be a very simple exercise, as illustrated in Technique 7.1. However, more often than not, regions are required that cover a substantial area of the scene rather than a small group of pixels. For example, a red car body region is unlikely to be gleaned from the crude region detection below, which will simply identify many regions of differing shading. Somehow these regions have to be combined to give the whole car body. This is covered in Technique 7.2.

### Technique 7.1 Crude region detection
USE To reconsider an image as a set of regions.

OPERATION There is no operation involved here. The regions are simply identified as containing pixels of the same grey level. The boundaries of the regions (contours) are at the cracks between the pixels rather than at pixel positions (see also Chapter 15 on compression, which covers contouring methods).

Such a region detection may give far too many regions to be useful (unless the number of grey levels is relatively small). So a simple approach is to group pixels into ranges of near values (quantizing or bunching), e.g. 0–24, 25–73, 74–160, 161–255. The ranges can be estimated by considering bunches of values on the grey-level histogram. Unfortunately, considering the image histogram in order to identify good bunching for region purposes results in a merging of regions based on *overall* grey-level statistics rather than on grey levels of pixels that are geographically near one another. (See Plate 2j for an illustration of region detection on 16 grey levels.)

## 7.2.1 Region merging

It is often useful to do the rough individual grey-level split and then to perform some technique on the cracks between the regions—not to enhance edges but to identify when whole regions are worth combining—thus reducing the number of regions from the crude region detection above.

### Technique 7.2 Region merging
USE Reducing the number of regions, combining fragmented regions, determining which regions are really part of the same area.

OPERATION Let $s$ be a crack difference, i.e. the absolute difference in grey levels between two adjacent (above, below, left, or right) pixels.
Then given a threshold value, $T$, we can identify, for each crack

$$w = \begin{cases} 1 & \text{if } s < T \\ 0 & \text{otherwise} \end{cases}$$

i.e. $w$ is 1 if the crack is below the threshold (suggesting that the regions are likely to be the same), or 0 if it is above the threshold.
Now measure the full length of the boundary of *each* of the regions that meet at the crack. These will be $b_1$ and $b_2$ say. Sum the $w$s that are along the length of the crack between the regions and calculate

$$\frac{\sum w}{\text{minimum}(b_1, b_2)}$$

If this is greater than a further threshold, deduce that the two regions should be joined.

EXAMPLE

```
1  1  1  2  2  2  2  4  4
1  1  1  1  2  2  2  4  4
1  1  1  1  1  1  2  2  2
1  1  1  1  1  1  1  1  1
```

If we make $T = 3$, then all the cracks are significant

```
1  1  1  2  2  2  2  4  4
1  1  1  1  2  2  2  4  4
1  1  1  1  1  1  2  2  2
1  1  1  1  1  1  1  1  1
```

|        |          | Sum of $w$s |        |        |
|--------|----------|-------------|--------|--------|
| Region | Boundary | With A      | With B | With C |
| A      | 17       | –           | 9      | 0      |
| B      | 10       | 9           | –      | 4      |
| C      | 4        | 0           | 4      | –      |

Giving sum/min$(b_1, b_2)$ for A, B, and C as follows:

| Region | A   | B   | C   |
|--------|-----|-----|-----|
| A      | –   | 0.9 | 0   |
| B      | 0.9 | –   | 1.0 |
| C      | 0   | 1.0 | –   |

If we take the threshold for combining as 0.95, then B will be combined with C. If the combining threshold is set lower, then A will also be combined giving the whole image as just one region.

Note that despite the differences between the pixels being bigger, the algorithm combines the small region with the larger region, rather than the two larger regions.

Effectively this is taking the number of cracks that suggest that the regions should be merged, and dividing by the smallest region boundary. Of course a particularly irregular shape may have a very long region boundary with a small area. In such circumstances it may be preferable to measure areas (count how many pixels there are in them), see Chapter 8.

Measuring *both* boundaries (as in the technique above) is better than dividing by the boundary length between the two regions as it takes into account the size of the regions involved. If one region is very small, then it will be added to a larger region, whereas if both regions are large, then the evidence for combining them has to be much stronger.

## 7.2.2 Region splitting

Just as it is possible to start from many regions and merge them into fewer, larger regions, it is also possible to consider the image as one region and split it into more and more regions.

One way of doing this is to examine the grey-level histograms. If the image is in colour, better results can be obtained by examination of the three colour value histograms.

### Technique 7.3 Region splitting

USE To subdivide sensibly an image or part of an image into regions of similar type.

OPERATION Identify significant peaks in the grey-level histogram and look in the valleys between the peaks for possible threshold values. Some peaks will be more substantial than others; find splits between the 'best' peaks first.

Regions are identified as containing grey levels between the thresholds. With colour there are three histograms to choose from. The algorithm halts when no peak is significant. This is a complex exercise. The try-it-and-see approach is worthwhile!

LIMITATIONS This techniques relies on the *overall* histogram giving good guidance as to sensible regions. If the image is a chessboard, then the region splitting works nicely. If the image is of 16 chessboards well spaced apart on a white background sheet, then instead of identifying 17 regions, one for each chessboard and one for the background, it identifies $16 \times 32$ black squares, which is probably not what is wanted.

EXAMPLE

### Image

```
0 0 0 0 0 0 2 0 3 3
0 0 0 1 0 0 0 2 4 2
0 0 2 0 2 4 3 3 2 3
0 0 1 3 3 4 3 3 3 3
0 1 0 4 3 3 2 4 3 2
0 0 1 2 3 3 4 4 4 3
```

### Histogram

```
0 ********************
1 ****
2 ********
3 *****************
4 ********
```

The valley is at 1. Which side should the 1s go?

Consider both options:

| (0), (1, 2, 3, 4) | (0, 1), (2, 3, 4) |
|---|---|
| ○○○○○○ . ○ . . | ○○○○○○ . ○ . . |
| ○○○ . ○○○ . . . | ○○○○○○○ . . . |
| ○○ . ○ . . . . . . | ○○ . ○ . . . . |
| ○○ . . . . . . . | ○○○ . . . . . . |
| ○ . ○ . . . . . . | ○○○ . . . . . . |
| ○○ . . . . . . . | ○○○ . . . . . . |

The second leaves less stragglers than the first but it is difficult to see this without trying it.

COMMENTS The histogram need not be of the whole image, it could just be of a region within the image. Also see Techniques 5.4 and 5.5.

## 7.3 BASIC EDGE DETECTION

Instead of discovering regions, looking for real edges (or lines) in an image may be a better first step to recognizing geometric shapes within an image. Edge detection, ideally, identifies all the lines that outline the objects in an image.

However, rarely does it work that well. Edges caused by poor lighting or poor capture equipment frequently appear where they are not required (type 2 error). On the other hand, edges of objects are often incomplete because the background is too like the foreground colour of the object and a clear line is not visible (type 1 error).

A basic edge detector (such as Sobel described in Technique 7.4 below) gives a measure of how likely each pixel is part of a 'real' edge. This measure is termed the *gradient magnitude*.

It then becomes necessary to decide what gradient magnitude values constitute a real edge and what do not. Depending on the application, thresholding might be at a high value if overidentification is preferred, or at a low value if only valid edges are to be identified.

### 7.3.1 Templates for edge detection

If we are looking for any horizontal edges it would seem sensible to calculate the difference between one pixel value and the next pixel value, either up or down from the first (called the crack difference), i.e. assuming top left origin

$$Y\_difference(x, y) = value(x, y) - value(x, y + 1)$$

In effect this is equivalent to convolving the image with a $2 \times 1$ template

$$\begin{matrix} 1 \\ -1 \end{matrix}$$

Likewise

$$X\_difference(x, y) = value(x, y) - value(x - 1, y)$$

**Table 7.1**

| Image | X_difference | Y_difference | Gradient direction |
|---|---|---|---|
| 1 1 1 1 1 | 0  0  0 0 * | 0 0 0 0 0 | * * * * * |
| 1 1 1 1 1 | 0  0  0 0 * | 0 0 0 1 1 | * * * ↕ ↕ |
| 1 1 1 0 0 | 0  0 −1 0 * | 0 0 1 0 0 | * * ↘ * * |
| 1 1 0 0 0 | 0 −1  0 0 * | 0 0 0 0 0 | * ↔ * * * |
| 1 1 0 0 0 | 0 −1  0 0 * | * * * * * | * ↔ * * * |

uses the template

$$-1 \quad 1$$

Occasionally it is useful to plot both X_difference and Y_difference, combining them to create the single measure of gradient magnitude (i.e. the strength of the edge).

Combining them by simply adding them could mean two edges cancelling each other out (one positive, one negative), so it is better to sum the absolute values (ignoring the sign) or sum the squares of them and then, possibly, take the positive square root of the result.

It is also useful to divide the Y_difference by the X_difference and identify a gradient direction (the angle of the edge between the regions).

$$\text{gradient\_direction}(x, y) = \tan^{-1}\left\{ \frac{Y\_\text{difference}(x, y)}{X\_\text{difference}(x, y)} \right\}$$

Consider the example shown in Table 7.1. It can be seen that the gradient direction is at right-angles to the edge itself and points towards (and away from) the centre of the areas whose edges have been detected. This can be used to detect the validity of an edge by looking at the continuity of gradient, as well as identifying the image centre for matching purposes (see Technique 9.3 The generalized Hough transform).

Clearly, such small templates do not take into account any of the surrounding pixels. In real images the lines are rarely so well defined as in the above figure. More often the change between regions is gradual and noisy.

The following image represents a typical read edge. A larger template is needed to average out the gradients over a number of pixels, rather than looking at two only.

```
0 0 0 0 0 0 2 0 3 3
0 0 0 1 0 0 0 2 4 2
0 0 2 0 3 4 3 3 2 3
0 0 1 3 3 4 3 3 3 3
0 1 0 4 3 3 2 4 3 2
0 0 1 2 3 3 4 4 4 3
```

**Technique 7.4 Sobel edge detection** The Sobel 3 × 3 templates are normally given as

| X-direction | Y-direction |
|---|---|
| −1  0  1 | 1   2   1 |
| −2  0  2 | 0   0   0 |
| −1  0  1 | −1  −2  −1 |

**Table 7.2**

| Image | | | | | | | | | | abs A + abs B | | | | | | | | Threshold at 12 | | | | | | | |
|---|---|---|---|---|---|---|---|---|---|---|---|---|---|---|---|---|---|---|---|---|---|---|---|---|---|
| 0 | 0 | 0 | 0 | 0 | 0 | 2 | 0 | 3 | 3 | 4 | 6 | 4 | 10 | 14 | 12 | 14 | 4 | 0 | 0 | 0 | 0 | 1 | 1 | 1 | 0 |
| 0 | 0 | 0 | 1 | 0 | 0 | 0 | 2 | 4 | 2 | 6 | 8 | 10 | 20 | 16 | 12 | 6 | 0 | 0 | 0 | 0 | 1 | 1 | 1 | 0 | 0 |
| 0 | 0 | 2 | 0 | 2 | 4 | 3 | 3 | 2 | 3 | 4 | 10 | 14 | 10 | 2 | 4 | 2 | 4 | 0 | 0 | 1 | 0 | 0 | 0 | 0 | 0 |
| 0 | 0 | 1 | 3 | 3 | 4 | 3 | 3 | 3 | 3 | 2 | 12 | 12 | 2 | 2 | 4 | 6 | 8 | 0 | 1 | 1 | 0 | 0 | 0 | 0 | 0 |
| 0 | 1 | 0 | 4 | 3 | 3 | 2 | 4 | 3 | 2 | | | | | | | | | | | | | | | | |
| 0 | 0 | 1 | 2 | 3 | 3 | 4 | 4 | 4 | 3 | | | | | | | | | | | | | | | | |

Table 7.2 shows Sobel edge detection with the threshold set at 12. Larger Sobel templates can be generated for wider image coverage giving more accurate likelihood measures for the existence or not of edges. See the images in Fig. 7.1.

## 7.4 SECOND-ORDER EDGE DETECTION

In an image such as

$$
\begin{array}{ccccccccc}
1 & 2 & 3 & 4 & 5 & 6 & 7 & 8 & 9 \\
1 & 2 & 3 & 4 & 5 & 6 & 7 & 8 & 9 \\
1 & 2 & 3 & 4 & 5 & 6 & 7 & 8 & 9 \\
1 & 2 & 3 & 4 & 5 & 6 & 7 & 8 & 9 \\
1 & 2 & 3 & 4 & 5 & 6 & 7 & 8 & 9
\end{array}
$$

The basic Sobel vertical edge operator (as described above) will yield a value right across the image. For example, if

$$
\begin{array}{ccc}
-1 & 0 & 1 \\
-2 & 0 & 2 \\
-1 & 0 & 1
\end{array}
$$

is used, then the result is

$$
\begin{array}{ccccccc}
8 & 8 & 8 & 8 & 8 & 8 & 8 \\
8 & 8 & 8 & 8 & 8 & 8 & 8 \\
8 & 8 & 8 & 8 & 8 & 8 & 8
\end{array}
$$

Implementing the same template on this 'all eights' image would yield

$$
\begin{array}{ccccc}
0 & 0 & 0 & 0 & 0
\end{array}
$$

This is not unlike the differentiation operator applied to a straight line, e.g. if $y = 3x - 2$

$$\frac{dy}{dx} = 3$$

and

$$\frac{d^2 y}{dx^2} = 0$$

(a)

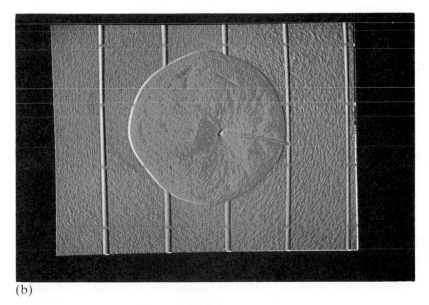

(b)

**Figure 7.1** Original apple. (b) Vertical Sobel.

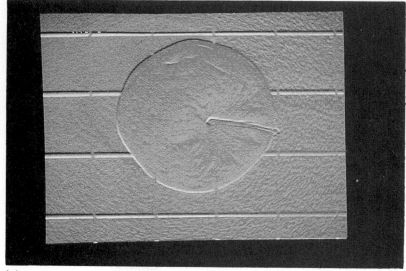

(c)

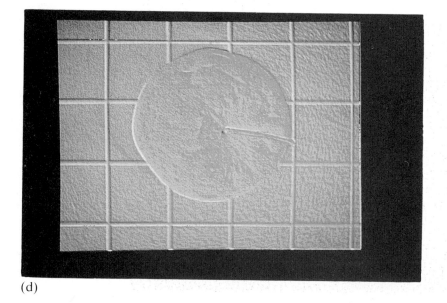

(d)

**Figure 7.1** (*continued*) (c) Horizontal Sobel. (d) Halved and added: $[a/2 - 64] + [b/2 - 64] + 128$.

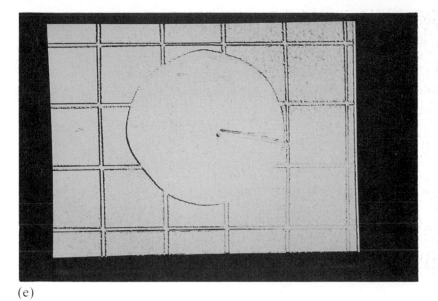

(e)

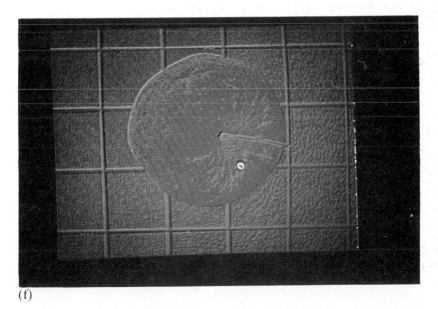

(f)

**Figure 7.1** (*continued*) (e) Part (d) negated and thresholded. (f) Gradient directions.

Once we have the gradient, if the gradient is then differentiated and the result is zero, it shows that the original line was straight.

Images often come with a grey-level 'trend' on them, i.e. one side of a region is lighter than the other but there is no 'edge' to be discovered in the region, the shading is even, indicating, perhaps, a light source that is stronger at one end, or a gradual colour change over the surface.

In such circumstances it is useful to use a second-order edge detector template, such as one from the Laplacian set, for example

$$\begin{matrix} 0 & -1 & 0 \\ -1 & 4 & -1 \\ 0 & -1 & 0 \end{matrix} \quad \text{or} \quad \begin{matrix} -1 & -1 & -1 \\ -1 & 8 & -1 \\ -1 & -1 & -1 \end{matrix}$$

The Laplacian set of operators is widely used. Since it effectively removes the general gradient of lighting or colouring from an image it only discovers and enhances much more discrete changes than, for example, the Sobel operator. It does not produce any information on direction which is seen as a function of gradual change. It enhances noise, though larger Laplacian operators and similar families of operators attempt to ignore noise.

One example of their use is in paint defect identification as described in Chapter 18.

## 7.5 PYRAMID EDGE DETECTION

Often it happens that the significant edges in an image are well spaced apart from each other and relatively easy to identify. However, there may be a number of other strong edges in the image that are not significant (from the user's point of view) because they are short or unconnected. The problem is how to enhance the substantial ones but ignore the other shorter ones.

One approach to this scenario is to create a pyramid of images.

**Technique 7.5  Pyramid edge detection**
USE To enhance substantial (strong and long) edges but to ignore the weak or short edges.

THEORY The image is cut down to quarter of the area by halving the length of the sides (both horizontally and vertically).

Each pixel in the new quarter-size image is an average of the four corresponding pixels in the full-size image.

This is repeated until an image is created where the substantial edges are still visible but the other edges have been lost.

Now the pyramid is traversed in the other direction. An edge detector is applied to the small image and where edge pixels have been found, an edge detector is applied to the corresponding four pixels in the next larger image—and so on to the full-size image.

OPERATION Let the original image be of size $m \times n$.

Create a second image of size $m/2 \times n/2$ by evaluating for each $0 < i < m$ and $0 < j < n$

$$\text{new } I(\tfrac{i}{2}, \tfrac{j}{2}) = \tfrac{1}{4}[I(i, j) + I(i + 1, j) + I(i, j + 1) + I(i + 1, j + 1)]$$

i.e. the corresponding square of four elements in the original image are averaged to give a value in the new image.

This is repeated (possibly recursively) $x$ times, and each generated image is kept. (The generated images will not be larger, in total, than the original image, so only one extra plane is required to hold the image.)

Now, with the smallest image, perform some edge detection operation—such as Sobel.

In pixels where edges are discovered (some threshold is required to identify an 'edge' pixel) perform an edge detection operation on the group of four corresponding pixels in the next largest image.

Continue to do this following the best edges down through the pyramid of images until the main edges in the original image have been discovered.

## 7.6 CRACK EDGE RELAXATION

Crack edge relaxation is also a popular and effective method of edge enhancement. This involves, at a simple level, allocating a likelihood value to all of the cracks *between* pixels as to whether they lie either side of an edge. Consider, for example, the following grid:

| 6 | 8 | 7 |
|---|---|---|
| 7 | 7 | 4 |
| 3 | 2 | 3 |

if the grey-level range is 0–9, then the crack probabilities in ninths are

```
  6 2 8 1 7
  1 + 1 + 3
  7 0 7 3 4
  4 + 5 + 1
  3 1 2 1 3
```

(thresholding at 2 gives)

### Technique 7.6 Crack edge relaxation

USE A technique that will find substantial edges from an original image, and, depending on the number of iterations that can be selected by the user, will find edges not only by simple statistics on a small local group, but will make sensible decisions about edges being connected to one another.

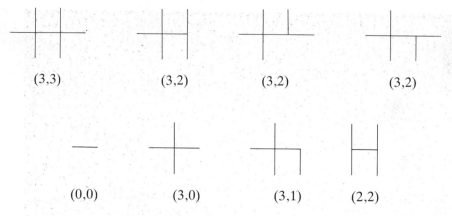

**Figure 7.2** A selection of crack edge types.

OPERATION Determine the values of the cracks between the pixels. This is $|I(x, y) - I(x + 1, y)|$ for the vertical cracks and $|I(x, y) - I(x, y + 1)|$ for the horizontal cracks.

Now we classify every pixel crack depending on how many of the cracks connected to it at both ends are likely to be 'significant' cracks, i.e. likely to represent real edges on the picture. Since there are three continuation cracks at each end of every crack, each crack can be classified as having 0, 1, 2, or 3 significant cracks hanging off it at each end. Figure 7.2 shows a selection of crack edge types.

If $a$, $b$, and $c$ are the values of the hanging-off cracks at one end of the crack being classified, and they are ordered such that $a \geq b \geq c$, and $m = \max(a, b, c, N/10)$, where $N$ is the number of grey levels supported by the system, then calculate the maximum of

$$(m - a)(m - b)(m - c) \qquad \text{likelihood value for 0 'significant' cracks}$$
$$a(m - b)(m - c) \qquad \text{likelihood value for 1 'significant' crack}$$
$$ab(m - c) \qquad \text{likelihood value for 2 'significant' cracks}$$
$$abc \qquad \text{likelihood value for 3 'significant' cracks}$$

Choose the most likely number of cracks—i.e. the one with the highest likelihood value. Do this for both ends, allocating a class such as $(3, 2)$ to the crack being considered.

Increment the crack value if the crack is of type $(1, 1)$, $(1, 2)$, $(2, 1)$, $(1, 3)$, $(3, 1)$. Intuitively these will probably be parts of an edge.

Decrement the crack value if the crack is of type $(0, 0)$, $(0, 2)$, $(0, 3)$, $(2, 0)$, $(3, 0)$. Do nothing for the others.

Repeat this enhancement process until adequate edge detection has been performed.

Create an edge detected image by allocating to each pixel a value dependent on the value of the crack above it and the crack to the right of it. This could be a simple sum or the maximum of the two or a binary value from some combined threshold.

This is edge enhancement, using as the initial estimate of edges the cracks between the pixels. It then removes the unlikely ones, enhancing the more likely ones (see the images in Fig. 7.3 (a) opposite and (b) on page 98).

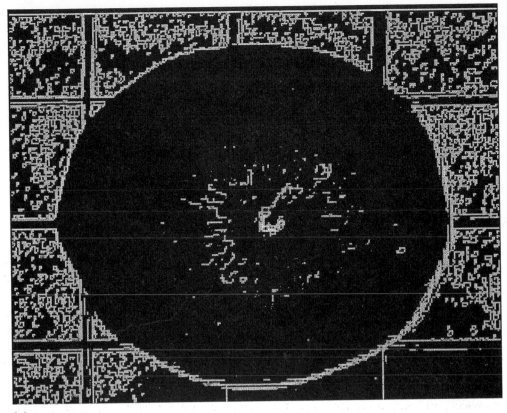

(a)

**Figure 7.3** (a) Crack edge detection (after five iterations) of apple.

## 7.7 EDGE FOLLOWING

If it is known that an object in an image has a discrete edge all around it, then it is possible, once a position on the edge has been found, to follow it around the object and back to the beginning.

Edge following is a very useful operation, particularly as a stepping stone to making decisions by discovering region positions in images. This is effectively the dual of segmenting by region detection.

There are a number of edge-following techniques. A simple one is outlined (only), below, but there are many levels of sophistication associated with edge following and the reader may well see how sophistication can be added to the simple technique described.

### Technique 7.7 Simple edge following

USE Knowing that a pixel is on an edge (point to it using a mouse pointer, for instance), the edge will be followed so that an object (a cell, for example) is outlined. This is useful prior to calculating the area of a particular shape. It is also useful if the enclosed region is made up of many regions that the user wishes to combine.

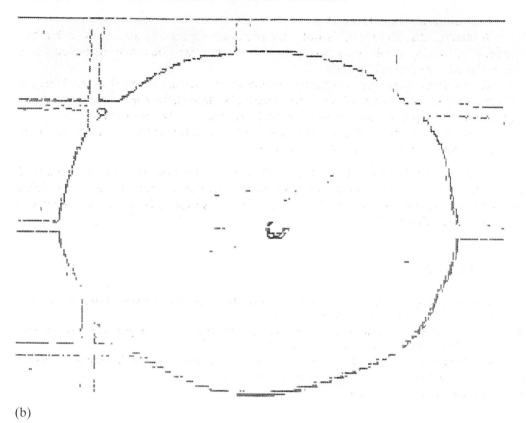

(b)

**Figure 7.3** (*continued*) (b) Crack edge detection (after five iterations) of apple. Thresholded and negated.

OPERATION  It is assumed that a position on the edge of a region has been identified, call it $(x, y)$.

Now flag this position as 'used' (so that it is not used again) and evaluate all the $3 \times 3$ (or larger) Sobel gradient values centred on each of the eight pixels surrounding $(x, y)$.

Choose the three pixels with the greatest absolute (neglecting the sign) gradient magnitude. Put these three pixel positions in a three-column array, one column for each pixel position, order them in the row according to gradient magnitude.

Choose the one with the greatest gradient magnitude.

Now this pixel will be in one of the directions 0–7 with respect to the pixel $(x, y)$ given by the following map, where * is the position of pixel $(x, y)$:

$$
\begin{array}{ccc}
0 & 1 & 2 \\
7 & * & 3 \\
6 & 5 & 4
\end{array}
$$

For example, if the maximum gradient magnitude was found from the Sobel operator centred round the pixel $(x + 1, y)$, then the direction would be '3'.

Call the direction of travel $d$.

Assuming that the shape is not very irregular, repeat the above algorithm but instead of looking at all the pixels around the new pixel, look only in directions $d$, $(d + 1)\bmod 8$, and $(d - 1)\bmod 8$.

If no suitably high value of gradient magnitude is found, remove the pixel from the list and choose the next one of the three stored. If all three have been removed from the list, then move up a row and choose the next best from the previous row.

Stop when the travel reaches the original pixel, or execution has gone on too long, or the number of rows in the list is very large.

As suggested in the description of the technique, the problem may be the amount of time it takes to reach a conclusion. Various heuristic techniques, including adding weights and creating more substantial trees, can be included. This routine is used in cell identification described in Chapter 18.

## 7.8 EXERCISES

**7.1** Implement crack edge detection on an image and compare the results after a different number of iterations. Does equalization of the original image affect the result?

**7.2** Compare the segmentation of an image by region merging and region splitting. Suggest an iterative scheme in which both might feature to give a better segmented image.

**7.3** Compare Sobel edge detection with crack edge detection. Which performs better under what conditions?

**7.4** How can gradient direction information be got from crack edge detection?

**7.5** Code an edge-following routine and assess its operation.

# 8

## MORPHOLOGICAL AND OTHER AREA OPERATIONS

### 8.1 INTRODUCTION

Morphology is the science of form and structure. In computer vision it is about regions or shapes—how they can be changed and counted, and how their areas can be evaluated. An early reference to the mathematics of morphology is Matheron (1975).

Morphology can be used for the following tasks:

1. Smoothing the edges of a region. This is useful if, say, it is required to create a line drawing of a face from an image. Using standard segmentation techniques, the edges will be noisy because the lighting or capture equipment makes the outline inaccurate. Morphology cannot add information to this, but since it is known that the edges of a face are normally curved, then the unlikely hills and valleys can be smoothed away.
2. Forcing shapes onto region edges. Instead of edges being curved it may be that prior knowledge is available that regions are square—e.g. in the image of a chessboard. Morphology can be used to force a shape onto a region so that where it was noisy and approximately square it becomes more square and less noisy.
3. The same morphological operations can be used to count regions (or granules in morphological terms). For example, how many dark cells are there in the image? Using morphological operations is just one way of region or granule counting. Others are also discussed in this chapter.
4. Morphological operations can be used to estimate sizes of regions (or granules). This is clearly essential as a tool for the image processor. Two area-calculating operations are described in this chapter.

Morphological operations are most easily seen on binary images (that is 1s and 0s only). Indeed, the early mathematics of morphology was concerned purely with position rather than intensity. This chapter approaches morphology by looking at the binary operations and then extending the work to practical grey-level operations. (In the images below, 1 and * are used. For all practical purposes the * may be seen to be a 0, thus making the images binary.)

## 8.2 BASIC MORPHOLOGICAL OPERATIONS

Consider the following image:

```
1  *  1  *  1
*  1  *  1  *
1  *  1  *  1
```

This could effectively be represented as a set (in mathematical terms) of all those pixels in $5 \times 3$ image that have value '1', namely

$$\{(0, 0), (0, 2), (0, 4), (1, 1), (1, 3), (2, 0), (2, 2), (2, 4)\}$$

And now it is possible to do set operations on images

```
        1  *  1  *  1              *  *  *  1  1
A =     *  1  *  1  *      B =     *  *  *  1  1
        1  *  1  *  1              *  *  *  1  1
```

Giving

```
                          1  *  1  1  1
A ∪ B   (A union B) =     *  1  *  1  1
                          1  *  1  1  1

                                  *  *  *  *  1
A ∩ B   (A intersection B) =      *  *  *  1  *
                                  *  *  *  *  1
```

Note here that the matrix really represents a set of known pixels (value '1') in among a set of unknown pixels (represented by '*'). The set of unknown pixels theoretically extends infinitely up, down left, and right, so that image A above could also be written as follows:

```
*  *  *  *  *  *  *  *  *  *  *
*  *  *  *  *  *  *  *  *  *  *
*  *  *  *  *  *  *  *  *  *  *
*  *  * (1) *  1  *  1  *  *  *
*  *  *  *  1  *  1  *  *  *  *
*  *  *  1  *  1  *  1  *  *  *
*  *  *  *  *  *  *  *  *  *  *
*  *  *  *  *  *  *  *  *  *  *
*  *  *  *  *  *  *  *  *  *  *
```

where the circle around the top left 1 indicates the position of the origin.

Two set operations (using an image and a template) that are fundamental to morphology are called dilation and erosion. The first has the effect of filling in the valleys between spiky regions edges, while the second has the effect of deleting spiky edges. These operations derive from Minkowski addition and Minkowski subtraction respectively, and are defined as follows.

### Technique 8.1 Dilation (Minkowski addition)

USE Region edge valley filling. The technique described here is on binary images. Later in this chapter it is extended to images with many grey levels.

OPERATION A template (made from 1s and *s) is created with a known origin, denoted by a circle around it.

The origin of this template is stepped over every element in the whole of the image.

Where the origin of the template corresponds to a 1 in the image, the template is 'unioned' with that part of the image. The resulting template-sized matrix is then unioned with all the other template-sized results *using their original image positions* and giving a resulting image that is larger (unless the template is 1 × 1) than the original.

EXAMPLE

Image                                                          Template

```
*  *  *  *  *  *  1  *  *  1  *                               1   *
*  *  *  *  *  *  1  *  *  *  1                              (1)  1
*  *  *  *  *  1  1  *  1  1  *
*  *  *  *  1  1  1  1  1  1  1
*  *  *  *  1  1  1  1  1  *  1
*  *  *  *  1  1  1  1  1  1  1
*  *  *  *  1  1  1  1  1  1  1
```

The 'first' 1 in the image is on the top line

```
*  *  *  *  *  *  1  *  *  1  *
```

When the template is applied to this 1, the following results:

```
*  *  *  *  *  *  1  *  *  *  *        ← new top line
*  *  *  *  *  *  1  1  *  1  *
```

And then application of the template to the second 1 gives

```
*  *  *  *  *  *  1  *  *  1  *
*  *  *  *  *  *  1  1  *  1  1
```

Application across the whole image gives

```
*  *  *  *  *  1  *  *  1  *  *        ← new row
*  *  *  *  *  1  1  *  1  1  *
*  *  *  *  1  1  1  1  1  1  1
*  *  *  *  1  1  1  1  1  1  1
*  *  *  *  1  1  1  1  1  1  1
```

↑<br>new column

Continually applying this to the image fills out all the holes and makes the image grow, one row and one column at a time.

### Technique 8.2  Erosion (Minkowski subtraction)

USE  This time the operation removes spikes from the edges of regions.

OPERATION  Creation of the template is done as per dilation. The template is stepped over the image but this time only in positions where the whole of the template lies on top of the image, i.e. it is now allowed to go off the edge. This means that the resulting matrix will be smaller than the image (unless the template is $1 \times 1$).

For every stepped position in the image the template is compared with the corresponding window to the image. If the template is exactly the same as the image window, then the element corresponding to the template origin in the resulting matrix is set to a 1.

This is particularly useful when the template is all 1s. It is also effectively equivalent to correlation. This is clear with a template containing a * as follows:

```
               Image                    Template
  *  *  *  *  *  *  1  *  *  1  *         1  *
  *  *  *  *  *  *  1  *  *  *  1        (1) 1
  *  *  *  *  *  1  1  *  1  1  *
  *  *  *  *  1  1  1  1  1  1  1
  *  *  *  *  1  1  1  1  1  *  1
  *  *  *  *  1  1  1  1  1  1  1
  *  *  *  *  1  1  1  1  1  1  1
```

The first 'match' is at (6, 3), there being only two other matches, so the result is:

```
  *  *  *  *  *  *  *  *  *  *  *     ← unused row
  *  *  *  *  *  *  *  *  *  *  *
  *  *  *  *  *  *  *  *  *  *  *
  *  *  *  *  *  *  1  *  *  1  *
  *  *  *  *  *  *  *  *  *  *  *
  *  *  *  *  *  *  *  *  1  *  *
  *  *  *  *  *  *  *  *  *  *  *
```

↑<br>unused column

This shows that the template matches the image in only three places. However, with a 'all 1s' template the spike removal becomes apparent. For example, with the same image and the template

$$
\begin{array}{cc}
1 & 1 \\
1 & 1
\end{array}
$$

the result is

```
*   *   *   *   *   *   *   *   *   *   *      ← unused row
*   *   *   *   *   *   *   *   *   *   *
*   *   *   *   *   *   *   *   *   *   *
*   *   *   *   *   1   *   *   1   *   *
*   *   *   *   1   1   1   1   1   *   *
*   *   *   *   1   1   1   1   *   *   *
*   *   *   *   1   1   1   1   1   1   *
```

↑
unused column

This clearly reduces the image, cutting out the spiky edges.

The techniques above have been applied to normal grey-level images. One way is to associate all the elements that have a constant grey-level value with binary 1 and all other pixels with * or binary 0. A better approach uses the actual values in grey-level morphological operations defined slightly differently to the binary/unary operations defined above. Refer to Haralick *et al.* (1987) for further details.

### Technique 8.3 Grey-level erosion and dilation

USE Flattening spikes and filling valleys on region edges in grey-level images.

OPERATION Let $I(x, y)$ be an image of grey levels and $R(x, y)$ be the resulting image after $I(x, y)$ has been dilated/eroded with $m \times n$ template $T(i, j)$.

$$0 \leq i \leq m - 1, \quad 0 \leq j \leq n - 1$$

Grey level dilation is defined as

$$R(x, y) = \operatorname*{maximum}_{\substack{0 \leq i \leq m-1 \\ 0 \leq j \leq n-1}} \{I(x - i, y - j) + T(i, j)\}$$

and grey level erosion is

$$R(x, y) = \operatorname*{minimum}_{\substack{0 \leq i \leq m-1 \\ 0 \leq j \leq n-1}} \{I(x + i, y + j) - T(i, j)\}$$

Both of the above definitions use locations outside of an $M \times N$ image, so where $I(x, y)$ is not defined, for the purposes of implementing the above calculations $I(x, y) = 0$.

The dilation example uses $(x - i, y - j)$ coordinates, which are not ideal in that the template is effectively rotated about both diagonals and then operates on the elements to the left and above the 'home' position. This can be avoided by defining the coordinates on the template to be $0 \geq i \geq -(m - 1)$ and $0 \geq j \geq -(n - 1)$.

Note that dilation is precisely the dual of the erosion operation. In some circumstances this mathematical relationship is important (e.g. with hardware to perform an erosion, a dilation can also be performed by reflecting the template and negating the original image and then negating the result.)

**Examples** Consider the following initial image:

```
0  0  0  0  0  0  0  0
0  0  2  4  4  2  0  0
0  0  4  8  8  4  0  0
0  0  2  4  4  2  0  0
0  0  0  0  0  0  0  0
```

Dilating by the template

```
1  1
1  1
```

gives

```
1  1  1  1  1  1  1  1
1  1  3  5  5  5  3  1
1  1  5  9  9  9  5  1
1  1  5  9  9  9  5  1
1  1  3  5  5  5  3  1
1  1  1  1  1  1  1  1
```

or subtracting 1 throughout

```
0  0  0  0  0  0  0  0
0  0  2  4  4  4  2  0
0  0  4  8  8  8  4  0
0  0  4  8  8  8  4  0
0  0  2  4  4  4  2  0
0  0  0  0  0  0  0  0
```

Showing that dilation with a constant (all 1s) template is equivalent to a stepping spatial operation that takes the maximum of a pixel window.

Conversely, eroding by the same template gives

```
-1  -1  -1  -1  -1  -1  -1  -1
-1  -1   1   3   1  -1  -1  -1
-1  -1   1   3   1  -1  -1  -1
-1  -1  -1  -1  -1  -1  -1  -1
-1  -1  -1  -1  -1  -1  -1  -1
```

or if 1 is subtracted throughout

```
0  0  0  0  0  0  0  0
0  0  2  4  2  0  0  0
0  0  2  4  2  0  0  0
0  0  0  0  0  0  0  0
0  0  0  0  0  0  0  0
```

Showing that erosion with a constant template is equivalent to taking a spatial minimum. The values in the template (or structuring element) effectively define the set of pixels which are searched for the maximum (dilation) or the minimum (erosion).

Note that dilation gives a larger image, while erosion gives a smaller image; in both cases, however, the original structure of the image is maintained.

If the template is not constant, say

$$
\begin{array}{cc}
1 & 0 \\
0 & 1
\end{array}
$$

the results are as follows:

| Original | | | | | | | | Dilated $-1$ | | | | | | | | Eroded $+1$ | | | | | | | |
|---|---|---|---|---|---|---|---|---|---|---|---|---|---|---|---|---|---|---|---|---|---|---|---|
| 0 | 0 | 0 | 0 | 0 | 0 | 0 | 0 | 0 | 0 | 0 | 0 | 0 | 0 | 0 | 0 | 0 | 0 | 0 | 0 | 0 | 0 | 0 | 0 |
| 0 | 0 | 2 | 4 | 4 | 2 | 0 | 0 | 0 | 0 | 2 | 4 | 4 | 3 | 1 | 0 | 0 | 0 | 2 | 4 | 3 | 0 | 0 | 0 |
| 0 | 0 | 4 | 8 | 8 | 4 | 0 | 0 | 0 | 0 | 4 | 8 | 8 | 7 | 3 | 0 | 0 | 0 | 3 | 4 | 2 | 0 | 0 | 0 |
| 0 | 0 | 2 | 4 | 4 | 2 | 0 | 0 | 0 | 0 | 3 | 7 | 8 | 8 | 4 | 0 | 0 | 0 | 0 | 0 | 0 | 0 | 0 | 0 |
| 0 | 0 | 0 | 0 | 0 | 0 | 0 | 0 | 0 | 0 | 1 | 3 | 4 | 4 | 2 | 0 | 0 | 0 | 0 | 0 | 0 | 0 | 0 | 0 |

Showing how dilation skews the image in favour of the higher values in the template. If the range of values in the template is small (0 to 1 in the above example) the shape of the template has much less effect on the final result than if the range is large, e.g. 0 to 100. Generally, if $T$ is the template used for dilation and erosion, $D(I)$ is the dilated image of $I$, and $E(I)$ is the eroded image of $I$, then

$$D(E(D(I))) = D(I)$$

i.e. the result of eroding and then dilating a previously dilated image is a return to that original dilated image.

Similarly

$$E(D(E(I))) = E(I)$$

Clearly, changing the templates for erosion and dilation gives different results.

## 8.3 OPENING AND CLOSING OPERATIONS

These are dilating after eroding (OPEN) and eroding after dilating (CLOSING). These two operations are more useful as means to an end rather than useful in themselves.

### Technique 8.4 Opening and closing operations
USE As a step towards the skeleton, counting, and size-estimating operations below.

OPERATION Let OPEN $(I, T)$ be the opening of image $I$ by some template $T$. Then, using previous terminology and the template $T$ throughout

$$\text{OPEN}(I, T) = D(E(I))$$

This gives

| Original | Opened with 1 1 / 1 1 | Opened with 1 0 / 1 1 |
|---|---|---|

| | | | | | | | | | | | | | | | | | | | | | | | | |
|---|---|---|---|---|---|---|---|---|---|---|---|---|---|---|---|---|---|---|---|---|---|---|---|---|
| 0 | 0 | 0 | 0 | 0 | 0 | 0 | 0 | 0 | 0 | 0 | 0 | 0 | 0 | 0 | 0 | 0 | 0 | 0 | 0 | 0 | 0 | 0 | 0 |
| 0 | 0 | 2 | 4 | 4 | 2 | 0 | 0 | 0 | 0 | 2 | 4 | 4 | 2 | 0 | 0 | 0 | 0 | 2 | 4 | 3 | 2 | 0 | 0 |
| 0 | 0 | 4 | 8 | 8 | 4 | 0 | 0 | 0 | 0 | 2 | 4 | 4 | 2 | 0 | 0 | 0 | 0 | 2 | 4 | 4 | 3 | 0 | 0 |
| 0 | 0 | 2 | 4 | 4 | 2 | 0 | 0 | 0 | 0 | 2 | 4 | 4 | 2 | 0 | 0 | 0 | 0 | 2 | 4 | 4 | 2 | 0 | 0 |
| 0 | 0 | 0 | 0 | 0 | 0 | 0 | 0 | 0 | 0 | 0 | 0 | 0 | 0 | 0 | 0 | 0 | 0 | 0 | 0 | 0 | 0 | 0 | 0 |

Clearly this restores the image to its original size and avoids the scaling of the result. It introduces the shaping of the template into the original.

More interesting is its operation on clear edges

| Original | Opened with 1 / 1 |
|---|---|

| | | | | | | | | | | | | | | | | |
|---|---|---|---|---|---|---|---|---|---|---|---|---|---|---|---|---|
| 0 | 0 | 0 | 0 | 0 | 0 | 0 | 0 | 0 | 0 | 0 | 0 | 0 | 0 | 0 | 0 |
| 0 | 0 | 0 | 0 | 0 | 0 | 1 | 4 | 0 | 0 | 0 | 0 | 0 | 0 | 1 | 4 |
| 0 | 0 | 0 | 0 | 1 | 2 | 4 | 5 | 0 | 0 | 0 | 0 | 1 | 2 | 4 | 4 |
| 0 | 0 | 1 | 1 | 2 | 5 | 5 | 4 | 0 | 0 | 0 | 0 | 1 | 2 | 4 | 4 |
| 0 | 0 | 0 | 0 | 0 | 1 | 2 | 3 | 0 | 0 | 0 | 0 | 0 | 1 | 2 | 3 |
| 0 | 0 | 0 | 0 | 0 | 0 | 1 | 3 | 0 | 0 | 0 | 0 | 0 | 0 | 1 | 3 |
| 0 | 0 | 0 | 0 | 0 | 1 | 2 | 3 | 0 | 0 | 0 | 0 | 0 | 1 | 2 | 3 |
| 0 | 0 | 0 | 0 | 1 | 2 | 2 | 3 | 0 | 0 | 0 | 0 | 0 | 1 | 2 | 3 |

Note how the peak (1 1 2 5 5 4) has been smoothed to the shape of the template but that the trough (1 3) has been left alone.

Closing is defined as

$$CLOSE(I) = E(D(I))$$

with $E$ and $D$ using $T'$ where $T'$ is the 180° rotation of $T$.

| Original | Closed with 1 / 1 |
|---|---|

| | | | | | | | | | | | | | | | | |
|---|---|---|---|---|---|---|---|---|---|---|---|---|---|---|---|---|
| 0 | 0 | 0 | 0 | 0 | 0 | 0 | 0 | 0 | 0 | 0 | 0 | 0 | 0 | 0 | 0 |
| 0 | 0 | 0 | 0 | 0 | 0 | 1 | 4 | 0 | 0 | 0 | 0 | 0 | 0 | 1 | 4 |
| 0 | 0 | 0 | 0 | 1 | 2 | 4 | 5 | 0 | 0 | 0 | 0 | 1 | 2 | 4 | 5 |
| 0 | 0 | 1 | 1 | 2 | 5 | 5 | 4 | 0 | 0 | 1 | 1 | 2 | 5 | 5 | 4 |
| 0 | 0 | 0 | 0 | 0 | 1 | 2 | 3 | 0 | 0 | 0 | 0 | 0 | 1 | 2 | 3 |
| 0 | 0 | 0 | 0 | 0 | 0 | 1 | 3 | 0 | 0 | 0 | 0 | 0 | 0 | 1 | 2 | 3 |
| 0 | 0 | 0 | 0 | 0 | 1 | 2 | 3 | 0 | 0 | 0 | 0 | 0 | 1 | 2 | 3 |
| 0 | 0 | 0 | 0 | 1 | 2 | 2 | 3 | 0 | 0 | 0 | 0 | 1 | 2 | 2 | 3 |

Now the trough has been filled in but the peak has been left.

### 8.3.1 Properties of open and close operations

The open operation forces the shape of the template (structuring element) on the convex parts of an edge. The close operation forces its shape on the concave parts of an edge.

It is possible to combine the erode and open operations to produce a skeleton operation. This is useful to reduce a region to a basic edge that corresponds to the region shape.

#### Technique 8.5 Skeleton operations

USE To create a skeleton of a region. This will consist of a set of lines corresponding to complete thinning of the region without losing the essential shape.

OPERATIONS Let $D_1, D_2, \ldots, D_n$ be structuring templates that are square, with sides $1 \times 1, 2 \times 2, \ldots, n \times n$, all of them filled with 1s.

With image $I$, using templates $D_1, D_2, \ldots, D_n$, in turn, evaluate

$$\text{result}_i = E(I) - \text{OPEN}(E(I))$$

Then determine

$$SK(I) = \underset{\text{for all } i}{\text{maximum}}(\text{result}_i)$$

EXAMPLE For the original above, this gives

```
0  0  0  0  0  0  0  0  0
0  0  0  0  0  0  1  0  0
0  0  0  0  1  1  3  0  0
0  0  0  0  0  0  1  0  0
0  0  0  0  0  0  1  0  0
0  0  0  0  0  0  1  0  0
0  0  0  0  0  1  2  0  0
0  0  0  0  0  0  0  0  0
0  0  0  0  0  0  0  0  0
```

using only $D_1, D_2, D_3,$ and $D_4$.

Intuitively, this corresponds to a skeleton of the image, retaining length but reducing thickness.

APPLICATION This technique has been used in one project to find out about the migration of cells in a fluid. Images of the cells were taken and their centres were found by a skeleton method similar to the one described above. The centres formed the basis of movement estimation.

Another useful operation is granule sizing and counting. How many widgets are there currently on the production line? How big are the chocolate blobs on the conveyer belt? One approach might be to use morphological techniques as follows.

#### Technique 8.6 Granule sizing and granule counting

USE To *estimate* the number of bright regions in an image. To *estimate* the size of the regions in an image.

OPERATION Using templates such as a set of vertical or horizontal 1s with increasing length, enables the 'granular sizes' to be estimated. Using vertical and horizontal templates with binary strings having values $2^n + 1$ (i.e. 1, 11, 101, 1001, 10001, 100001, etc.) allows the number of granules to be estimated. In both cases the image is eroded by the structuring template and a measure of how many elements are now non-zero, or a sum of the power in the system is calculated. This is plotted against the template structure length to give a covariance curve, the peaks of which indicate the size and number of granules in the image.

EXAMPLE The following image was eroded with the templates as shown below. After each erosion the number of pixels > 0 was counted (COUNT) and the power of the resulting image was summed (POWER).

Original image

```
0  0  2  3  0  0  0  0  4  4
0  0  1  1  2  0  0  5  6  3
0  1  4  4  3  0  0  0  5  6
0  0  0  2  2  0  0  0  0  1
0  0  0  0  4  0  0  0  0  0
0  0  0  0  0  0  0  0  0  0
```

Note that the image contains two blobs (or granules), horizontally separated. Taking any image, normally both vertical and horizontal erosion would be done to test for vertically different granules (see Table 8.1).

A variety of information can be deduced from Table 8.1:

1. From the 11. . . 1 series it can be seen that there are no horizontal runs of more than four pixels where all the values are greater than zero.
2. From the 10 . . . 01 series it can be seen that the peak at length 6 and 7 corresponds to

**Table 8.1**

| Length of string | Type | | | |
|---|---|---|---|---|
| | 11 . . . 1 | | 10 . . . 01 | |
| | POWER | COUNT | POWER | COUNT |
| 1 | 63 | 20 | 63 | 20 |
| 2 | 31 | 11 | 31 | 11 |
| 3 | 8 | 4 | 8 | 4 |
| 4 | 1 | 1 | 2 | 2 |
| 5 | 0 | 0 | 3 | 3 |
| 6 | | | 7 | 7 |
| 7 | | | 7 | 7 |
| 8 | | | 4 | 4 |
| 9 | | | 1 | 1 |
| 10 | | | 0 | 0 |

the distance between the blobs, while the consistent POWER = COUNT for this series is a good indicator that the blobs are separated by zeros.

For example, given the above image slightly altered to join the two blobs on the bottom line, the following new image is obtained:

```
0  0  2  3  0  0  0  0  4  4
0  0  1  1  2  0  0  5  6  3
0  1  4  4  3  0  0  0  5  6
0  0  0  2  2  2  0  2  2  1
0  0  4  2  2  2  4  3  3  2
0  0  0  0  0  0  0  0  0  0
```

which eroded with the 10 . . . 01 pattern gives

| | Length | | | | | | | | |
|---|---|---|---|---|---|---|---|---|---|
| | 1 | 2 | 3 | 4 | 5 | 6 | 7 | 8 | 9 |
| COUNT | 30 | 21 | 13 | 9 | 10 | 11 | 9 | 5 | 1 |
| POWER | 87 | 52 | 25 | 14 | 15 | 15 | 12 | 6 | 1 |

The peak comes at 5 and 6, suggesting two blobs; however, with POWER ≠ COUNT for most of the peak period, it suggests that the blobs may not be separate.

The reader can find considerable literature on this subject, a good start is Dougherty and Giardina (1986).

## 8.4 AREA OPERATIONS

A frequent requirement in image processing is to determine accurately the size of an area that is either bounded by a particular range of grey levels or consists of a particular range of grey levels. If the area is a known geometric shape, then this process can be trivial: a box-shaped region is known to be square and upright; the topmost pixel in the box is at $y = 20$, the bottommost pixel is at $y = 30$. Therefore the area of the box is 100 pixels.

It is less easy to find the areas of a region if the region is not regular. The problem can, however, be mapped onto a classic graphics problem of flood filling an irregular shape. Here a pixel is identified as being inside the contour and a rule is given for what is defined to be the edge of the contour (i.e. either a change in grey level from a known level, or the reaching of a pixel that has a specified grey level).

Some clinical trials required that the cross-sectional area of bone on a large number of skull X-rays needed to be measured. The shape of the bone made the measurements particularly difficult to do by hand in any way. The X-rays were scanned and, with an initial point given by an operator using a mouse, the bone region was flood filled with a new colour and the number of pixels counted as the filling progressed.

Flood fill routines normally fill, from the start pixel, until the contour is reached, testing all possible directions. The counting routine moves in the same way and has to 'fill' as it moves, otherwise it does not know which pixels have been counted so far. Two issues are problematic for the image processor in this approach.

First, it may be that the region contains useful information. For example, we may wish to determine the area of one particular dark blob with grey levels 100–120 that lies on a light background of grey levels 240–255. If the dark blob is filled as it is counted (say with a single grey level 0), then the information inside that dark blob is irrecoverably lost.

One approach is to make a copy of the screen *before* filling the blob, so that the blob may be restored when counting is done. Another is to fill a background array instead of filling the original. Finally, if memory is at a premium it may be possible to identify a range of grey levels independent from the background range and the blob range into which the grey levels can be transposed. In the above example we may choose 0–20, say, so that as a new pixel in the blob is found, 100 is subtracted from the grey level.

If this last approach is used then the fill has to be implemented twice in order to reset the values back to their original values by searching for grey levels in the range 0–20 and adding 100.

Secondly, image filling usually involves many more 'internal' boundaries than graphics filling.

Flood fill routines scan a new pixel and, if they fill it (i.e. it is in the region for counting), then they have to choose which direction to proceed to look. If there is a choice of directions, then they have temporarily to store the pixel position and come back to it later so as to try the other directions. This does not need to be done for every pixel. If we can guarantee that coming back to pixel A will mean that pixel B's alternatives will also be processed, then we need only store pixel A for future reference. Implementing this in software is tricky.

Graphics images are often binary images with complete boundaries without anything inside them. Images of real life are not like that. Figure 8.1 shows a very difficult image to count, assuming that the 'connected' 0s are to be counted starting at a specific zero pixel. It contains boundary-value pixels 'inside' the region whose area is to be counted. In fact, given any zero pixel, it is not possible to travel more than two zero pixels in any direction without having a choice of routes available. Note that a zero is connected to another zero if it is immediately above, below, to the left, or to the right of the other zero.

```
1 1 1 1 1 1 1 1 1 1 1 1 1 1 1 1 1 1 1 1 1 1 1
1 0 1 0 0 0 1 0 0 0 1 0 0 0 1 0 0 0 1 0 0 0 1 1
1 0 0 0 1 0 0 0 1 0 0 0 1 0 0 0 1 0 0 0 1 0 0 1
1 0 0 1 0 0 0 1 0 0 0 1 0 0 0 1 0 0 0 1 0 0 0 1
1 0 1 0 0 0 1 0 0 0 1 0 0 0 1 0 0 0 1 0 0 0 1 1
1 0 0 0 1 0 0 0 0 1 0 0 0 1 0 0 0 1 0 0 0 1 0 1
1 0 0 1 0 0 0 1 0 0 0 1 0 0 0 1 0 0 0 1 0 0 0 1
1 0 1 0 0 0 1 0 0 0 1 0 0 0 1 0 0 0 1 0 0 0 1 1
1 0 0 0 1 0 0 0 1 0 0 0 1 0 0 0 1 0 0 0 1 0 0 1
1 0 0 1 0 0 0 1 0 0 0 1 0 0 0 1 0 0 0 1 0 0 0 1
1 1 1 1 1 1 1 1 1 1 1 1 1 1 1 1 1 1 1 1 1 1 1
```

**Figure 8.1**

In order to avoid storing every position where a choice has to be made, the algorithm should store a first pixel position and then only store another pixel position when it has passed by the side of an internal boundary value. For example:

```
1  1  1  1  1  1  1  1  1  1  1  1  1  1  1  1
0  0  0  0  0  0  0  0  0  1  0  0  0  0  0  0
0  0  0  0  0  0  0  0  0  1  0  0  0  0  0  0
0  0  ←  ←  ←  S  ←  ←  S  ←  ←  ←  ←  ←  S  0
0  0  0  0  0  0  1  0  0  0  0  0  0  0  0  0
0  0  0  0  0  0  1  0  0  0  0  0  0  0  0  0
1  1  1  1  1  1  1  1  1  1  1  1  1  1  1  1
```

Here the algorithm saves the start pixel (the rightmost S) and then moves left, filling and counting as it goes. It does not need to store any further pixel positions until it encounters the internal boundary value (the 1 above the row). It has to store the next pixel position because there may not be a route from the first S to be able to deal with the 0s now above the filled line since there has been a boundary value in the way. Similarly, when it encounters a boundary value below the line, it needs to store the position of the next pixel so that the lower 0s will be filled.

The first of the three Ss will be reconsidered when the present line has been filled and then new start points, above and below the S, will be processed. The number of stored points can therefore be a problem. On the 'difficult to fill' diagram above, it is necessary to store at least every other pixel position every third row. In the worst case, with $640 \times 480$ VGA, that would amount to $50\,000$ pixel positions. Given 4 bytes per position, that is 200K for maximum storage size. Rarely does it actually require anything like that, but if a fill routine is used that uses the stack to store the positions, a 64K stack size is frequently too small.

This leads to a choice of fills. The classic 'forest fire' fill can be adapted but is extremely wasteful in terms of storage.

```
int start_fill(x,y)
int x,y;
{
int count=0;
 fill(x,y);
 return(count);
}

fill(x,y)
int x,y;
{
 if(not_boundary(x,y) && not_filled(x,y))
 {
  setpixel(x,y);
  count++;
  if(x>0)fill(x-1,y);
  if(x<XMAX)fill(x+1,y);
  if(y>0)fill(x,y-1);
  if(y<YMAX)fill(x,y+1);
 }
}
```

For a full VGA screen fill this would require a stack size of at least 1 Mbyte, even if the screen was not 'difficult to fill'.

A more intelligent fill is given in a number of texts. One used by the author, which still incorporates the stack as the storage mechanism, is as follows.

### Technique 8.7 Row search fill and count
USE To find the area of a region in an image.

OPERATION Having identified a start pixel, store its position and fill as far as possible to the right and left.

Now, starting at the stored position move right.

If the pixel above the current pixel does not require filling, continue to move right until a pixel is found that does require filling.

If it does require filling, perform this function recursively starting from the found pixel.

Repeat the operation, looking below the line of filled pixels.

Throughout, increment a counter whenever a pixel is filled.

CODE

| | |
|---|---|
| (xa,ya) | is the pixel start point |
| ccol | is the grey-level that requires filling |
| fcol | is the final fill grey level |
| LEFT | is the leftmost x-coordinate of the screen (typically 0) |
| TOP | is the topmost y-coordinate of the screen (typically 0) |
| BOT | is the bottommost y-coordinate of the screen (typically 479 on VGA) |
| RIGHT | is the rightmost x-coordinate of the screen (typically 639 on VGA) |
| oldxa | is global temporary storage |
| screen[ya][xa] | is the grey level at (xa,ya) |

```
fill(int xa,int ya)
{
int xleft,xright;

 oldxa=xa;

/*fill to the left*/

 while(ccol==screen[ya][xa] && xa>=LEFT)screen[ya][xa--]=fcol;
 xleft=xa+1;

/*fill to the right*/

 xa=oldxa+1;
 while(ccol==screen[ya](xa] && xa<=RIGHT)screen[ya][xa++]=fcol;
 xright=xa;

/*Check above row and*/
/*Recursive fill if new area above is found for filling*/

 for(xa=xleft;xa<xright;xa++)
 if(ya>TOP && ccol==screen[ya-1][xa])fill(xa,ya-1);
```

```
/*Check below row and*/
/*Recursive fill if new area below is discovered for filling*/
  for(xa=xleft;xa<xright;xa++)
  if(ya>BOT && ccol==screen[ya+1][xa])fill(xa,ya+1);
}
```

PROBLEMS Stack requirements are still heavy. For example, with a 10 per cent random snow on a $640 \times 480$ screen, a 64K stack is too small to fill the background. With a 1 per cent random snow, 64K is adequate, with a 60 per cent random snow, 64K is adequate, but only because not all of the background is connected so that the fill does not cover every dark pixel.

This 'filling' approach to counting generates two further techniques that can be used to count granules, i.e. discovering how many blobs are there in the image.

### Technique 8.8  Granule counting (2)
USE  To determine exactly how many regions there are of a particular type in an image.

OPERATION This process involves scanning the image for the first pixel in a granule, typically by raster scanning left to right and top to bottom.

When a granule pixel is found, the flood fill/count routine is implemented to eliminate that granule from the image.

Scanning then continues so as to find the next granule, and so on.

### Technique 8.9  Granule counting given edges only

USE  To count the number of enclosed areas in an image.

OPERATION The best approach is to fill the background first and then use granule counting as above. The top left pixel is therefore used as the start pixel for a flood fill. The scanning procedure is then implemented. (See Chapter 1 for application.)

## 8.5  EXERCISES

**8.1** Using open and close operations, determine the skeleton of the following array:

$$
\begin{array}{cccccccc}
3 & 3 & 4 & 4 & 7 & 7 & 7 & 7 \\
3 & 3 & 2 & 4 & 4 & 4 & 2 & 0 \\
0 & 0 & 4 & 8 & 8 & 8 & 4 & 0 \\
0 & 0 & 0 & 0 & 0 & 0 & 4 & 0 \\
3 & 0 & 0 & 0 & 0 & 4 & 2 & 0 \\
3 & 3 & 5 & 5 & 6 & 6 & 6 & 0 \\
\end{array}
$$

**8.2** Show how the row-search fill works on the following image (filling the 0 starting at position *).

```
1 1 1 1 1 1 1 1 1 1 1 1 1 1
1 1 0 0 0 0 0 0 0 1 1 1 1 1
1 1 0 * 0 0 1 1 0 0 0 0 1 1
1 1 0 1 0 0 0 1 0 0 1 0 0 1
1 1 1 1 0 1 1 1 0 1 1 1 1 1
1 1 1 1 0 0 0 1 1 0 0 0 0 1
1 1 1 1 1 1 1 1 1 1 1 1 1 1
```

# 9

---

# FINDING BASIC SHAPES

## 9.1 INTRODUCTION

Whereas Chapters 5–8 dealt with purely statistical and spatial local operations, this chapter is mainly concerned with looking at the whole image and processing the image with the information generated by the algorithms in the previous chapters.

The chapter deals with methods for finding basic two-dimensional shapes or elements of shapes by putting edges detected in earlier processing together to form lines that are likely to represent real edges.

Towards the end of the chapter there is also a basic discussion about character recognition. This uses histogram operations and thresholding on small areas, and is an example of applied image processing.

## 9.2 COMBINING EDGES

Bits of edges, even when they have been joined up in some way by using, for example, crack edge relaxation, are not very useful in themselves unless they are used to enhance a previous image. From an identification point of view it is more useful to determine structure of lines, equations, lengths, thicknesses, and so on. These facts form building blocks for the labelling that appears in the next chapter.

There are a variety of edge-combining methods in the literature. These include edge following (covered in Section 7.6) and Hough transforms.

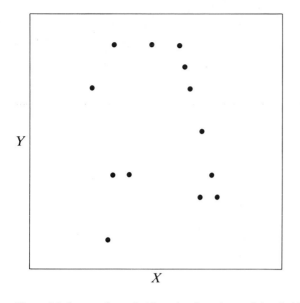

**Figure 9.1** Screen after primitive edge detection and thresholding (only significant edge pixels shown).

## 9.3 HOUGH TRANSFORMS

This technique allows you to discover shapes from image *edges*. It assumes that a primitive edge detection has already been performed on an image. It attempts to combine edges into lines where a sequence of edge pixels in a line indicates that a real edge exists.

As well as detecting straight lines, versions of the Hough transform can be used to detect regular or non-regular shapes, though, as will be seen, the most generalized Hough transform, which will detect a two-dimensional specific shape of any size or orientation, requires a lot of processing power in order to be able to do its work in a reasonably finite time.

### 9.3.1 Basic principle of the straight-line Hough transform

After primitive edge detection and then thresholding to keep only pixels with a strong edge gradient, the screen may look like Fig. 9.1.

A straight line connecting a sequence of pixels can be expressed in the form

$$y = mx + c$$

If we can evaluate values for $m$ and $c$ such that the line passes through a number of the pixels that are set, then we have a usable representation of a straight line.

The Hough transform takes the above image and converts it into a new image in (what is termed) a new space. In fact, it transforms each significant edge pixel in $(x, y)$ space into a straight line in this new space.

When this has been done for all pixels, the intersections of the lines in the new space indicate real edges in the original $(x, y)$ space.

Consider an example. The $(x, y)$ space line equation is

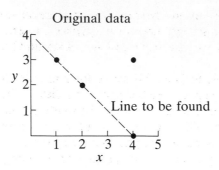

| y | x | Gives | Transposed |
|---|---|-------|------------|
| 3 | 1 | $3 = m.1 + c$ | $c = -1m + 3$ |
| 2 | 2 | $2 = m.2 + c$ | $c = -2m + 2$ |
| 3 | 4 | $3 = m.4 + c$ | $c = -4m + 3$ |
| 0 | 4 | $0 = m.4 + c$ | $c = -4m$ |

(a)

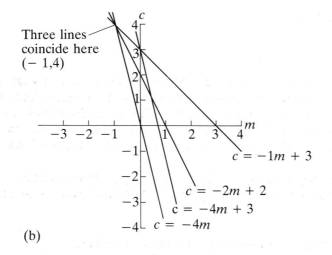

(b)

**Figure 9.2** (a) Illustration of the effect of the straight-line Hough transform in $(m, c)$ space. (b) Accumulator array in $(m, c)$ space. Maximum in the accumulator array is 3 at $(-1, 4)$, suggesting that a line $y = -1x + 4$ goes through three of the original data points.

$$y = mx + c$$

Clearly, many lines go through a single point $(x, y)$, e.g. a horizontal line can be drawn through the point, a vertical line, and all the lines at different angles between these. However, each line will have a slope $(m)$ and an intercept $(c)$ such that the above equation holds true.

A little manipulation of the above equation gives

$$c = (-x)m + y$$

We know the values of $x$ and $y$ (the position where the pixel may be on an edge), but, in this form, the equation now represents a straight line in $(m, c)$ space, i.e. with a horizontal $m$-axis and a vertical $c$-axis, each $(x, y)$ edge pixel corresponds to a straight line on this new $(m, c)$ graph.

We need spare store to be available to hold this set of lines in an array (called the accumulator array). Then for every $(x, y)$ point, each element that lies on the corresponding line in the $(m, c)$ accumulator array can be incremented. (So that after the first point in the $(x, y)$ space has been processed there will be a line of 1s in the $(m, c)$ array.)

This 'plotting' in the $(m, c)$ array is done using an enhanced form of Bresenham's algorithm, which will plot a wide, straight line (so that at the ends crossing lines are not missed).

At the end of processing all the $(x, y)$ pixels, the highest value in the $(m, c)$ accumulator array indicates that a large number of lines cross in that array at some point $(m', c')$. The value in this element corresponds to the same number of pixels being in a straight line in the $(x, y)$ space, and the position of this element gives the equation of the line in $(x, y)$ space, namely

$$y = m' x + c'$$

Figure 9.2 illustrates this method

### 9.3.2 Problems

There are serious problems in using $(m, c)$ space. For each pixel, $m$ may properly vary from minus infinity to infinity (i.e. a straight line upwards). Clearly this is unsatisfactory; no accumulator array can be set up with enough elements. There are alternatives, such as using two accumulator arrays, with $m$ ranging from $-1 \le m \le +1$ in one and $-1 < 1/m < +1$ in the second. The reader is left to determine the other problems with this approach.

It is safer, though requiring more calculations, to use angles, transforming to polar coordinates $(r, \theta)$, where $x \cos \theta + y \sin \theta = r$. Figure 9.3 illustrates the polar coordinate connection.

### Technique 9.1  Real straight-edge discovery using the Hough transform
USE To find out and connect substantial straight edges from partial edges already found using an edge detector.

OPERATION For each edge pixel value $I(x, y)$, vary $\theta$ from $0°$ to $360°$ and calculate $r = x \cos \theta + y \sin \theta$.

Given an accumulator array size $(N + M, 360)$, increment those elements in the array that lie in a box $(b \times b)$ with centre $(r, \theta)$. Clearly, if the box is $1 \times 1$, only one element of the array is incremented; if the box is $3 \times 3$, nine elements are incremented. This gives a 'thick' line in the new space so that intersections are not missed.

Finally, look for the highest values in the accumulator $(r, \theta)$ array and thus identify the pairs $(r, \theta)$ that are most likely to indicate a line in $(x, y)$ space.

This method can be enhanced in a number of ways:

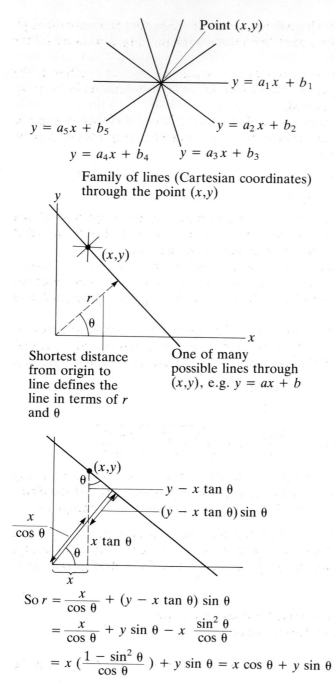

Point $(x,y)$

$y = a_1 x + b_1$

$y = a_5 x + b_5$

$y = a_2 x + b_2$

$y = a_4 x + b_4$

$y = a_3 x + b_3$

Family of lines (Cartesian coordinates)
through the point $(x,y)$

$(x,y)$

$r$

$\theta$

$y$

$x$

Shortest distance
from origin to
line defines the
line in terms of $r$
and $\theta$

One of many
possible lines through
$(x,y)$, e.g. $y = ax + b$

$(x,y)$

$\theta$

$y - x \tan \theta$

$(y - x \tan \theta) \sin \theta$

$\dfrac{x}{\cos \theta}$

$x \tan \theta$

$\theta$

$x$

So $r = \dfrac{x}{\cos \theta} + (y - x \tan \theta) \sin \theta$

$\qquad = \dfrac{x}{\cos \theta} + y \sin \theta - x \dfrac{\sin^2 \theta}{\cos \theta}$

$\qquad = x \left( \dfrac{1 - \sin^2 \theta}{\cos \theta} \right) + y \sin \theta = x \cos \theta + y \sin \theta$

**Figure 9.3** Relationship between Cartesian straight line and polar defined line.

1. Instead of just incrementing the cells in the accumulator array, the gradient of the edge, prior to thresholding, could be added to the cell, thus plotting a measure of the likelihood of this being an edge.
2. Gradient direction can be taken into account. If this suggests that the direction of the real edge lies between two angles ($\theta_1$ and $\theta_2$, say), then only the elements in the $(r, \theta)$ array that lie in $\theta_1 < \theta < \theta_2$ are plotted.
3. The incrementing box does not need to be uniform. It is known that the best estimate of $(r, \theta)$ is at the centre of the box, so this element is incremented by a larger figure than the elements around that centre element.

Note that the line length is not given, so that the lines go to infinity as it stands.

Three approaches may be considered:

1. Foglein *et al.* (1984) suggest passing a $3 \times 3$ median filter over the image original and subtracting the value of the centre pixel in the window from the result. This tends to find some corners of images, thus enabling line endings to be estimated.
2. Set up four further accumulator arrays. The first pair can hold the most north-east position on the line and the second pair the most south-west position, these positions being updated as and when a pixel contributes to the corresponding accumulating element in the main array.
3. Again with four further accumulator arrays, let the main accumulator array be increased by $w$ for some pixel $(x, y)$. Increase the first pair by $wx$ and $wy$ and the second by $(wx)^2$ and $(wy)^2$. At the end of the operation a good estimate of the end of the line is

$$\text{mean of line } \pm 2\sigma$$

where $\sigma$ is the standard deviation, i.e.

$$\text{End of line estimate} = \frac{\Sigma wx}{\Sigma w} \pm 2 \times \sqrt{\frac{\Sigma (wx)^2}{\Sigma w} - \left(\frac{\Sigma wx}{\Sigma w}\right)^2}$$

for the $x$ range and a similar expression for the $y$ range. This makes some big assumptions regarding the distribution of edge pixels, e.g. it assumes that the distribution is not skewed to one end of the line, and so may not always be appropriate.

The Hough technique is good for finding straight lines. It is even better for finding circles. Again the algorithm requires significant edge pixels to be identified, so some edge detector must be passed over the original image before it is transformed using the Hough technique.

### Technique 9.2  Real circle discovery using the Hough transform
USE  Finding circles from an edge-detected image.

OPERATION  If the object is to search for circles of a known radius $R$, say, then the following identity can be used:

$$(x - a)^2 + (y - b)^2 = R^2$$

where $(a, b)$ is the centre of the circle. Again in $(x, y)$ space all pixels on an edge are identified (by thresholding) or every pixel with $I(x, y) > 0$ is processed. A circle of

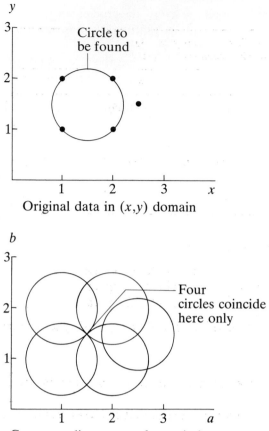

Original data in $(x,y)$ domain

Corresponding accumulator circles
in $(a,b)$ domain

Maximum in accumulator array is value 4 at
position (1.5, 1.5) => probable
circle at (1.5, 1.5) centre, with radius $\dfrac{1}{\sqrt{2}}$

**Figure 9.4** Illustration of Hough circle transform (looking for circles radius $1/\sqrt{2}$)

elements is incremented in the $(a, b)$ accumulator array centre $(0 < a < M - 1,$
$0 < b < N - 1)$, radius $R$ for each edge pixel to be processed. Bresenham's circle-
drawing algorithm can be used to increment the circle elements quickly. Finally, the
highest values in the $(a, b)$ array indicate coincident edges in $(a, b)$ space corresponding
to a number of pixels on the edge of the same circle in $(x, y)$ space.

Again it is possible to reduce the amount of work by using the gradient direction to
indicate the likely arc within which the circle centre is expected to lie.

Figure 9.4 illustrates this technique.

**Table 9.1**

| Boundary angle w.r.t horizontal (degrees | Relative distance readings (dx, dy) of boundary point from 'centre' | | | | |
|---|---|---|---|---|---|
| | 1 | 2 | 3 | 4 | 5 |
| 0 | (− 36, 23) | (38, − 12) | (− 27, 33) | (84, 85) | |
| 1 | (44, − 32) | (20, 92) | | | |
| 2 | (91, 24) | (− 12, 49) | | | |
| 3 | | | | | |
| 4 | (53, − 89) | (54, − 82) | (55, − 74) | (66, − 48) | (67, 13) |
| 5 | (24, 10) | | | | |
| ⋮ | | | | | |
| 359 | (13, − 14) | (19, − 9) | | | |

It is possible to look for the following types of circle:

| different radii | plot in $(a, b, R)$ space |
|---|---|
| different radii, same vertical centres | plot in $(b, R)$ space |
| different radii, same horizontal centres | plot in $(a, R)$ space |

If the circle radius is known to be one of three values, say, then $(a, b, R)$ space can be three planes of $(a, b)$ arrays.

The following points are important:

1. As the number of unknown parameters increases, the amount of processing increases exponentially.
2. The Hough technique above can be used to discover any edge that can be expressed as a simple identity.
3. The generalized Hough transform can also be used to discover shapes that are not able to be represented by simple mathematical identities. This is described below.

**Technique 9.3 The generalized Hough transform**

USE Find a known shape—in its most general form—of any size or orientation in an image. In practice it is best to go for a known size and orientation.

OPERATION Some preparation is needed prior to the analysis of the image. Given the object boundary, and assuming that the object in the image is of the same size and orientation (otherwise a number of accumulator arrays have to be set up for different sizes and orientations), a 'centre' $(x, y)$ is chosen, somewhere within the boundary of the object.

The boundary is then traversed and after every step $d$ along the boundary the angle of the boundary tangent with respect to horizontal is noted, and the $x$ difference and $y$ difference of the boundary position from the centre point are also noted.

The differences are entered into a table of the type shown in Table 9.1.

For every pixel $I(x, y)$ in the edge-detected image, the gradient direction is found and the row of elements in the array shown in Table 9.1 then refer to a set of elements relative to this boundary point which may be possible 'centres' of the object. The accumulator array (same size as the image) is then incremented by 1 for each such element.

Finally, the highest-valued element(s) in the accumulator array point to the possible 'centres' of the object in the image.

## 9.4 BRESENHAM'S ALGORITHMS

Bresenham's algorithms have been referred to in a number of places in this book, particularly in the work with Hough transforms. The reader should refer to a standard computer graphics text (such as Foley and Van Dam, 1984) for a theoretical description of why these operate as they do. The techniques for plotting are described below.

The algorithms are methods for plotting on an incremental plotter system (such as an array of pixels). In most cases image processing does not need plotting, but incrementing pixels in a straight line or circle is required for implementing algorithms such as Hough. Both straight-line and circular plotting algorithms are described below.

**Technique 9.4  Bresenham's straight-line drawing algorithm**
USE To fill the accumulator array in the Hough transform for straight lines using an $(m, c)$ array, also for drawing straight lines on images.

OPERATION Assuming that the pixels between $x_1$, $y_1$ and $x_2$, $y_2$ are to be incremented.
    Determine the steepness of the line

$$dx = |x_1 - x_2| \quad dy = |y_1 - y_2|$$

If $dx < dy$, we classify the line as steep and swap the values for $dx$ and $dy$, $x_1$ and $y_1$, and $x_2$ and $y_2$.
    Determine the direction of incrementation (i.e. 1 if $x_1 \to x_2$ is the same direction as $y_1 \to y_2$, $-1$ otherwise).
    Set $incr_1 = 2dy$, $incr_2 = 2(dy - dx)$ and $d = 2dy - dx$.
    Set $x$ and $y$ to the leftmost point of $(x_1, y_1)$, $(x_2, y_2)$.
    Finally, the incrementing loop

        while $x$ is still in range of $x_1 : x_2$
        {
        If steep then increment $I(y, x)$ else increment $I(x, y)$
            If $d \geq 0$ then increment $y$ and add $incr_2$ to $d$ else add $incr_1$ to $d$

        increment $x$
        }
    If steep then increment $I(y, x)$ else increment $I(x, y)$

CODE
```
void line(x1,y1,x2,y2)
int x1,x2,y1,y2;
{
  int dx,dy,steep,d,x,y,xlast,dir;
  dx=abs(x2-x1); dy=abs(y2-y1); steep=(dy>dx);
  if(steep)
```

```
{
  d=dx; dx=dy; dy=d; d=x1; x1=y1; y1=d; d=x2; x2=y2; y2=d;
}
i1=2*dy; i2=2*dy-2*dx; d=2*dy-dx;
if(x1>x2){x=x2; y=y2; xlast=x1;} else {x=x1; y=y1; xlast=x2;}
if((x1>x2)==(y1>y2))dir=1; else dir=-1;
while(x<xlast)
{
  if(steep)arr[y][x]++; else arr[x][y]++;
  if(d>=0){y+=dir; d+=i2;} else d+=i1;
  x++;
}
if(steep)arr[y][x]++; else arr[x][y]++;
}
```

This routine may be used to draw a line from $(x_1, y_1)$ to $(x_2, y_2)$ instead of just incrementing the array, in which case all the occurrences of arr[ ][ ] + +; should read arr[ ][ ] = 255; or similar.

With both circle and straight-line cumulation it is important to remember the following points:

1. When incrementing the array (arr[ ][ ] + +; in this case) a block may need to be incremented to give a thick line and the incrementing value (here it is 1) could usefully be related to the edge gradient.
2. If the array is of type 'unsigned char', then a check needs to be made that the value 255 has not already been reached, otherwise further incrementation will reset this back to zero.
3. Clearly, the accumulator arrays must be initialized to zero to start with.

### 9.4.1 Circle incrementation

This circle cumulation algorithm uses only shift and add in its main loop so that a circle is quickly obtained. It assumes that the centres of the circle is at $(cx, cy)$ with radius $r$ pixels. Also, prior to incrementation it may be necessary to check whether the position to be incremented is actually a valid position in the array. C programmers will know that most C compilers do not automatically check for access of elements outside of a defined array area. This simply creates other, difficult-to-solve run-time errors instead.

**Technique 9.5 Bresenham's circle drawing algorithm**
USE To fill the circle accumulator array in the Hough transform, and for drawing circles in images.

CODE

```
void circle(cx,cy,r)
int cx,cy,r;
{
  int x,y=0,d;
  x=r; d=3-(r<<1);
  while(x>y)
  {
    increment_circle(cx,cy,x,y);
    if(d<0)d+=(y<<2)-6; else {d+=((y-x)<<2)+10; x--;}
    y++;
  }
  increment_circle(cx,cy,x,y);
}
void increment_circle(cx,cy,x,y)
int cx,cy,x,y;
{
  arr[cx+x][cy+y]++; arr[cy+y][cx+x]++;
  arr[cx-x][cy+y]++; arr[cy-y][cx+x]++;
  arr[cx+x][cy-y]++; arr[cy+y][cx-x]++;
  arr[cx-x][cy-y]++; arr[cy-y][cx-x]++;
}
```

The Hough transform is very close in operation to template matching; however, except in the generalized case, the template is replaced by a function which makes the operation considerably cheaper than convolution/correlation with a large template image.

## 9.5 USING INTEREST POINTS

The previous chapter described how interest points might be discovered from an image. From these, it is possible to determine whether the object being viewed is a 'known' object. Here the two-dimensional problem, without occlusion (objects being covered up by other objects), is considered. We assume that the interest points from the known two-dimensional shape are held on file in some way and that the two-dimensional shape to be identified has been processed by the same interest point finding routine and delivered a set of interest points that now have to be compared with the known shape.

We further assume that the shape may have been rotated, scaled, and/or translated from the original known shape. Hence it is necessary to determine a matrix that satisfies

$$\text{discovered interest points} = \text{known shape interest points} \times M$$

or

$$D = KM$$

where $M$ is a two-dimensional transformation matrix of the form

$$\begin{pmatrix} a & b & 0 \\ c & d & 0 \\ e & f & 1 \end{pmatrix}$$

and the interest point sets are of the form

$$\begin{pmatrix} x_1 & y_1 & 1 \\ x_2 & y_2 & 1 \\ x_3 & y_3 & 1 \\ x_4 & y_4 & 1 \\ x_5 & y_5 & 1 \\ \dots & \dots & \dots \\ x_n & y_n & 1 \end{pmatrix}$$

The $M$ matrix described above does not allow for sheering transformations because this is essentially a three-dimensional transformation of an original shape.

There is usually some error in the calculations of interest point positions so that

$$D = KM + \epsilon$$

and the purpose is to find $M$ with the least error and then determine whether that error is small enough to indicate that the match is correct or not. A good approach is to use a least-squares approximation to determine $M$ and the errors, i.e. minimize $F(D - KM)$, where $F(Z) = x_i^2 + y_i^2$.

This gives the following normal equations:

$$\begin{pmatrix} \Sigma x^2 & \Sigma xy & \Sigma x \\ \Sigma xy & \Sigma y^2 & \Sigma y \\ \Sigma x & \Sigma y & n \end{pmatrix} \begin{pmatrix} a \\ c \\ e \end{pmatrix} = \begin{pmatrix} \Sigma xX \\ \Sigma yX \\ \Sigma X \end{pmatrix} \quad \text{or } L\mathbf{a} = \mathbf{s}_1$$

and

$$\begin{pmatrix} \Sigma x^2 & \Sigma xy & \Sigma x \\ \Sigma xy & \Sigma y^2 & \Sigma y \\ \Sigma x & \Sigma y & n \end{pmatrix} \begin{pmatrix} b \\ d \\ f \end{pmatrix} = \begin{pmatrix} \Sigma xY \\ \Sigma yY \\ \Sigma Y \end{pmatrix} \quad \text{or } L\mathbf{b} = \mathbf{s}_1$$

where lowercase letters denote the known points and uppercase letters the unknown points. $n$ is the number of pairs of matched points.

Using the alternative notation

$$L\mathbf{a} = \mathbf{s}_1$$

$$L\mathbf{b} = \mathbf{s}_2$$

If the inverse of the square $L$ matrix is calculated, then the values for $a$ to $f$ can be evaluated and the error determined. That is, calculate

$$L^{-1}L\mathbf{a} = L^{-1}\mathbf{s}_1$$

and

$$L^{-1}L\mathbf{b} = L^{-1}\mathbf{s}_2$$

giving

$$\mathbf{a} = L^{-1}\mathbf{s}_1$$

and

$$\mathbf{b} = L^{-1}\mathbf{s}_2$$

An image of a known four-sided object was passed through an interest point algorithm which discovered a set of points (corners) as follows:

$$\{(30, 50), (40, 50), (30, 10), (50, 10)\}$$

An image of a second unknown object was passed through the same interest point algorithm and this discovered the following set of points:

$$\{(35, 150), (78, 210), (254, 25), (330, 129)\}$$

The $L$ matrix evaluated to

$$\begin{pmatrix} 5900 & 4300 & 150 \\ 4300 & 5200 & 120 \\ 150 & 120 & 4 \end{pmatrix}$$

and inverted to

$$\begin{pmatrix} 0.004 & 0.0005 & -0.165 \\ 0.0005 & 0.0007 & -0.039 \\ -0.165 & -0.393 & 7.618 \end{pmatrix}$$

This was multiplied by each of the **s** vectors, giving the final $M$ matrix

$$\begin{pmatrix} a & b & 0 \\ c & d & 0 \\ e & f & 1 \end{pmatrix} = \begin{pmatrix} 3.9 & 5.4 & 0 \\ -5.4 & 3.2 & 0 \\ 190 & -170 & 1 \end{pmatrix}$$

When this was applied to the unknown image points, the results were within 4 pixels radius of the known image points, the error sum of squares/4 being 4.45. This was, therefore, likely to be the object originally described.

## 9.5.1 Problems

There are some problems with this approach. First, coordinates must be paired beforehand. That is, there are known library coordinates, each of which must correspond to the correct unknown coordinate for a match to occur. This can be done by extensive searching, i.e. by matching each known coordinate with each captured coordinate, all possible permutations have to be considered. For example, consider an interest point algorithm that delivers five interest points for a known object. Also let there be $N$ images, each containing an unknown object, the purpose of the exercise being to identify if any or all of the images contain the known object.

A reduction on the search can be done by eliminating all those images that do not have five interest points. If this leaves $n$ images there will be $b \times 5! = 120n$ possible permutations to search. Clearly any mechanism to reduce this work is advantageous. One search reduction method is to order the interest points. The interest operator itself may give a value which can place that interest point at a particular position in a list. Alternatively, a simple sum of the brightness of the surrounding pixels can be used to give a position. Either way, if the order is known, the searches are reduced from $O(n \times i!)$ to $O(n)$, where $i$ is the number of interest points in the image.

An alternative ordering scheme for silhouette images makes the assumption that the interest points held will only be those on the outer circumference of the object and that these are ordered according to their sequence around the edge. This requires an edge-following algorithm to discover the sequence (see Section 7.6).

The second problem is that the system cannot deal with occlusion or part views of objects, nor can it deal with three-dimensional objects in different orientations.

## 9.6 EXERCISES

**9.1** Using standard graph paper, perform a straight-line Hough transform on the binary pixel array shown in Figure 9.5, transforming into $(m, c)$ space.

**9.2** A library object has the following ordered interest point classification:

$$\{(0, 0), (0, 3), (1, 0), (2, 4)\}$$

Identify, using the above technique, which of the following two sets of interest points represent a translation, rotation, and/or scaling of the above object:

$$\{(1, 1), (6, 12), (2, 5), (12, 23)\}$$

$$\{(1, 3), (1, 12), (-1, 8), (3, 6)\}$$

Check your answer by showing that a final point maps near to its corresponding known point.

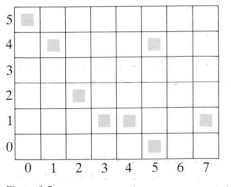

Figure 9.5

# 10

## LABELLING LINES AND REGIONS

### 10.1 INTRODUCTION

Having identified lines, regions, textures, interest points, or whatever, the computer vision process often requires some labelling of the elements that have been found as a kind of forerunner to recognition and then image description proper. We need to move from the position of having, for instance, a set of lines with no idea as to if and where they join, to some concept of corner, object edge, object surface, background, object orientation, lighting position, etc.

We have already touched on this subject towards the end of the last chapter. However, recognition often requires a set of small, processor-intensive labelling and searching steps.

Furthermore, a single set of algorithms will not do all the labelling work. What might work well in the laboratory for an image of a right-angled box may not work in real life for a car or a coin. Whereas edge labelling is relatively easy to perform with objects with straight edges (and flat surfaces), it is much harder to do with objects with curved edges and curved surfaces. In these cases edge labelling might be an inappropriate route to take. Region labelling might be more valuable.

The extent of labelling depends on the number of different possibilities in the set to be recognized. If there are only two 'types' of item to be identified, it is not worth labelling if a simple area, size, or colour test will do the job.

> Matches were checked for an adequate amount of combustible coating by a vision system which looked at the top of the match. The system determined whether the width was within an acceptable range of widths, and it also checked the colour of the coating, that it was also within a given wavelength range. This enabled the matches to be labelled good or reject.

If the task is to identify an object as being one of a number of possibilities held in a library, or recognize, label (and in some way understand) an object that is unknown previously to the system, then labelling can be a very useful tool.

This chapter outlines some techniques for labelling, and then methods for storing the results of labelling in some form in a library.

## 10.2 FLAT-SURFACE AND STRAIGHT-LINE LABELLING

A good first move is to try and identify the vertices in the image. These are the positions where straight lines converge to make a corner. If the equations of the lines have been found using a Hough transform, then we also need data about where, precisely, lines stop and start.

### Technique 10.1 Finding vertices from Hough transform results

USE As a first step in the labelling process, to identify where the corners of objects are likely to be in a given image.

OPERATION This can be done by searching the found direction using an edge-detection operator (such as Sobel), looking for gradient magnitudes on the original, or summing the pixels on an image that is the result of an edge detection of the original.

Lines can then be expected in a parameter form. If $(x_0, y_0)$ is the 'start' and $(x_1, y_1)$ is the end of a line (the typical data pair that will be delivered by the earlier Sobel searching operation) and the line is known to be straight, then the line can be written as

$$y = y_0 + a(y_1 - y_0), \ x = x_0 + a(x_1 - x_0) \quad \text{where } 0 \le a \le 1$$

A second, different, line can also be written as

$$y = y_2 + b(y_3 - y_2), \ x = x_2 + b(x_3 - x_2) \quad \text{where } 0 \le b \le 1$$

Two lines intersect if there exists $a$ and $b$ in the range 0 to 1 such that

$$y_2 + b(y_3 - y_2) = y_0 + a(y_1 - y_0) \quad \text{and} \quad x_2 + b(x_3 - x_2) = x_0 + a(x_1 - x_0)$$

This gives

$$b = \frac{(y_2 - y_0)(x_1 - x_0) - (y_1 - y_0)(x_2 - x_0)}{(x_3 - x_2)(y_1 - y_0) - (y_3 - y_2)(x_1 - x_0)}$$

and then

$$a = \frac{(y_2 - y_0) + b(y_3 - y_2)}{(y_1 - y_0)}$$

It therefore remains to evaluate $a$ and $b$ to check whether they are between 0 and 1 inclusive. In practice, it is worth looking just outside that range in case the edges have not been identified well near the corners. The position of the vertex can be evaluated from

$$y = y_1 + a(y_1 - y_0) \quad \text{and} \quad x = x_0 + a(x_1 - x_0)$$

Having identified the vertices, it is necessary to determine how many lines arrive at

**Table 10.1**

| Line number | Start vertex | End vertex | $\theta$ (from Hough) (in range 0–179°) |
|---|---|---|---|
| 0 | 2 | 5 | 50 |
| 1 | 7 | 1 | 82 |
| 2 | 1 | 3 | 50 |
| ⋮ | ⋮ | ⋮ | ⋮ |

| Vertex number | Position | (Order) (lines coming out of it) |
|---|---|---|
| 0 | (23, 50) | 2 |
| 1 | (100, 278) | 3 |
| ⋮ | ⋮ | ⋮ |

*Notes:*

1. $\theta$ and order can be derived from the rest of the table but are useful in the following labelling routine.
2. Order indicates the number of straight lines intersecting or ending at the vertex, not necessarily the number of lines into/out of a vertex, since a straight line can go through a vertex and could be counted only once.
3. An approach needs to be agreed on when a line seems to stop without being at a vertex. One of two possible errors will have occurred, namely the line is not really a line, or the real line needs extending to a vertex. The reader is left to think of a solution to each of these!

each corner. Using the above technique, three lines arriving at one corner will create three corners, i.e. the corner between (1, 2), (1, 3), and (2, 3). An exhaustive search can be made to eliminate unnecessary corners from the list of corners.

Ideally the algorithm should finish with two arrays of the form shown in Table 10.1.

Labelling can now start. It is possible to do a labelling on any scene with flat surfaces, but the complications go considerably beyond this text, see Ballard and Brown (1982) or Shirai (1987) for good descriptions.

To make it easy we will consider only basic planar polyhedra with no more than three surfaces arriving at any vertex. Given this, it becomes possible to identify all the vertices as 'L', 'T', 'Y', or 'arrow', purely on the geometry of the system.

### Technique 10.2 Labelling the vertices

USE To classify the corners so that the combination of classification of the vertices can then be identified as a specific shape.

OPERATION

1. If vertex is of order 2 (i.e. two lines intersect at the vertex), then

$$\text{if both terminate at the vertex} \rightarrow \text{L type vertex}$$
$$\text{otherwise} \rightarrow \text{T type vertex}$$

2. To determine whether the vertex is an arrow or a Y we have to look at the angles between the lines that terminate at that vertex.

Label the lines coming into the vertex as follows. If the vertex is at $(x_v, y_v)$ and the other end of the line is at $(x_e, y_e)$, then if $y_e < y_v$ or $y_e = y_v$ and $x_e < x_v$, call the line 'entering', otherwise call it 'leaving'.

If all three lines are entering or all three lines leaving, then the vertex is an arrow.

Evaluate the angles of the lines with respect to the horizontal by taking the $\tan^{-1}$ of the slope (between $0°$ and $180°$) and if the line is entering the vertex, add $180°$. (This may have already been held in Table 10.1).

Let the angles be $a$, $b$, and $c$ such that $a < b < c$. Now evaluate

$$\text{minimum}(c - a, a + 360 - b, b + 360 - c)$$

If this is $< 180$, then the vertex is an arrow. T and Y types follow automatically.

(Clowes (1971) and Huffman (1971) identified a line-labelling method that is now particularly well documented, based on the labelling of vertices similar to that done above. Shirai (1987) contains substantial descriptions of this, and other related line-labelling methods.

An exhaustive search will identify the 'L' two-dimensional vertex as having four possible three-dimensional interpretations, namely

> 3 convex edges but only 1 surface visible
> 2 convex edges and 1 concave edge with only 1 surface visible
> 2 convex edges and 1 concave edge with 2 surfaces visible
> 1 convex edge and 2 concave edges with all 2 surfaces visible

We use the notation 3/1, 2/1, 2/2, and 1/2 to represent convex edges/surfaces visible.

The following is an exhaustive list of all possible real interpretations (given the earlier assumptions) of visible vertices:

| | |
|---|---|
| arrow | 3/2 2/3 1/3 |
| L | 3/1 2/1 2/2 1/2 |
| Y | 3/3 0/3 3/3 |
| T | 3/2 |

To make the model complete it is necessary to introduce some (the minimum number) of invisible vertices. These may take the following form

'invisible'   3/1 2/0 1/0 0/0 1/1 0/1 0/2

The labelling exercise now proceeds by allocating to one vertex a single possible label. By doing this we are allocating convexity or concavity to the lines, and visibility or invisibility to the surfaces. It is quite possible to look at all the instances of each $a/b$ to see where the visible surfaces could lie with respect to the concave and convex lines.

Having made a first 'jab' at labelling the vertex, the next vertex must be consistent with the previous one, i.e. the convex line must not have become concave, the visible surface must not have become invisible, and so on. Consistency can be maintained by using invisible vertices to explain the surfaces and edges that are occluded from the viewer. It is thus possible to label the edges in a shape.

However, it will soon be found that there is more than one consistent labelling for most shapes, and labelling can also be produced that is nonsense. To find a unique labelling method, more information is needed. Waltz (1975) includes shadows in the labelling process. This is consistent with human perception.

**Table 10.2**

| Absolute | Relative |
|---|---|
| A car has reflective subregions | A car region is smaller than a road region |
| A car is between 5 feet and 15 feet long | Reflective sub-regions on a car will be less than half |
| A car has four black tyres | the size of the car |
| Trees are green and between 3 feet and 300 feet tall | A car will be shinier than a road and shinier than |
| Grass is between 1 inch and 10 inches tall | grass |
| Grass is green | Grass is greener than a road |
| | Trees are greener and darker than grass |

Further information can be gleaned from the image with out too much extra work. It can be shown that if it is known that the whole of an object is visible in an image, then the outside edges of the object must be convex and must be occluding planes behind them. This gives labels to the outside lines immediately so that only consistent vertex labels may be put at the end of them.

## 10.3 DEALING WITH CURVES

This is a much more difficult problem. Furthermore, it may not be apparent that the image contains curves in the first place. For example, an image of an upright circular cylinder will have two vertical edges. How does the machine tell if they are edges that are purely caused by a curved surface going into occlusion or the edges of an upright box? This work is beyond the scope of this book but the reader might like to look at papers by Nalwa (1988) and Besl and Jain (1986) for examples of how this might be done.

## 10.4 LABELLING REGIONS

An alternative approach to edge and line labelling is to label regions. If an image is of a sea scene, for example, there will be two distinct regions, sky and sea, with possible sub-regions in each. This is a far more meaningful labelling procedure for scene work than edge labelling.

This procedure is a reflection of what is done by the brain. The human viewer rarely knows the precise shape of what he or she is seeing (a car, for example), yet identifies it by its position, texture, and sub-regions (it is on a road, it is smaller than the road, it is red compared to the road, it has black circular things between the body and the road, it has a number of sheets of reflective surface, i.e. glass, etc.).

Of these points, some are due to reasoning, others due to perception, and in particular *relative* perception (i.e. comparing one region with another rather than accumulating facts about regions as if they were not related in any way.)

One possible process to adopt is to regionalize the image and then make absolute and relative information available about the regions. Absolute constraints can be about size, colour, texture—or whatever measure seems sensible for a particular object, though often relative constraints give a better reasoned statement. Table 10.2 gives examples of relative and absolute constraints (see also Fig. 10.1).

If the system has an image that contains a road, some trees, some grass, and a car, it is going to be easier to label the regions by relative constraints rather than absolute ones since use of the absolute ones implies that the system has knowledge of the real three-dimensional colours, heights, areas, etc. This means a vast amount of preprocessing before this stage. It is better to use a form of relative labelling that relaxes into the best solution. This is one solution to the classic labelling problem. Presented below is a summary of a technique due to Carlotto (1988).

### Technique 10.3 Classification of regions by relaxation labelling

USE To determine 'best' labelling for regions based on the labelling for other regions.

THEORY The 'relaxation' technique relies on making wrong labelling decisions and then discovering that the penalty for the wrong decision is so high that it has to retrace its steps and makes a different decision.

OPERATION Asume that there are $L$ possible labels (such as CAR, ROAD, SKY, ...), $l_1$ to $l_L$.

Assume that there are $R$ regions to be labelled $r_1$ to $r_R$.

Assume that data is available on $P$ properties for each region (such as colour, area, texture, luminosity, ...).

Finally assume that there are $K$ relative rules, relating the known labels one to another according to the properties (such as SKY is bluer than ROAD).

It is useful to draw these in a digraph (directed graph) form (see Fig. 10.1, for example).

Now create a search tree (see Fig. 10.2) of all possible allocations to all possible

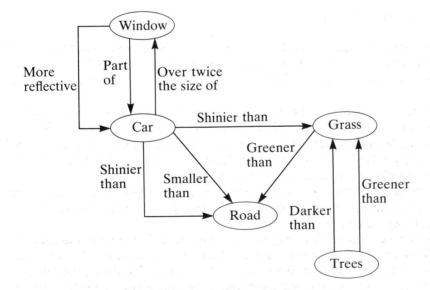

**Figure 10.1** Digraph of relative constraints.

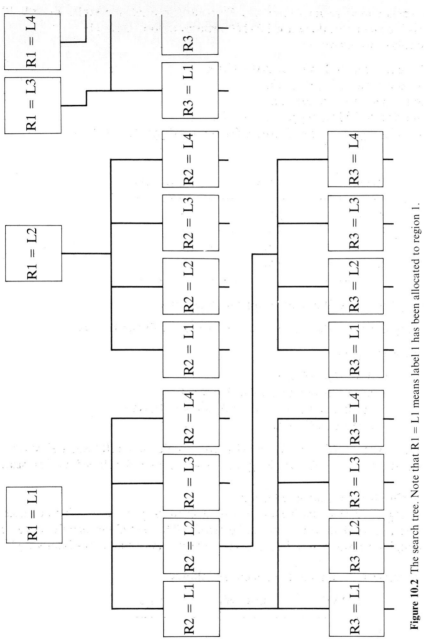

**Figure 10.2** The search tree. Note that R1 = L1 means label 1 has been allocated to region 1.

regions. Traverse the tree looking for inconsistences in possible allocations, removing the inconsistent allocation and all the branches below it.

Clearly, with $L$ labels and $R$ regions there are $R^L$ routes through the table, so with 10 regions and 6 possible labellings there are 1 000 000 routes to look through.
Consider the following example:

with three labels (GRASS, ROAD, CAR)
With four regions (A, B, C, D)
With properties (area, greenness)
With rules (ROAD is bigger than CAR,
  GRASS is greener than ROAD, GRASS is bigger than CAR)

With data

| Region | Area | Greenness |
|--------|------|-----------|
| A      | 200  | 5         |
| B      | 600  | 5         |
| C      | 250  | 5         |
| D      | 600  | 30        |

Careful filtering (similar to Waltz filtering) can determine

Nothing is smaller than a CAR, so neither B nor D can be cars.

The depth-first search goes:

If A = GRASS then
  since B is bigger than A, B ≠ CAR
  but B is not greener than A, so B ≠ ROAD
  B must be GRASS

So remove the branches B = CAR and B = ROAD from under A = GRASS, and so on.
This is time consuming. A useful, working, heuristic has been developed by Carlotto.

### Technique 10.4 Heuristic for search reduction

USE The above algorithm can involve a very long drawn-out process. If it is to be used in real life a shortening of that process would be helpful. This technique usually shortens the process, though no proof exists that it always works (hence the term—heuristic).

OPERATION AND EXAMPLE Tabulate the system as follows:

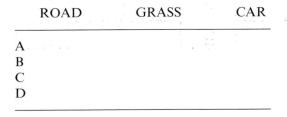

|   | ROAD | GRASS | CAR |
|---|------|-------|-----|
| A |      |       |     |
| B |      |       |     |
| C |      |       |     |
| D |      |       |     |

Now in turn assume that one region is labelled (initially A = ROAD), then count the number of other labellings that cannot occur, i.e.

If A = ROAD
   Can B = ROAD   Yes
   Can B = GRASS? No
   Can B = CAR?    No
   Can C = ROAD?  Yes
   Can C = GRASS? No
   Can C = CAR?    No
   Can D = ROAD?  Yes
   Can D = GRASS? Yes
   Can D = CAR?    No

Giving a total of five no's. Put this value in the box.

Do the same with all the alternatives and then search the tree beginning with the allocation of the label with the lowest number of no's to the first region, the lowest number to the second region, and so on.

The above example gives the following hypothesis table:

|   | ROAD | GRASS | CAR |
|---|------|-------|-----|
| A | 5    | 0*    | 6   |
| B | 3*   | 6     | 4   |
| C | 2*   | 2*    | 4   |
| D | 4    | 6     | 1*  |

\* Minimum in each row.

Therefore start by assuming that A = CAR, B = ROAD, C = ROAD or CAR, and D = GRASS. This gives a feasible solution straight away.

The technique of labelling is only one of many techniques available for the recognition of objects in an image. As has already been shown, labelling uses reasoning to get the labels right. Reasoning deserves a substantial discussion on its own, and this appears in the next chapter.

## 10.5 EXERCISES

**10.1** Label the following shape vertices. How many consistent labellings are possible?

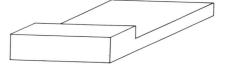

**10.2** Use Carlotto's heuristic to determine a feasible solution to the following labelling problem:

Labels      = {BOOK, BISCUIT, PEN}
Regions    = {A, B, C, D}
Properties = {area, shininess}
Rules        = {BOOK and PEN are shinier than BISCUIT, PEN is smaller than BOOK}

Data:

| Region | Area | Shininess |
|--------|------|-----------|
| A      | 10   | 3         |
| B      | 20   | 74        |
| C      | 6    | 420       |
| D      | 12   | 300       |

# 11

## REASONING, FACTS, AND INFERENCES

## 11.1 INTRODUCTION

Chapter 10 began to move beyond the standard 'image-processing' approach to computer vision to make statements about the geometry of objects and allocate labels to them. This is enhanced by making reasoned statements, by codifying facts, and making judgements based on past experience.

Here we delve into the realms of artificial intelligence, expert systems, logic programming, intelligent knowledge-based systems, etc. All of these are covered in many excellent texts and are beyond the scope of this book; however, this chapter introduces the reader to some concepts in logical reasoning that relate specifically to computer vision. It looks more specifically at the 'training' aspects of reasoning systems that use computer vision.

Reasoning is the highest level of computer vision processing. Reasoning takes facts together with a figure indicating the level of confidence in the facts, and concludes (or infers) another fact. This other fact is, in a sense, at a higher level than the original facts presented to the system. These inferences themselves have levels of confidence associated with them, so that subsequent to the reasoning strategic decisions can be made.

A computer vision security system analyses images from one of a number of cameras. At one point in time it identifies that from one particular camera there are 350 pixels in the image that have changed by more than $\pm 20$ in value over the last 30 seconds.

Does it flag an intruder?

On a simple system these facts might be the threshold at which the system does flag an intruder. However, a reasoning system takes much more into account before the decision to telephone for assistance is made. The computer vision system might check for the movement as being wind in the trees, or the shadows from moving clouds. It might attempt to identify the object that moved, was it human or an animal; could the change have been caused by a firework lighting the sky?

These kind of questions need to be answered with a calculated level of confidence so that the final decision can be made. This is a significant step beyond the geometry, the regions, and the labelling; it is concerned with reasoning about the facts known from the image.

In the above case prior knowledge, about the world, is essential. Without a database of knowledge, the system cannot make a confident estimate as to the cause of the change in the image.

Consider another example:

An image subsystem, called SCENE ANALYSIS, produces, as output, a textual description of a scene. The system is supplied with labelled objects and their probable locations in three-dimensional space. Rather than simply saying that A is to the right of B, which is above C, the system has to deliver a respectable description of the scene, for example: 'The telephone is on the table; the hanging light, in the centre of the ceiling, is on. The vase has fallen off the table. The apple is in the ash tray.'

These statements are most difficult to create. Even ignoring the complexities of the natural language produced, the system still needs to have knowledge of what 'on' (*on* the table and the light is *on*),'in', and 'fallen off' mean. It has to have rules about each of these.

When is something on something else and not suspended above it? These are difficult notions. For example, if you look at a closed door, it is not on the ground but suspended just above it. Yet what can a vision system see? Maybe it interprets the door as another piece of wall of a different colour. Not to do so implies that it has a reason for suspecting that it is a door. If it is a door, then there have to be rules about doors that are not true for tables or ashtrays or other general objects. It has to know that the door is hanging from the wall opposite the handle. This is essential knowledge if the scene is to be described.

This level of reasoning is not normally necessary for vision in manufacturing, but may be essential for a vision system on an autonomous vehicle, or in an X-ray diagnosis system.

## 11.2 FACTS AND RULES

There are a number of ways of expressing rules for computers. Languages exist for precisely that kind of operation. PROLOG, for instance, lends itself to expressing rules in a form that the computer can process—i.e. reason with.

Expert systems, normally written in a rule-like language, allow the user to put their knowledge onto a computer. In effect the computer is programmed to learn, and may also be programmed to learn further, beyond the human knowledge, by implementing the knowledge and updating its confidence in the inferences it makes according to the result of its decisions. The computer can become better than the expert in making reasoned decisions.

With computer vision, however, the problem is not the technology but the sheer volume of information required to make expert judgements, unless the scene is very predictable.

Going back to the example in the last chapter. If it is discovered that a region is a road and that that region is next to another region now labelled a car, it would be reasonable to suggest that the car is on the road.

Expressed in a formal manner

$$
\begin{aligned}
\text{IF} \quad & \text{region}(x) \ \textbf{is} \ \text{A\_CAR} \\
\&\& \ & \text{region}(y) \ \textbf{is} \ \text{A\_ROAD} \\
\&\& \ & \text{region}(x) \ \textbf{is next to} \ \text{region}(y) \\
\text{THEN} & \\
& \text{A\_CAR} \ \textbf{is on} \ \text{A\_ROAD}
\end{aligned}
$$

This notation is not the normal notation used in logic programming, but reads more easily for those unused to the more formal notation. Note that && means logical AND. Logic programming would write the above as something like

IS(A_CAR, region $x$)
& IS(A_ROAD, region $y$)
& IS_NEXT_TO(region $x$, region $y$) $\Rightarrow$ IS_ON(A_CAR, A_ROAD);

Given this rule, consisting of two assumptions and an inference, and given that the assumptions are, in fact, true, the system can now say that a car is on a road.

However, pure, discrete logic operations do not correspond to what is, after all, a continuous world. These rules are not exactly watertight. They are general rules and either we include every possibility in the set of rules we use (known as the rule base)—a most difficult option—or we generate a measure of confidence in the truth of the rule. This represents how often the inference, generated by the rule, is going to be true.

It may be that we know the image-labelling system makes mistakes when it identifies a CAR region and a ROAD region. For example, out of 100 CAR regions identified, 90 were real CARS and the others were not. We therefore have a confidence of 90 per cent in the statement

region($x$) **is a** CAR

In fact the confidence in the statement can be variable. The image-labelling system may be able to give a confidence value for each statement about the region being a car. Sometimes the labelling system may be quite sure, such as when there are no other feasible solutions to the labelling problem in the last chapter. In these cases the confidence will be high, say 99 per cent. In other cases the confidence will be low.

Therefore, a variable confidence level is associated with the above statement. We might write

region($x$) **is a** CAR   [a]

to indicate that the confidence we have in the statement is value $a$.

Now, looking at the whole rule

$$
\begin{aligned}
\text{IF} \quad & \text{region}(x) \ \textbf{is} \ \text{A\_CAR} & [a] \\
\&\& \ & \text{region}(y) \ \textbf{is} \ \text{A\_ROAD} & [b] \\
\&\& \ & \text{region}(x) \ \textbf{is next to} \ \text{region}(y) & [c] \\
\text{THEN} & \\
& \text{A\_CAR} \ \textbf{is on} \ \text{A\_ROAD}
\end{aligned}
$$

we should be able to give a confidence to the final fact (the inference) based on the confidences we have in the previous statements *and* on the confidence we have in the rule itself.

If $a$, $b$, and $c$ were probability values between 0 and 1 inclusive, and the rule was 100 per cent watertight, then the inference would be

A_CAR **is on** A_ROAD  $[a \times b \times c]$

For example

| | | |
|---|---|---|
| IF | region($x$) **is** A_CAR | [90%] |
| | && region($y$) **is** A_ROAD | [77%] |
| | && region($x$) **is next to** region($y$) | [100%] |
| THEN | | |
| | A_CAR **is on** A_ROAD | [69%] |

Note that

region($x$) **is next to** region($y$)   [100%]

was given as 100 per cent because this is a fact the system can deduce exactly.

Of course the car may be on the grass in the foreground with the road in the background with the roof of the car being the area of the two-dimensional region that is touching the road region. This means that the rule is not 100 per cent watertight, so the rule needs to have a confidence of its own, say $k$. This now makes the formal rule

| | | |
|---|---|---|
| IF | region($x$) **is** A_CAR | $[a]$ |
| | && region($y$) **is** A_ROAD | $[b]$ |
| | && region($x$) **is next to** region($y$) | $[c]$ |
| THEN | | |
| | A_CAR **is on** A_ROAD | $[a \times b \times c \times k]$ |

If $k$ is small, e.g. if only 55 per cent of the time is the rule true given that all the three assumptions are true, it implies that more evidence is needed before the inference can be made. More evidence can be brought in by including further facts before the inference is made

| | | |
|---|---|---|
| IF | region($x$) **is** A_CAR | $[a]$ |
| | && region($y$) **is** A_ROAD | $[b]$ |
| | && region($x$) **is next to** region($y$) | $[c]$ |
| | && region($x$) **is above** region($y$) | $[d]$ |
| THEN | | |
| | A_CAR **is on** A_ROAD | |

Here the new fact, which at least at first glance seems to be able to be given a 100 per cent confidence value by the earlier labelling routine, knocks out the unreasonable case that the touching part of the two-dimensional regions corresponds to the roof of the car. Hence the confidence in the inference now increases. There is a limit to this. If the added evidence is not watertight, then the overall confidence value of the rule may be reduced. This is illustrated in Fig. 11.1 where the **is above** evidence is not clear.

In the example below, the confidence value of the rule is reduced by adding an extra evidence requirement.

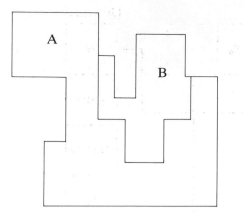

**Figure 11.1** Is region A above region B, or is B above A?

| | | Original values with three facts only | New values with four facts |
|---|---|---|---|
| IF | region(x) **is** A_CAR | [90%] | [90%] |
| | && region(y) **is** A_ROAD | [77%] | [77%] |
| | && region(x) **is next to** region(y) | [100%] | [100%] |
| | && region(x) **is above** region(y) | | [80%] |
| THEN | | | |
| | A_CAR **is on** A_ROAD | [$k$ = 55% rule = 38%] | [$k$ = 65% rule = 36%] |

Despite the extra, good-quality (80 per cent) fact, and the improvement in the confidence of the system given the fact is true—from 55 to 65 per cent—the whole rule becomes less useful, simply because the 80 and 65 per cent were not high enough to jump up the overall figure.

This gives us a good guideline for adding facts to rules. Generally only add a fact if by doing so the confidence of the rule, as a whole, is increased.

Note that the $k$ value is the confidence in the inference *given that the facts are true*.

The technique below describes how these rule bases can be held in normal procedural language.

### Technique 11.1 Constructing a set of facts

Use A set of facts is a description of the real world. It may be a description of a scene in an image. It may be a list of things that are true in real life that the processor can refer to when reasoning about an image. It is necessary to hold these in a sensible form that the processor can access with ease. Suggestions as to the best form are described in this technique.

OPERATION This is best done using a proprietary language, such as PROLOG, but, assuming that the reader has not got access to this or experience in programming in it, the following data structure can be implemented in most procedural languages, such as Pascal, ADA, C, etc.

Identify a set of constants, e.g.

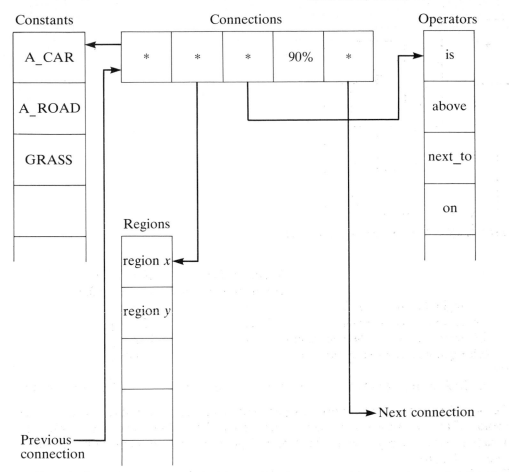

**Figure 11.2** Illustration of the facts implementation discussed in the text.

{CAR, ROAD, GRASS}

a set of labelled image parts

{region *x*, region *y*}

a set of operators

{ **is, above, on, next to** }

Put each of these sets into its own array. Finally create an array (or linked list) of connection records that point to the other arrays and hold a value for each connection. Figure 11.2 illustrates this.

Rule bases can be constructed along similar lines.

**Technique 11.2  Constructing a rule base**
USE  Rules connect facts. If one or more fact is true, then a rule will say that they imply

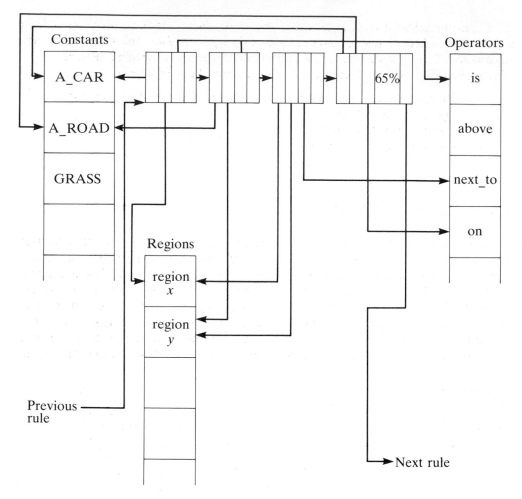

**Figure 11.3** Illustration of the implementation of the rule discussed in the text.

that another fact will be true. The rule contains the assumptions (the facts that drive the rule, and the fact that is inferred from the assumptions—or implied by the assumptions).

OPERATION Using the above descriptions of facts, a rule base consists of a set of linked lists, one for each rule. Each linked list contains records, each pointing to the arrays, as above, for the assumed facts, and a record with a $k$ value in it for the inferred facts. Figure 11.3 illustrates this.

It now remains to implement an algorithm that will search the facts for a match to a set of assumed facts so that a rule can be implemented. When the assumed facts are found for a particular rule, the inferred fact can be added to the facts list with a confidence value.

The whole process is time consuming, and exhaustive searches must be made, repeating the searches when a new fact is added to the system. The new fact may enable other rules to operate that have not been able to operate before.

It is sometimes useful to hold an extra field in the facts that have been found from rules. This extra field contains a pointer to the rule that gave the fact. This allows backward operations enabling the system to explain the reasoning behind a certain inference.

For example, at the end of reasoning the system may be able to print

> I discovered that A_CAR is on A_ROAD (38% confident) because:
> region($x$) is a A_CAR
> region($y$) is a A_ROAD
> and    region($x$) is next to region($y$)

## 11.3 STRATEGIC LEARNING

This section could arguably appear in the next chapter, which is more concerned with training; however, this training is at a higher level than that associated with pattern recognition. Indeed, it depends far more on reasoned argument than a statistical process.

Winston (1972), in a now classic paper, describes a strategic learning process. He shows that objects (a pedestal and an arch are illustrated in his paper) can have their structures taught to a machine by giving the machine examples of the right structures and the wrong structures. In practice only one right structure need be described for each object, providing there is no substantial variation in the structures between 'right' structured

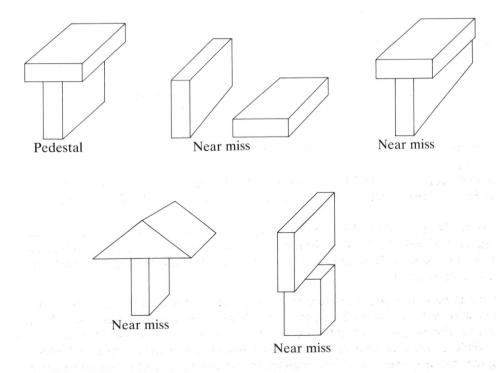

Figure 11.4 A pedestal training sequence. (*Source*: Winston, 1972.)

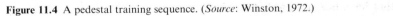

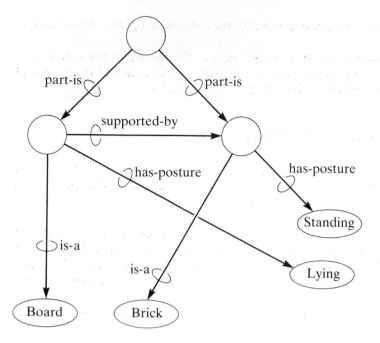

**Figure 11.5** A pedestal description. (*Source*: Winston, 1972.)

objects. However, a number of wrong structures (or near misses as he calls them) need to be described to cope with all possible cases of error in the recognition process. Figure 11.4 shows Winston's structures for a pedestal training sequence.

The process of learning goes as follows:

1. Show the system a sample of the correct image. Using labelling techniques and reasoning, the system creates a description of the object in terms of labels, constants and connections between them. Figure 11.5 illustrates Winston's computer description of the pedestal.
2. Supply near misses for the system to analyse and deduce the difference between the network for a correct image and the network for a wrong image. When it finds the difference (preferably only one difference—hence the idea of a near miss), then it supports the right fact or connection in the correct description by saying that it is essential.

For example, the first pedestal 'near-miss' is the same as the pedestal except that the top is not supported by the base. So the 'supported-by' operator becomes an essential part of the description of the pedestal, i.e. without it, the object is not a pedestal. Winston suggests that the 'supported-by' connection becomes a 'must-be-supported-by' connection.

Here the training has been done by the analysis of *one* image only, rather than many images averaged out over time. Training continues by supplying further near misses.

What happens when a near miss shows two differences from the original? A set of rules is required here. One approach is to strengthen both connections equally. Another is to rank the differences in order of their distance from the origin of the network. For example, the connection 'supported-by' is more important to the concept of a pedestal than 'is-a' or 'has-posture'.

These networks are called 'semantic nets' because they describe the real known structure of an object. There has been much development in this area and in the area of neural nets, which can also lend themselves to spatial descriptions.

## 11.4 NETWORKS AS SPATIAL DESCRIPTORS

Networks can be constructed with the property that objects which are spatially or conceptually close to each other are close to each other in the network. This closeness is measured by the number of arcs between each node.

**Note on networks** A node is like a station on a railway. The arcs are like the rails between the stations. A node might represent a fact, an object, or a stage in reasoning. An arc might represent the connection between facts (as in rules, for example), a geographical connection between objects ('on', for example), or an activity required, or resulting from the movement along the arc.

Networks may be directed (only one route is available along the arcs), in which case they are referred to as digraphs.

Figure 11.6 illustrates a network that is modelling a spatial relationship. The notation on the arcs is as follows:

$$\varepsilon \quad \text{is an element of}$$
$$\subset \quad \text{is a subset of}$$
$$\mathbb{P} \quad \text{with the visual property of}$$
$$\mathbb{R} \quad \text{at this position with respect to}$$

This relates well to the rules discussed earlier in this chapter, each of which can be represented in this network form.

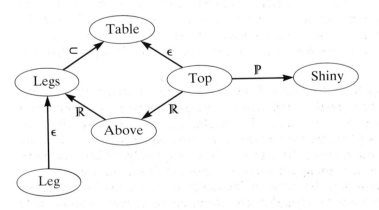

**Figure 11.6** Elementary network of spatial relationships.

## 11.5 RULE ORDERS

Post-boxes (in the United Kingdom, at any rate) are red. This is a general rule. We might supply this rule to a vision system so that if it sees a red object it will undertake processing to determine whether it is a post-box and will not undertake to determine whether it is a duck, because, generally, ducks are not red.

However, what if the post-box is yellow, after rag week at the university? Does this mean that the system never recognized the object because it is the wrong colour?

Intuitively, it feels right to check out the most probable alternatives first and then try the less possible ones. Sherlock Holmes said 'once we have eliminated the possible, the impossible must be true, however improbable'. This is precisely what is going on here.

Rules can therefore be classed as general (it is light during the day) and exceptional (it is dark during an eclipse of the sun, during the day). If these are set up in a vision system, the processor will need to process the exceptional rules first so that wrong facts are not inferred from a general rule when an exceptional rule applies. This is fine if there are not too many exceptions. If, however, the number of exception rules is large, and testing is required for each exception, a substantial amount of work is needed before the system is able to state a fact.

If the exceptions are improbable, then there is a trade-off between testing for exceptions (and therefore spending a long time in processing), or making occasional errors by not testing.

## 11.6 EXERCISES

**11.1** Express the ROAD/CAR rule as a network.

**11.1** Develop a general rule for the operator 'is on'.

*12*

---

# PATTERN RECOGNITION AND TRAINING

## 12.1 INTRODUCTION

In the previous chapter we looked at some methods used in reasoning about facts from images. These facts were determined from some recognition of edges or textures, colours, or surface positions.

Some problems are better described as problems of determining a high-level fact from a pattern of some kind. The term 'pattern' has a wide range of meanings, but here we are particularly interested in sets of values that describe things, normally where the set of values is of a known size. This is different to looking at a scene of a flat-surfaced object where we do not know how many corners there are, how many edges or how many surfaces.

However, in attempting to recognize one signature from another, we might measure its height/width ratio, the number of peaks, take a set of samples from the histogram of its horizontal and vertical density, count the number of loops, and so on. A finite number of similar tests can be applied to particular recognition problems so that a set of values is discovered. It then becomes necessary to identify what real signature that set of values is pointing at.

This is a broad description of what pattern recognition is about.

## 12.2 THE GENERAL PROBLEM

Figure 12.1 illustrates the general problem. The 'decision function generator' creates a set of values based on the image. The set of values is fed into a decision-making process which,

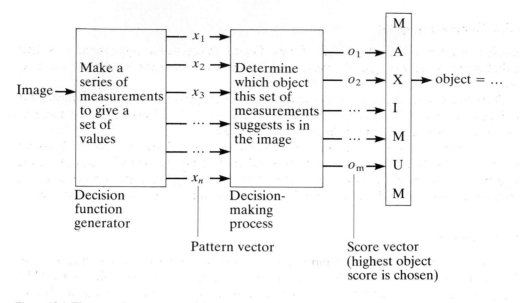

**Figure 12.1** The general pattern recognition problem.

typically, allocates a score to a number of boxes, indicating the likelihood that the image contains the object associated with that box. The box with the highest value in it will be chosen as the most likely object in the image.

The whole system above can be enhanced by including subsystems that will change the decision-making processes if the context of the image changes, and change the decision function generator if it becomes apparent that one or more of the functions does not perform well, e.g. it gives the same value whatever the image.

Also a feedback subsystem can be introduced that will 'learn' the best weighting to be placed on the elements of the pattern vector, and the best measurements to be taken so as to give the right answer as often as possible.

## 12.3 APPROACHES TO THE DECISION-MAKING PROCESS

### 12.3.1 Simple comparison

Simply make a library of all the objects that are likely to be encountered and put the values of the pattern vector for each object in the library. Then when an unknown object needs to be recognized, generate all the elements of the pattern vector and compare the vector with each vector in the library. When one is exactly the same, then the object can be labelled.

This is fine providing there is no noise or possible adjustment to the object. If there is a slight error in capture when compared with the value in the library, this simple method will not work. In practice it is not overuseful.

### 12.3.2 Common property

Identify one distinct thing about each of the different objects in library that has to be true for that object to be that type of object, e.g. all 0s have a hole in the middle and no loose lines.

Then make sure that one of the decision functions gives a 1 or 0 to indicate the presence or absence of a hole in the middle, and a 1 or a 0 to indicate the presence or absence of a loose line. Then the decision can be made.

If, however, we have to discriminate between 'A' and 'R' and 'Q', then it becomes much more difficult to make statements about a definite property for each one. In fact, the properties become valued ones like what angles are the lines, if they are between $x$ and $y$, then it must be the letter 'R', and so on. Thus the common property cannot be applied.

### 12.3.3 Clusters

Of course, the vector above can be plotted in a multidimensional space. If it only had two values in the vector, then we could plot it on an $x-y$ graph. With three values it could be plotted on an $x-y-z$ three-dimensional plane. With many values, though unable to visualize it, it can be plotted in multidimensional space. If it is possible to get lots of sets of measurements for one object, say for example the vector for the letter 'A', then these will form a kind of cluster surrounding the average 'A' values. We can do this with all the letters and have 26 capital letter clusters. Now when an unknown letter is measured, the 'distance' from each cluster is measured and the nearest cluster is the best estimate of the letter.

A 'distance' measurement can be simply

$$|x_1 - u_1| + |x_2 - u_2| + |x_3 - u_3| + |x_4 - u_4| + \ldots + |x_n - u_n|$$

where $x_1, \ldots, x_n$ represents the position of the cluster centre (or average of each of these measurements for all of the different tries), and $u_1, \ldots, u_n$ represent the decision vector values from the unknown image.

Of course, simple comparison, common property and clusters can all be used in part or in full for a particular recognition problem. It might be that software is designed with an intuitive solution identifying which letter corresponds to the unknown pattern (heuristic approach). Alternatively, a purely mathematical/statistical set of operations can be performed to make the decision.

## 12.4 DECISION FUNCTIONS

One way of implementing a decision on the pattern vector is to use what are termed decision vectors. These are weights that are applied to the pattern vectors, which then produce values upon which the decisions can be made. Ideally they produce just one value and the decision is made on whether, for example, the value produced is greater or less than zero. For example

$$\mathbf{w} = (w_1, w_2, w_3, \ldots, w_n)$$

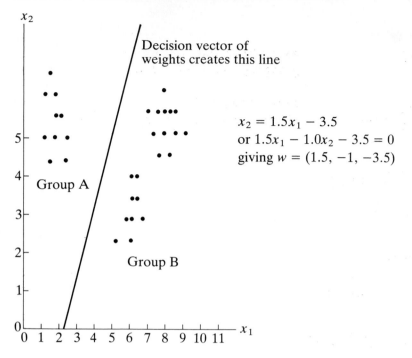

**Figure 12.2** The decision vector.

A two-dimensional decision vector is illustrated in Fig. 12.2.
So, if the pattern vector is

$$\mathbf{x} = \begin{pmatrix} x_1 \\ x_2 \\ x_3 \\ \vdots \\ x_n \\ 1 \end{pmatrix}$$

with a 1 appended on the bottom for convenience, then $\mathbf{w}'\mathbf{x}$ will give a value which, if it is greater than 0, suggests that the unknown pattern is in group A, otherwise is in group B. For example, taking point (pattern vector) (8, 4)

$$(1.5, -1.0, -3.5) \begin{pmatrix} 8 \\ 4 \\ 1 \end{pmatrix} = 8 \times 1.5 - 4 - 3.5 = 4.5$$

4.5 > 0, so the point is in group B

and, taking point (pattern vector) (4, 4)

$$(1.5, -1.0, -3.5) \begin{pmatrix} 4 \\ 4 \\ 1 \end{pmatrix} = 4 \times 1.5 - 4 - 3.5 = -1.5$$

$-1.5 < 0$, so the point is in group A

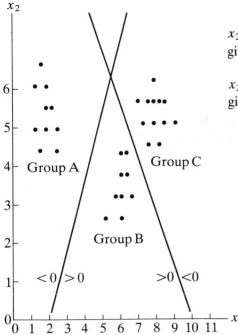
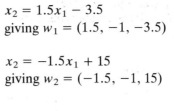

$x_2 = 1.5x_1 - 3.5$
giving $w_1 = (1.5, -1, -3.5)$

$x_2 = -1.5x_1 + 15$
giving $w_2 = (-1.5, -1, 15)$

**Figure 12.3** The four regions created by two decision vectors.

Of course, normally the number of groups is greater than two (e.g. there are 26 capital letters in the alphabet). There should preferably be more measurements than just two, but the example that follows explains how more than one decision function can be used on two dimensions to distinguish between more than two groups.

Figure 12.3 shows four regions created by two decision vectors, and Table 12.1 is the decision table created from this figure.

Of course, there are times when clusters overlap each other. Then the process becomes a probability exercise, trying to identify which cluster centre is nearest. The linear decision functions are not, of themselves, satisfactory.

## 12.5 DETERMINING THE DECISION FUNCTIONS

This is easily done in two dimensions by plotting and inspection; however, if a number of measurements are taken, then it is necessary to create multidimensional planes, and a

**Table 12.1**

| Result of $w_1$ | Result of $w_2$ | Implication |
| --- | --- | --- |
| $< 0$ | $< 0$ | no group |
| $< 0$ | $> 0$ | group A |
| $> 0$ | $< 0$ | group C |
| $> 0$ | $> 0$ | group B |

method is needed to do this. See a selection of algorithms for this in Chapter 6 of Tou and Gonzalez (1974).

## 12.6 NON-LINEAR DECISION FUNCTIONS

Decision functions need not be straight lines. A curved decision function, or a sphere, might be appropriate for some applications. However, if the system can be kept linear (perhaps by implementing two straight lines instead of one curved line), it may reduce significantly the arithmetic activity involved in recognition.

## 12.7 USING THE CLUSTER MEANS

We have already indicated that one way of classifying a new pattern vector is to find its Euclidean distance from the means of the clusters that have already been identified. The vector corresponding to the cluster mean consists of elements that are themselves means of the corresponding elements in the pattern vectors of all the entries in the cluster. For example, if the cluster consists of

$$\begin{pmatrix} 3 \\ 4 \\ 8 \\ 2 \end{pmatrix} \begin{pmatrix} 2 \\ 9 \\ 5 \\ 1 \end{pmatrix} \begin{pmatrix} 5 \\ 7 \\ 7 \\ 1 \end{pmatrix} \text{ then the mean is } \begin{pmatrix} 3.33 \\ 6.67 \\ 6.67 \\ 1.33 \end{pmatrix}$$

This represents the centre of the four-dimensional cluster.

The Euclidean distance from the centre of a new pattern vector can be calculated as follows:

New vector     Euclidean distance =

$$\begin{pmatrix} 3 \\ 5 \\ 7 \\ 0 \end{pmatrix} \quad \begin{aligned} &(3-3.33)^2 \\ &+(5-6.67)^2 \\ &+(7-6.67)^2 \\ &+(0-1.33)^2 = 4.78 \end{aligned}$$

We may know that there are $N$ clusters but not know which pattern vector belongs to each cluster. This requires an algorithm to find the best $N$ cluster means so that the pattern vectors each become members of a suitable cluster.

The example in Fig. 12.4 gives six points that are easily clustered by hand. In order to do this automatically the following technique may be used.

### Technique 12.1 Automatic clustering (the $K$-means algorithm)
USE TO find automatically the best groupings and means of $K$ clusters. This is a learning exercise. The pattern vectors of $K$ different items are given to the system, which then classifies them as best it can without knowing *a priori* which vector corresponds to which item.

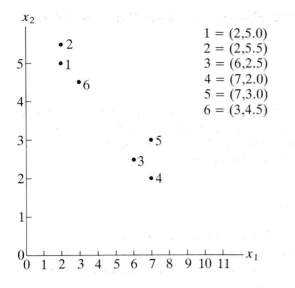

$x_2$

```
•2
5   •1
      •6
4
3                •5
              •3
2              •4
1
0
  0 1 2 3 4 5 6 7 8 9 10 11    x_1
```

1 = (2,5.0)
2 = (2,5.5)
3 = (6,2.5)
4 = (7,2.0)
5 = (7,3.0)
6 = (3,4.5)

**Figure 12.4** Data for automatic clustering.

OPERATION Let the pattern vectors be $\mathbf{X}_1, \ldots \mathbf{X}_n$. Take the first $K$ points as the initial estimation of the cluster means.

$$\mathbf{M}_1 = \mathbf{X}_1, \mathbf{M}_2 = \mathbf{X}_2, \ldots, \mathbf{M}_k = \mathbf{X}_k$$

'A'. Now allocate each pattern vector to a group corresponding to the nearest group mean.

Calculate the new cluster centres as the average of all the pattern vectors in each cluster group.

If they are all the same as the old cluster centres, STOP, otherwise go to 'A'.

EXAMPLE Using the numbers in Fig. 12.4

$$\mathbf{M}_1 = (2, 5.0), \quad \mathbf{M}_2 = (2, 5.5)$$

(The two first cluster centre estimates.)

Allocating each pattern vector to the nearest centre gives

$$
\begin{array}{lll}
1 & (2, 5.0) & \text{group 1} \\
2 & (2, 5.5) & \text{group 2} \\
3 & (6, 2.5) & \text{group 1} \\
4 & (7, 2.0) & \text{group 1} \\
5 & (7, 3.0) & \text{group 1} \\
6 & (3, 4.5) & \text{group 1}
\end{array}
$$

i.e. group 1 = {1, 3, 4, 5, 6}, group 2 = {2}

The group means now become

$$\text{group 1 } (5, 3.4), \quad \text{group 2 } (2, 5.5)$$

This gives new groupings as follows:

$$
\begin{array}{lll}
1 & (2, 5.0) & \text{group 2} \\
2 & (2, 5.5) & \text{group 2} \\
3 & (6, 2.5) & \text{group 1} \\
4 & (7, 2.0) & \text{group 1} \\
5 & (7, 3.0) & \text{group 1} \\
6 & (3, 4.5) & \text{group 2}
\end{array}
$$

i.e. group $1 = \{3, 4, 5\}$, group $2 = \{1, 2, 6\}$
This gives means of

$$\text{group 1 } (6.67, 2.5), \quad \text{group 2 } (2.33, 5.0)$$

Groupings now stay the same and the means are therefore the same, so the algorithm stops with the above final means and groupings.

## 12.8 SUPERVISED AND UNSUPERVISED LEARNING

So the system can be trained. More often than not we have some prior knowledge so, effectively, we can tell the system what we know. The technique below, which uses Bayes' theorem, incorporates prior probabilities into the recognition process.

Probabilities can be updated as the system works, so that it can constantly be within some kind of training mode. This is supervised training (i.e. a pattern is shown to the system and the answer is also told to the system so that it can place the pattern in the right place in the cluster or library).

Maybe the system has to learn for itself (as in the above example). In this case unsupervised learning has to occur. The system determines where clusters are occurring and classifies based on a belief that objects with similar decision vectors are the same.

### 12.8.1 Statistical learning

When a vision system is doing a repetitive process, at the end of which it gets feedback indicating whether it performed correctly or not (feedback is usually in the form of the latter), then it has every element necessary to learn. Learning can be simply an updating of the confidences it has in certain rules when they perform well. Equally, it may update the confidences in the facts supplied to it by the labelling routines. It may, also, be able to combine rules so that one rule is able to replace a number of rules, with a consequent reduction in processing.

> A security system looking at a scene would update the 'base' scene from time to time as gradual changes occurred. Had it not learnt the gradual changes, the system would have had to be reset regularly by hand, or would have had to be significantly less sensitive to any change. As it is, the system was very sensitive to sudden abnormal changes, but ignored frequently moving items such as tree branches. It was also not affected by gradual changes from night light to day light.

Bayes' theorem can be used effectively to classify regions under a training system called Bayesian maximum likelihood supervised classification.

**Technique 12.2 Bayesian maximum likelihood supervised classification**

USE Training a system to identify/classify regions can be done using this powerful technique. It is particularly powerful when each region has more than one measure associated with it (such as intensity, colour, size, texture measure, etc.)

OPERATION

**1** Identify, on an image, a training area for each class or label. For example, given a ROAD/CAR/GRASS image (similar to that in Chapter 9), the system is trained first by specifying exactly what area is ROAD, what is CAR, and what is GRASS.

**2** For each of these areas the grey-level histogram is evaluated and all the frequencies in the histogram are divided by the number of pixels in the corresponding area. (This is called normalizing the histogram.) It may be that more than one histogram is available for each area, e.g. there may be red, green, and blue planes for a colour image, in which case each of them can deliver a histogram—with the ROAD/CAR/GRASS image it would mean nine histograms altogether, three for each label.

The values in the normalized histograms now correspond to conditional probabilities.

Thus, if the ROAD/CAR/GRASS image is used as a monochrome image (only one histogram), it may give, for the sake of argument, the following frequencies:

| Label | Grey levels | | | | |
|---|---|---|---|---|---|
| | 0 | 1 | 2 | 3 | Total |
| ROAD | 50 | 12 | 0 | 0 | 62 |
| CAR | 14 | 30 | 28 | 2 | 74 |
| GRASS | 0 | 10 | 34 | 20 | 64 |

Dividing the rows by the totals gives the following conditional probabilities:

| Label | Grey levels | | | | |
|---|---|---|---|---|---|
| | 0 | 1 | 2 | 3 | Total |
| ROAD | 0.81 | 0.19 | 0 | 0 | 1.00 |
| CAR | 0.19 | 0.41 | 0.38 | 0.03 | 1.00 |
| GRASS | 0 | 0.16 | 0.53 | 0.31 | 1.00 |

For example, 0.41 in the CAR row means that given we are analysing a car region on an image, the probability that any pixel in that region has the value 1 is 0.41 (got from 30/74). Or formally

$$P(\text{grey-level 1} \mid \text{region is a CAR}) = 0.41$$

**3** Estimate the probability that a pixel on the image belongs to the CAR, ROAD and GRASS regions. One way of doing this is to say that if there are 200 pixels in the image in total, the probability that a pixel is a CAR pixel is

$$P(\text{a pixel is a CAR pixel}) \quad = 62/200 = 0.31$$
$$P(\text{a pixel is a ROAD pixel}) = 74/200 = 0.37$$
$$P(\text{a pixel is a GRASS pixel}) = 64/200 = 0.32$$

Multiply these values into the rows in the conditional probabilities, giving

| | Grey levels | | | |
|---|---|---|---|---|
| Label | 0 | 1 | 2 | 3 |
| ROAD | 0.25 | 0.06 | 0 | 0 |
| CAR | 0.07 | 0.15 | 0.14 | 0.01 |
| GRASS | 0 | 0.05 | 0.17 | 0.10 |

Now give each pixel the label corresponding to the highest probability for that grey level, as follows:

| | Grey levels | | | |
|---|---|---|---|---|
| Region | 0 | 1 | 2 | 3 |
| ROAD | * | | | |
| CAR | | * | | |
| GRASS | | | * | * |

So every pixel of grey level 0 will be labelled ROAD, 1 will be labelled CAR, and 2 and 3 will be labelled GRASS.

As this stands it seems a rather weak technique. This is because the example used only a small number of labels and grey levels and only one feature (grey level). The technique really comes into its own when more than one plane (or feature) of the image is available, such as red, green, and blue, or range and intensity; in other words, when the pattern vector is extended.

A similar operation with glossiness and intensity is illustrated in the following example:

| | Grey levels: glossiness | | | | |
|---|---|---|---|---|---|
| Label | 0 | 1 | 2 | 3 | Total |
| ROAD | 50:8 | 12:30 | 0:22 | 0:2 | 62 |
| CAR | 14:0 | 30:0 | 28:18 | 2:56 | 74 |
| GRASS | 0:10 | 10:24 | 34:30 | 20:0 | 64 |

Giving the following normalized histograms:

| | Grey levels: glossiness | | | |
|---|---|---|---|---|
| Label | 0 | 1 | 2 | 3 |
| ROAD | 0.81:0.13 | 0.19:0.48 | 0.00:0.35 | 0.00:0.03 |
| CAR | 0.19:0.00 | 0.41:0.00 | 0.38:0.24 | 0.03:0.76 |
| GRASS | 0.00:0.16 | 0.16:0.38 | 0.53:0.47 | 0.31:0.00 |

The conditional probabilities are more complicated. For example, the probability that, if a pixel is a ROAD pixel it had grey level 1 *and* glossiness $2 = 0.19 \times 0.35 = 0.0665$. This gives the following three matrices:

**ROAD**

| | Grey level | | | |
|---|---|---|---|---|
| Gloss | 0 | 1 | 2 | 3 |
| 0 | 0.11 | 0.02 | 0 | 0 |
| 1 | 0.39 | 0.09 | 0 | 0 |
| 2 | 0.28 | 0.07 | 0 | 0 |
| 3 | 0.02 | 0 | 0 | 0 |

**CAR**

| | Grey level | | | |
|---|---|---|---|---|
| Gloss | 0 | 1 | 2 | 3 |
| 0 | 0 | 0 | 0 | 0 |
| 1 | 0 | 0 | 0 | 0 |
| 2 | 0.05 | 0.10 | 0.09 | 0.01 |
| 3 | 0.14 | 0.31 | 0.29 | 0.02 |

**GRASS**

| | Grey level | | | |
|---|---|---|---|---|
| Gloss | 0 | 1 | 2 | 3 |
| 0 | 0 | 0.03 | 0.08 | 0.05 |
| 1 | 0 | 0.06 | 0.20 | 0.12 |
| 2 | 0 | 0.07 | 0.25 | 0.15 |
| 3 | 0 | 0 | 0 | 0 |

Now multiply all of the elements in the appropriate matrix by the probabilities that any one pixel in the image is a CAR, a ROAD, or GRASS and then identify the highest value from the three matrices. This then gives

| | Grey level | | | |
|---|---|---|---|---|
| Gloss | 0 | 1 | 2 | 3 |
| 0 | ROAD | ROAD | GRASS | GRASS |
| 1 | ROAD | ROAD | GRASS | GRASS |
| 2 | ROAD | CAR | GRASS | GRASS |
| 3 | CAR | CAR | CAR | CAR |

Thus each pixel is classifiable by its grey level and its glossiness.

PROBLEMS The main problem with the technique as it stands is the amount of memory required to hold the tables. For example, with three features, red, green, and blue planes, with 0–255 levels in each plane, the final labelling matrix has $256 \times 256 \times 256$ entries = 1.7 million entries.

One way of reducing this is to use functions to approximate to the histograms. Then only the function parameters need be held. This approximation technique is beyond this text. (See Niblack (1986) for further details.)

For only two features such as range and intensity, this system works well.

## 12.9 OPTICAL CHARACTER RECOGNITION (ENGLISH SCRIPT)

There are a number of measures that can be identified for the purposes of recognizing a character. Some of these are discussed in outline in Chapter 18, where recognition of Chinese characters is considered. This section illustrates how to create a pattern vector for a real character using a simple area count.

### 12.9.1 Initial problems

Rarely does the image processor have the luxury of having an image of the character totally separated from other characters, in an array of suitable resolution (at least $10 \times 10$ per character), oriented and lit correctly—such an image can be thresholded into a perfectly shaped binary character image.

Orientation can often be arranged physically by putting the sheet onto the scanner at the right angle. Isolating a character is the first exercise.

#### Technique 12.3 Isolation of a character in an OCR document
USE To create a window containing only one character onto an array containing a text image.

OPERATION Assuming that the image is correctly orientated and that the text is dark on a white background, calculate row sums of the pixel grey-level values. Significantly high row sums are indicators of a space between the rows.

Now calculate column sums on a row of letters found by the above technique. Significantly high column sums are indicators of a space between the characters. (Note that this is not necessarily true of non-English script.)

Thus isolate a character.

A thresholding exercise is useful at this point as it effectively normalizes the pixels—say to 0 for background white and 1 for ink dark. Automatic thresholding can be done using the algorithm in Chapter 5. Finally, a scaling exercise may be needed. In order to process the character we need to put it in a matrix of known size, moving it from a window of variable size.

Additionally, we may need to process smaller characters more carefully. For example, it is worth expanding the full stop into the full matrix to ensure that the system is not actually viewing a comma.

Scaling may be done by keeping the aspect ratio or changing it. Keeping the aspect ratio is fine for a character like 'o', which is as high as it is wide, but a character like 'l', for example, will be difficult to distinguish from a '['. In this case it would be better not to keep the aspect ratio.

### 12.9.2 Establishing the pattern vector

We assume that each character has been moved into a $28 \times 12$ matrix. In this simple illustration, the pattern vector is created by passing a $4 \times 4$ grid over the matrix and counting the number of dark pixels in each square. The pattern vector then consists of 16 values corresponding to each element in the grid.

### 12.9.3 The library

In this case a 'distance' operation is used. The pattern vector is compared with a library of all the characters likely to be found. The nearest match is flagged as the correct character. If the nearest match is still significantly in error, the character is flagged as unknown.

**Technique 12.4 Creating the pattern vector**
USE To create the pattern vector for a character so that it can be compared with the library.

OPERATION Having isolated the character, it is now necessary to place a grid over the character and count the number of 'ink' pixels in each square. This is then divided by the total number of pixels in the square and the figures are then compared with the library. An example of this is illustrated in Fig. 12.5.

The library of characters may be ordered according to the values in different squares. For example, the characters that have the top left square empty (0 per cent) might be placed at the beginning of the list and those with the top left square full, at the end of the list. This

| | 11<br>111<br>111 | 11<br>111<br>111 | |
|---|---|---|---|
| | 111<br>111<br>111 | 111<br>111<br>111 | |
| 1<br>111<br>111 | 1111111<br>1111111 | 1111111<br>1111111 | 11<br>111<br>111 |
| 111<br>111<br>111 | | | 111<br>111<br>111 |

| 0% | 40% | 40% | 0% |
|---|---|---|---|
| 0% | 45% | 45% | 0% |
| 33% | 66% | 66% | 40% |
| 45% | 0% | 0% | 45% |

**Figure 12.5** Pattern vector from area calculations.

enables an index to be created so that if the unknown character has 37 per cent full in its top left square, the index points to a region that is compared first with the pattern vector. If a suitable match is made quickly, then the whole alphabet need not be searched.

The 'nearness' measure may simply be the sum of squares of the differences of the observed percentages with the expected percentages for each character in the library. The 'best' character is then the one with the smallest sum of squares.

Various statistical techniques can be performed in order to give a level of confidence in the final decision; however, these are not particularly useful. A simple threshold of acceptance or rejection is required in practice and this level is normally set manually.

## 12.10 EXERCISES

**12.1** Assuming a 4 × 4 grid, suggest ink percentage values for each square for the following characters:

$$I \quad 1 \quad / \quad ! \quad [$$

Comment on your results and the usefulness of the 4 × 4 grid.

**12.2** Implement the Bayesian likelihood operation on some figures of your own.

**12.3** The following pattern vectors belong to three groups as shown. Identify decision vectors and a decision table to classify further points.

group A (1, 5), (3, 7), (4, 7), (2, 6), (1, 3)
group B (5, 7), (7, 5), (7, 7), (8, 7), (8, 8)
group C (7, 3), (8, 4), (4, 1), (3, 1), (5, 3)

**12.4** Taking the points in 12.3 in row order, perform the automatic clustering algorithm on them.

# 13

# THE FREQUENCY DOMAIN

At first sight this chapter may appear daunting, particularly to those who are less than happy with summation signs, integral signs, and formulae in general. However, the frequency domain is important and any book that covers image processing without looking at the frequency domain somewhere is seriously flawed.

The chapter can be skimmed. There is an opportunity to implement frequency domain processing by using the C code in the text. There is, additionally, an opportunity to get a feeling for what frequency domain processing is about by reading the text but missing out the mathematics. Finally, for the dedicated, there is an opportunity to get into the maths and possibly obtain the references in order to do further reading on the whole subject.

## 13.1 INTRODUCTION

Transformations have already been shown to be useful in identifying lines, circles, and shapes using the Hough transform, which transforms $(x, y)$ space into another space—$(m, c)$, $(a, b)$ or similar. Some technique can then be performed in this other space which, when the inverse transformation is taken—to convert back to $(x, y)$ space—gives some useful results.

Transformations are particularly useful in elementary graphics. For example, the rotation of a two-dimensional image about a point $(a, b)$ is made simpler by translating the image by $(-a, -b)$ so that the rotation is now about the point $(0, 0)$. The solution is completed by translating the image back by $(a, b)$.

In both of the above cases the transformation from normal space is done purely to make subsequent computation or identification easier than it would have been in the

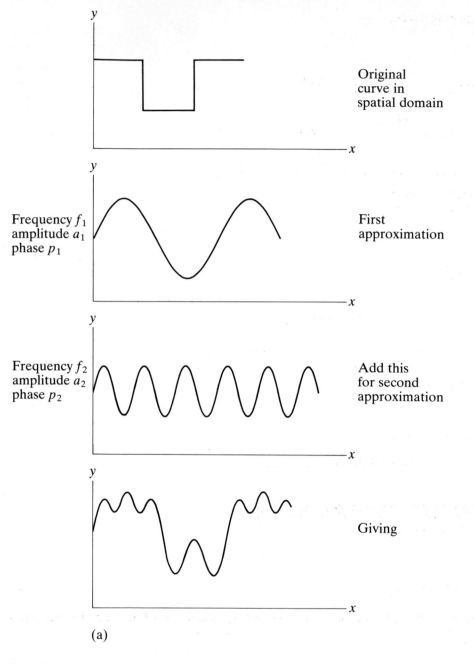

**Figure 13.1** The frequency domain.

So, ignoring phase,

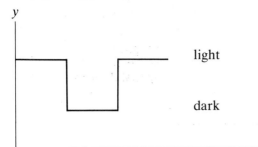

in the spatial domain
can be represented by

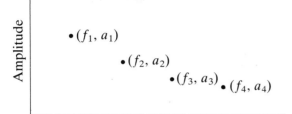

in the frequency domain

OR

a single row of pixels

by

a single row of amplitudes

(b)

**Figure 13.1** (*continued*)

normal space. The same purposes are fulfilled by transformations into the frequency
domain

## 13.2 THE FREQUENCY DOMAIN

Elementary mathematical analysis can be used to show that any wave shape can be
approximated by a sum of periodic (such as sine and cosine) functions. Figure 13.1
illustrates how this may be done. Here the wave to be approximated is a single flat

platform. With one sine wave the approximation is a long way away from the ideal, but with an increasing number of sine waves added together with different weights, the square platform gets nearer to the original.

We can write the combination of sine waves used to make up the platform as a certain amount ($u$ say) of sine wave at frequency $f$ at phase $p$.

The frequency, $f$, is the number of times the wave repeats itself in a given length (or time). A frequency of 0 means that the wave is simply a constant, a frequency of 1 means that the wave gets back to where it started in the given length.

The amplitude, $u$, is the size of the wave. This is how far it goes below and above the axis. If $u = 0$, then the wave is simply a constant line along the zero axis because it has no amplitude.

The phase is the position that the wave starts. Phase is usually measured in degrees; if the phase is $0°$, then the wave starts at its 'normal' point, e.g. the sine wave starts at $(x, y) = (0, 0)$ and is rising as $x$ increases. If the phase is $90°$, then the wave is shifted left by $90°$. In the case of a sine wave, this makes it into a cosine wave with phase $0°$.

In image processing, broadly speaking, phase is processed but ignored. For example, the image may contain some regular interference. Users are interested in how regular it is (the frequency) and how powerful it is (the amplitude). They are less interested in exactly what part of the regular interference wave is leftmost on the screen.

Both transforms below hold the phase information, though in different forms. In fact phase information is purposely removed when viewing the 'power spectrum' because it adds an unnecessary level of complexity.

Plotting amplitude ($u$) against frequency ($f$) gives a two-dimensional frequency representation of the original image (without phase). A trivial example is the frequency approximation of a sine wave.

The sine wave can be written $5 \sin 3\theta$ in the spatial domain, with the parameter $\theta$. Different frequencies would be $\theta$, $2\theta$, $3\theta$, and so on.

In the frequency domain the important terms are magnitude 5 and frequency 3. On magnitude $v$ frequency coordinates, this would be represented by a point at (3, 5).

Different spatial equations like a saw-tooth wave require combinations of frequency waves to make them up. So, for example

$$3f_1 + 2f_2 + 5.7f_3 + 9f_4$$

might approximate a saw-tooth wave. These frequencies can also be plotted: magnitude (3, 2, 5.7, and 9) versus frequency ($f_1$, $f_2$, $f_3$, and $f_4$).

## 13.3 IN THE IMAGE

Now take a single row of pixels from an image. This can be represented as a graph of light intensity versus $x$ coordinate. As a wave it can be approximated by sine and cosine waves of a variety of frequencies. These, in turn, can be represented in frequency space as frequency waves by plotting their magnitude versus frequency.

Conversion from a one-dimensional wave to a two-dimensional image depends on the particular transformation used (there are a number of possibilities). A simple approach is to perform the transformation on all the rows, creating an intermediate image, and then perform the transformation again on all the columns in the intermediate image to create a final output.

There are many applications for which transformation of the image to the frequency domain is useful. Initial image filtering can be done more easily in the frequency domain, particularly if the software tools are available to the image processor and the processing is human directed.

> An image was captured with a regular set of 'line' noise visible that ran from top to bottom and left to right. The lines reduced the intensity of the image, though the basic image under the lines was still visible.
>
> When converted into the frequency domain the lines appeared as two regions. These were removed (by setting them to zero). On converting back to the spatial domain the lines had been removed.

Specific transformations into the frequency domain can also be used to reduce the amount of computation required in convolving images (useful in solving registration problems) and identifying particular shapes and sizes of objects.

Two transformations are presented here. Both are presented in their discrete form (i.e. although they can be applied to continuous waves, it is assumed that the image consists of a number of individually placed pixels that represent samples of the continuous image). The first, the Hartley transformation, is the simpler to implement though less common than the Fourier transformation, which is covered more extensively later in the chapter. The Hartley transformation is less demanding in terms of mathematics and computer storage and is therefore presented first.

## 13.4 THE HARTLEY TRANSFORM

This transform is due to Hartley (1942) and is a real-valued frequency transformation using sines and cosines. As with many of these algorithms there is a basic way of doing the transformation (in this case called the discrete Hartley transform—DHT) and a fast way (fast Hartley transform—FHT). The DHT is presented first.

The $M \times N$ image ($M$ pixels wide by $N$ pixels high) is converted into a second image, also $M \times N$. Actual operation dictates that $M$ and $N$ should preferably be powers of 2, typically $256 \times 256$.

The basic transform depends on calculating the following *for each pixel in the new 256 × 256 array*:

$$H(u, v) = \frac{1}{MN} \sum_{x=0}^{M-1} \sum_{y=0}^{N-1} f(x, y) \cdot \left\{ \cos 2\pi \left( \frac{ux}{M} - \frac{vy}{N} \right) + \sin 2\pi \left( \frac{ux}{M} - \frac{vy}{N} \right) \right\}$$

where $f(x, y)$ is the intensity of the pixel at position $(x, y)$ in the image and $H(u, v)$ is the value (intensity if you like) of the element (pixel) in the frequency domain ($0 \leq u < M$, $0 \leq v < N$). The results are periodic, i.e. the value of the resulting transformation at position $(u, v)$ is the same as the value at position $(u \pm M, v \pm N)$, though, of course, the latter points are not stored. The axes $u$ and $v$ may be seen as representing frequencies in the horizontal ($x$) and vertical ($y$) directions, respectively, in the original image.

The cosine + sine term (cas) is called the kernel of the transformation. Other terms are used by other transformations (Fourier, for example), though the basic double summation is a central feature of transformations into the frequency domain.

## Technique 13.1 The discrete Hartley transform

USE To convert an ordinary image into the frequency domain so that some processing techniques, best done in the frequency domain, can be implemented. In practice, it is best not to use this technique as it is very slow. However, it is more easily understood than the fast Hartley transform decribed later.

OPERATION While this is a technique that can be used, it is not fast. The better technique is the FHT shown later. However, much of the work in this technique is necessary for the FHT.

Decide on the size of the input image $(M, N)$ and, therefore, the corresponding output image.

Fill an array with a set of cas values. Cas values are $\sin \theta + \cos \theta$. Use, say, 500 values of $\theta$ from 0 (result into arr[0]) to $2\pi$ (result into arr[499]). This avoids calculating them every time, which is time wasting. Note that the values are in radians.

Now the slog is to set up outer $u$ and $v$ loops (for the output array of pixels) and inner $x$ and $y$ loops (for the analysis of the input array for each output pixel). Then, within these loops calculate $(ux/M + vy/N)$, look up the cas value in the table and add it to the sum for that pixel:

```
for(u=0; u<640; u++)for(v=0; v<480; v++)
sum=0;
for(x=0; x<640; x++)for(y=0; y<480; y++)
sum+=image[x][y]*arr[500*u*x/640/640+500*v*y/480/480];
out_image[u][v]=sum;
```

It is impossible to get away from a minimum $N^2 M^2$ multiplications, even if the results of the calculations $ux/M$ and $vy/N$ are already calculated in two-dimensional tables. This means a lot of work is involved—in the above coding example 6 710 886 400 multiplications. If these are floating-point calculations a typical microcomputer would take, at the very least, some hours to complete, and probably, in practice, some days.

An approach that reduces this work considerably is to subdivide the work into a calculation of the row transforms and then column transformations, at the same time implementing a binary tree calculation approach. The subdivision of the work into rows and columns can be done if a temporary matrix of results is set up as follows:

$$T(u, v) = \frac{1}{MN} \sum_{x=0}^{M-1} \sum_{y=0}^{N-1} f(x, y) \cdot \text{cas } 2\pi \frac{ux}{M} \cdot \text{cas } 2\pi \frac{vy}{N}$$

so that

$$T(u, v) = \frac{1}{MN} \sum_{y=0}^{N-1} \text{cas } 2\pi \frac{vy}{N} \sum_{x=0}^{M-1} f(x, y) \cdot \text{cas } 2\pi \frac{ux}{M}$$

$$= \frac{1}{MN} \sum_{y=0}^{N-1} \text{cas } 2\pi \frac{vy}{M} \cdot H(u, y)$$

where $H(u, y)$ is the one-dimensional row transform for row $y$.

The Hartley transform is then calculated from the $T$ array by

$$H(u, v) = \tfrac{1}{2}\{T(u, v) + T(M - u, v) + T(u, N - v) - T(M - u, N - v)\}$$

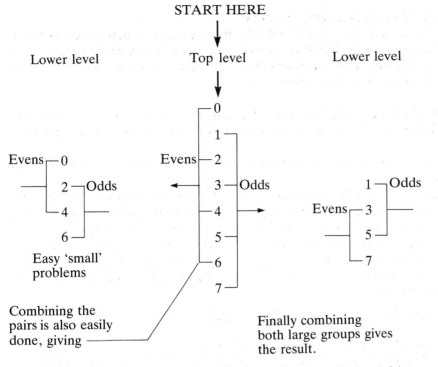

**Figure 13.2** Calculation of a one-dimensional Hartley transform over eight items of data.

This method still involves $N + 1$ multiplications per row for $M$ rows for each calculation of $T(u, v)$. However, a further technique, breaking the work down into a binary tree, reduces the number of calculations to $\log_2 N \cdot \log_2 M$ for each $T(u, v)$. It uses the following identity:

$$H(s) = H_{\text{evens}}(s) + H_{\text{odds}}(s)\cos\frac{2\pi s}{N} - H_{\text{evens}}(-s)\sin\frac{2\pi s}{N}$$

and

$$H(-s) = H_{\text{evens}}(-s) + H_{\text{odds}}(-s)\cos\frac{2\pi s}{N} - H_{\text{odds}}(s)\sin\frac{2\pi s}{N}$$

A calculation of a one-dimensional Hartley transform over eight items of data can therefore be done as shown in Fig. 13.2.

Thus do Hartley transforms on elements (0 & 4), (2 & 6), (1 & 5), and (3 & 7). Combine them to give Hartley transforms on (0 & 2 & 4 & 6) and (1 & 3 & 5 & 7). Finally combine them to give a Hartley transform on all the elements.

The concept is not an easy one to grasp, and it is not necessary to understand the intricacies of the system in order to be able to use it. If the reader feels like skipping this bit and implementing the code as if it were a 'black box', then do so.

Note that combining the transformations means using the above evens/odds identity and duplicating the length of each resulting transform. Thus if transform of (0 & 4) yielded {$a$ $b$} $a$ would be $H(0)$, $b$ would be $H(1)$; in order to be able to implement a combining

**Table 13.1**

| Number | Binary | Reversed bits | New position |
|---|---|---|---|
| 0 | 000 | 000 | 0 |
| 1 | 001 | 100 | 4 |
| 2 | 010 | 010 | 2 |
| 3 | 011 | 110 | 6 |
| 4 | 100 | 001 | 1 |
| 5 | 101 | 101 | 5 |
| 6 | 110 | 011 | 3 |
| 7 | 111 | 111 | 7 |

algorithm to get $H(0)$ to $H(3)$ with the transform of (2 & 6), the $\{a\ b\}$ needs to be lengthened to $\{a\ b\ a\ b\}$ so as to fulfil the above identity.

A program for one-dimensional Hartley transforms is presented later in the text.

### Technique 13.2 Bit reversal

USE If the user wishes to understand the 'fast' algorithms, then implementing them without using recursion requires identifying which elements need combining first. This technique labels the elements so that the correct pairings are made.

OPERATION The order of operations is identified by reversing the bits of the binary value representing the element number. Normally this is done in an array in the fast transform, as shown in Table 13.1.

Elements at position 0 and 1 are combined (0 & 4), 2 and 3 are combined (2 & 6), 4 and 5 are combined (1 & 5), and 6 and 7 are combined (3 & 7).

Then the top two pairs are combined, and so on.

This technique is not used in the presented program, instead a recursive technique is used to select groups.

Fast Fourier transforms are available as black box software routines. Fast Hartley transforms are not readily available. The FHT for a square array of size $N \times N$ where $N$ is a power of 2, is described in the following technique.

### Technique 13.3 Fast Hartley transforms

USE This is a description of the code that appears in this algorithm. The code is fast and enables the user to set up frequency domain processing without having to understand the fast Hartley concept. For an image, this algorithm will be applied to every row, giving a result; then, on those results, to every column. This then gives the $T$ array described earlier in this section. The $T$ array is then converted into the $H$ array by implementing the following formula on each element:

$$H(u, v) = \{T(u, v) + T(M - u, v) + T(u, N - v) - T(M - u, N - v)\}/2$$

OPERATION Create $\cos \theta$ and $\sin \theta$ tables as described in Technique 13.1.

Note that a one-dimensional Hartley transform of a single element is the element itself

$$H(1) = f(x), \quad \text{also} \quad H(-1) = f(x)$$

Select the top row and perform a one-dimensional FHT on that row.

Select the first two pairs of elements (either by using a permutation algorithm or recursive techniques), and apply the combining equation above. Perform this on all pairs of elements and then on fours, on eights, and so on.

Write the row back to the original array. (Note that it is floating point rather than integer.)

Do the same with each row in turn.

Now perform the same operations on the columns of the results from above.

Finally, create the Hartley transform for each element by converting the $T$ array (which has just been calculated) into an $H$ array (see above identity).

## CODE

```
/* Fast Hartley Transform */
/* This version uses global allocation of working storage */

#include<stdio.h>
#include<math.h>
char *malloc();
#define twopi 6.2831853
int size;
float *sn,*cs,*a,*AA,*work;

main()
{
 int i;
 /* initialisation is only needed once */

 initw();

 /* code required here to pass data sequence into array a[] */
 /* a[0] to a[size-1] */

 FHT(size,a,AA,1,work);
 /* shuffle and scale results */
 for (i=0; i<size; i++)a[i]=AA[(size-i)%size]/sqrt((float)size);

 /* results are now in AA[0] to AA[size-1] */
}
initw()
{
int i;
float k;

/* set up working areas */

 a=(float *) malloc(size*sizeof(float));
 AA=(float *) malloc(2*size*sizeof(float));
 work=(float *) malloc(4*size*sizeof(float));

/* define length of dataset */

 size=256;

/* prestores values of cs=cos 2pi.i/N and sn=sin 2pi.i/N */
/* so that these are obtained by simple look-up when needed */
```

```
    sn=(float *) malloc((size+1)*sizeof(float));
    cs=(float *) malloc((size+1)*sizeof(float));
    k=twopi/size;
    for(i=0; i<=size; i++)
    {
      sn[i]=sin(k*(float)i); cs[i]=cos(k*(float)i);
    }
}

FHT(N,f,F,step, warea)
int N;
float *f,*F;
int step;
float *warea;
{
  if (N==1)*F=(*(F+1))=*f;
  else
  {
   float *B,*C,*wa;
   register float *Bp,*Cp;
   int n,s;
   register int k;
   /* grab some temporary working space */
   Bp=B=warea;
   Cp=C=warea+N;
   wa=warea+(N<<1);
   n=N>>1;               /* halve problem size */
   s=step+step;          /* for use by w[k] later */
   FHT(n,f,B,s,wa);      /* recursive calls */
   FHT(n,f+step,C,s,wa); /* to set up B & C */
/* note that b and c are accessed from f implicitly via step */
/* ie the original input data */
/* now put the output together — note symmetry use */
   *(F+N)=(*F)=(*Bp++)+(*Cp++); F++; /* Hartley trans for H(0) */
   for (k=step; k<size; k+=step)
   {
     *(F+N)=(*F)=(*Bp)+cs[k]*(*Cp)-sn[k]*(*(C+N-Cp+C));
     F++; Cp++; Bp++;    /* Hartley trans for rest */
   }
  }
}
```

COMMENTS ON THE CODE This one-dimensional fast Hartley routine was developed from a fast Fourier algorithm described in Lipson (1981). It uses a recursive technique to select the elements to be processed and, while array arithmetic has been used in setting up the necessary tables, pointer arithmetic has been used to optimize the FHT routine where possible.

Readers who are not familiar with C and who wish to understand the code, should refer to one of the appropriate texts for information on pointers.

Further optimization is possible by using more register declarations.

Note that 'size' is the length of the data set which has to be given values before the routine FHT is called. The global declarations above have to be made to avoid a lot of stack work if they are made local.

The results need scaling, and can be held in one integer array when that has been done.

## 13.5 THE FOURIER TRANSFORM

The main drawback with the Fourier transform is the need to include a second array output, called the imaginary array. So each element actually has *two* values—a 'real' and an 'imaginary' value. In fact the 'phase' information is held in the weighting given to the real or imaginary part of each element. In practice the Fourier transform does not double the amount of output information compared to the Hartley transform but simply duplicates it, symmetrically, in each array.

When converting from an intensity image to the frequency domain, the imaginary input array initially contains zeros, though the transformed imaginary array contains values that must not be lost, hence the transformation creates two arrays that have to be stored. Dealing with both arrays is normally done in parallel, so that anything that is implemented on the real array is also implemented on the imaginary array.

The reverse Fourier transform is marginally different from the forward Fourier transform and it also produces an imaginary array. It is difficult to interpret the imaginary output from the reverse transform when no imaginary input was supplied, and the new values in the output have been created by altering the two frequency domain arrays.

The continuous function uses $i$ (the imaginary square root of $-1$) and instead of using cosine and sine as the kernel it uses the exponential function.

$$F(u, v) = \int\int f(x, y)e^{-2i\pi(ux + vy)}dxdy$$

Again, using the above notation, $f(x, y)$ is point $(x, y)$ in the original image and $F(u, v)$ is the point $(u, v)$ in the frequency image produced.

As with the Hartley transform, this has to be calculated for all possible values of $u$ and $v$. In discrete terms

$$F(u, v) = \frac{1}{MN} \sum_x \sum_y f(x, y)e^{-2i\pi\left(\frac{ux}{M} + \frac{vy}{N}\right)}$$

where $x = 0, 1, \ldots, M - 1$ and $y = 0, 1, \ldots, N - 1$.

This is simplified if DeMoivres theorem is used to

Imaginary part

$$F_i(u, v) = -\frac{1}{MN} \sum_x \sum_y f(x, y)\sin 2\pi\left(\frac{ux}{M} + \frac{vy}{N}\right)$$

real part

$$F_r(u, v) = \frac{1}{MN} \sum_x \sum_y f(x, y)\cos 2\pi\left(\frac{ux}{M} + \frac{vy}{N}\right)$$

The actual complex result is then $F_r(u, v) + iF_i(u, v)$. This is not particularly helpful so it is transformed into the power spectrum (as in the Hartley transform) by

Fourier power spectrum: $|F(u, v)| = F_r(u, v)^2 + F_i(u, v)^2$

The reverse Fourier transformation returns the Fourier back to the image. This is very similar to the forward Fourier

$$f(x, y) = \sum_u \sum_v F(u, v)e^{2i\pi\left(\frac{ux}{M} + \frac{vy}{N}\right)}$$

Because the discrete Fourier is also very slow, a fast Fourier transform (FFT) is normally used instead. This uses similar tactics to the fast Hartley transform above, creating a binary tree structure of the image rows and combining odds and evens. The combining of smaller transforms to create larger ones, although it does require complex arithmetic, is made easier by the simpler equations

$$F(s) = F_{\text{evens}}(s) + F_{\text{odds}}(s)e^{-2i\pi\left(\frac{s}{N}\right)}$$

This reduces computation from $M^2 N^2$ to $MN \log_2 M \cdot \log_2 N$ which in the earlier example brings the number of floating-point multiplications down to 5 898 240, i.e. about 1/1000th of the original weight of calculation.

## 13.6 OPTICAL TRANSFORMATION

It is common practice to transform the viewing output from the frequency transforms into an optical image with the frequency 0 in the centre. This is done by quartering the image and moving the quarters as shown in Fig. 13.3.

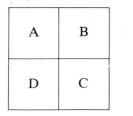

Original frequency
domain image

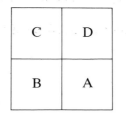

Optically
transformed

**Figure 13.3**

## 13.7  POWER AND AUTOCORRELATION FUNCTIONS

The power function can be obtained from either the Hartley or Fourier transform:

$$P(u, v) = |F(u, v)| = \tfrac{1}{2}[H(u, v)^2 + H(-u, -v)^2]$$

where if $F(u, v) = a + ib$, then $|F(u, v)| = a^2 + b^2$

Autocorrelation has been found to be useful in a number of applications (see Paik and Fox, 1988). This can be evaluated from the Fourier transform by calculating the inverse Fourier of $|F(u, v)|^2$ and from the Hartley transform by performing a further Hartley transform on $\tfrac{1}{2}[H(u, v)^2 + H(-u, -v)^2]$.

The power function typically generates figures that lie at great extremes. There may be a few values in the thousands, with 99 per cent of the values less than 1. It becomes necessary to do scaling on these results, normally involving some logarithmic function to bring them into a range that can be modelled as grey levels on the system being used. A scaling example for power function results is discussed in Chapter 4.

## 13.8  INTERPRETATION OF THE POWER FUNCTION

The typical power function has significantly brighter pixels at the centre (at a frequency of zero) and a gradual decrease in brightness towards the edge of the picture. An original image with little structure generates a power image with a circular haze in the centre, also with little structure. If there are spots off centre from the haze, then this may indicate a regular patterning on the original image. Such spots can be removed in a number of ways using filters. A simple discrete filter would be to set to zero those elements of the $F$ or $H$ spectrum that make up the power image for those dots. (This is two values in the $H$ array—$H(u, v)$ and $H(-u, -v)$—and the corresponding pair of values in the imaginary and real $F$ arrays.) More sophisticated filtering would include smoothing the dots into the surrounding area so that the overall power of the image is not decreased but the discontinuities are removed.

Figure 13.4 illustrates the process of image enhancement using one spatial domain, by Hartley and Fourier transforms.

Figure 13.5 shows a sealed power function of the X-ray of a breast.

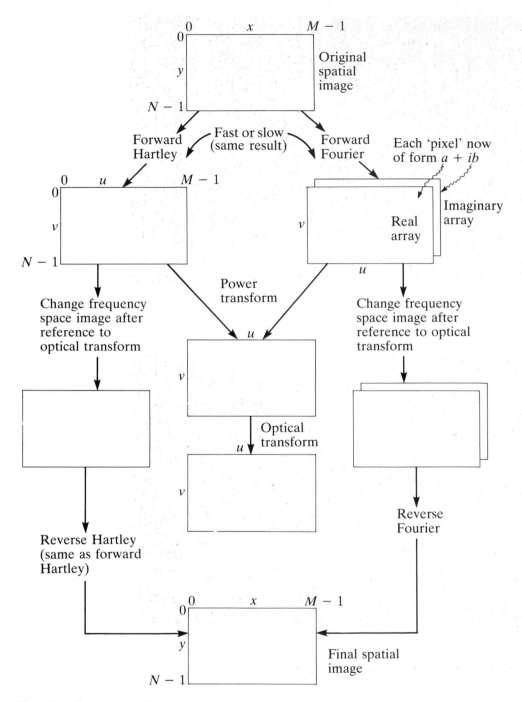

**Figure 13.4** Hartley versus Fourier transforms.

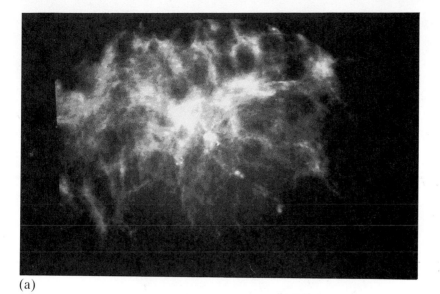

(a)

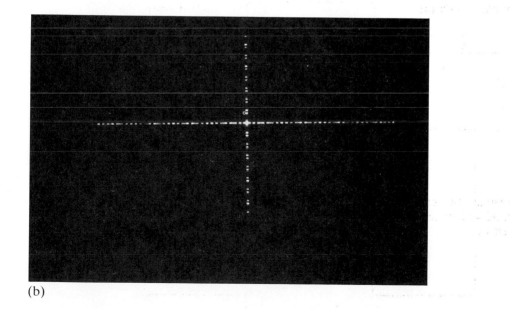

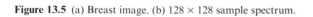

(b)

**Figure 13.5** (a) Breast image. (b) 128 × 128 sample spectrum.

## 13.9 EXERCISE

**13.1** Perform (i) a Hartley transform and (ii) a Fourier transform on the following $4 \times 4$ image:

$$
\begin{array}{cccc}
0 & 0 & 0 & 0 \\
0 & 2 & 2 & 0 \\
0 & 2 & 2 & 0 \\
0 & 0 & 0 & 0
\end{array}
$$

Show that the power transformation is the same from both calculations.

# APPLICATIONS OF FREQUENCY DOMAIN PROCESSING

## 14.1 INTRODUCTION

Having transformed the image into the frequency domain, what can be done with it? This chapter gives a brief summary of the kind of operations that might preferably be done in the frequency domain. The choice of domain for the processing can be an expensive one if the wrong decision is made, as is shown later in this chapter. It is true to say, however, that anything that can be done to an image in the frequency domain can be done in the spatial domain and vice versa. It may simply be easier in one or the other.

## 14.2 CONVOLUTION IN THE FREQUENCY DOMAIN

There are occasions when it is more profitable, in terms of speed, to do convolution in the frequency domain rather than the spatial domain. Figure 14.1 illustrates this. In fact, benefits, in terms of the number of multiplications required, become apparent on a $1024 \times 1024$ image when the template is $16 \times 16$ or larger.

## 14.3 PRACTICAL POINTS ABOUT CORRELATING IMAGES IN THE FREQUENCY DOMAIN

Before describing the algorithm, a few notes need to be made.

1. The initial image and template must be the same size. This normally means that the template has to be made larger by stuffing with zeros, so

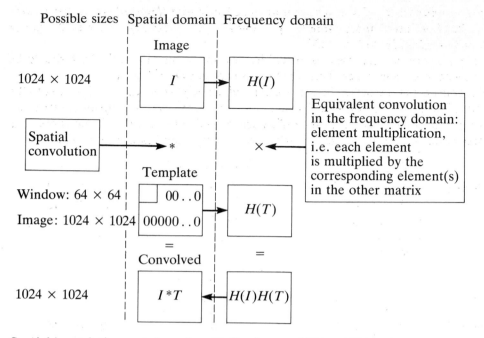

Spatial convolution: number of multiplications $= 1024 \times 1024 \times 64 \times 64 \simeq 4 \times 10^9$
Frequency domain convolution: number of multiplications $=$

| | | |
|---|---|---|
| $2 \times 1024 \times 1024 \times \log_2 1024$ | $= 20\ 971\ 520$ | conversion to $H(I)$ |
| $2 \times 1024 \times 1024 \times \log_2 1024$ | $= 20\ 971\ 520$ | conversion to $H(T)$ |
| $4 \times 1024 \times 1024$ | $=\ \ 4\ 194\ 304$ | element-by-element multiplication |
| $2 \times 1024 \times 1024 \times \log_2 1024$ | $= 20\ 971\ 520$ | conversion back to $I*T$ |

$$67\ 108\ 864 \simeq 7 \times 10^7$$

**Figure 14.1** Convolution in the frequency domain.

$$
\begin{matrix}
1 & 1 \\
1 & 1
\end{matrix}
$$

becomes

$$
\begin{matrix}
1 & 1 & 0 & 0 & 0 & \ldots & 0 \\
1 & 1 & 0 & 0 & 0 & \ldots & 0 \\
0 & 0 & 0 & 0 & 0 & \ldots & 0 \\
. & . & . & . & . & .. & . \\
0 & 0 & 0 & 0 & 0 & \ldots & 0
\end{matrix}
$$

This has to be done before converting the matrices into the frequency domain.
2. The 'fast' algorithms FHT and FFT work most efficiently (and are more easily

programmed) if the $N \times M$ matrix is arranged such that $N$ and $M$ are integer powers of 2. For even more simplicity, $N = M = 2^k$, typically $7 \le k \le 10$, giving $N = M = 128, 256, 512,$ or 1024.

3. Unless a very fast processor is available, or a lot of time is available, $k$ should be smaller rather than larger. Time for the transform is $O(N^2 \log_2 N)$.
4. The transform is periodic. This means that, effectively, when the template gets to the edge of the picture it wraps itself around to the other side. If the template is very small compared to the image, then the difference is negligible; however, if the template is large compared to the image the difference becomes significant. For example

```
              Image                    Template

Normal    1  2  3 │ 0 . . .         1  1  0              12  16   9
          4  5  6 │ 0 . . .         1  1  0      →       24  28  15
          7  8  9 │ 0 . . .         0  0  0              15   7   9

          0  0  0   0 . . .
          ⋮  ⋮  ⋮
```

```
              Image                    Template

Periodic  1  2  3 │ 1  2  3 . . .   1  1  0              12  16  14
          4  5  6 │ 4  5  6 . . .   1  1  0      →       24  28  26
          7  8  9 │ 7  8  9 . . .   0  0  0              18  22  20

          1  2  3   1  2  3 . . .
          ⋮  ⋮  ⋮
```

This means that to avoid wrapround problems caused by the assumption that the image and template are periodic, columns of rows and zeros need to be added to the image and the template. In practice, if the template is $n \times m$ and the image is $N \times M$, then pack out *both* images at the right and bottom with zeros to a minimum size of $(N + n - 1) \times (M + m - 1)$. See Gonzalez and Wintz (1977) for a fuller explanation of this packing.

5. As was stated in Chapter 6, convolution in the frequency domain is 'real' convolution, i.e.

$$I * T(X, Y) = T(i, j) \times I(X - i, Y - j)$$

This means that if 'commonly accepted' convolution (actually cross-correlation) is required, the template needs to be transposed, and the results are then out of step by the size of the template. The following example illustrates this:

```
        Image              Template
    0   1   2   0       1   2   0   0
    4   5   6   0       7   3   0   0
    8   9  10   0       0   0   0   0
    0   0   0   0       0   0   0   0
```

would 'normally' be expected to give

$$
\begin{array}{cccc}
45 & 58 & 44 & 12 \\
97 & 110 & 76 & 32 \\
26 & 29 & 10 & 16 \\
3 & 13 & 14 & 0
\end{array}
$$

However, this is in fact cross-correlation. 'Real' convolution automatically transposes the template to

$$
\begin{array}{cccc}
0 & 0 & 0 & 0 \\
0 & 0 & 0 & 0 \\
0 & 0 & 3 & 7 \\
0 & 0 & 2 & 1
\end{array}
$$

and cross-correlates that with the images, putting the result at the position corresponding to the bottom righthand corner of the template. It also performs the convolution periodically, producing an image the same size as the original.

$$
\begin{array}{cccc}
0 & 1 & 4 & 4 \\
4 & 20 & 33 & 18 \\
36 & 72 & 85 & 38 \\
56 & 87 & 97 & 30
\end{array}
$$

Thus, if 'normal' convolution (cross-correlation) is to be performed in the frequency domain, then the template has to be transposed first, as above, and then used. This effectively reverses the transposal, and 'normal' convolution takes place.

Given a non-symmetric image and template, there is little to choose between convolution using Fourier or Hartley transforms. Hartley is generally easier because it avoids the complex plane, but the code to run either application is very similar and involves a similar number of calculations.

### Technique 14.1 Convolution using the Fourier transform
USE If a two-dimensional Fourier 'black box' is available, and the template and image size are large (see below for definition of large), then this method performs a convolution faster than direct spatial convolution.

OPERATION Using the Fourier transform, convolution is simply multiplication, element by element, of the transformed image by the transformed template, i.e. $(N + n - 1) \times (M + m - 1)$ complex multiplications.

Multiplying element by element means taking the top left elements of both transformed images and multiplying them together and calling this the top left element of the output image. This multiplication has to be complex, i.e. there are two arrays (real and imaginary) for each of the template, image, and result. The elements in the result (real and imaginary arrays) are as follows:

$$
\begin{array}{ccc}
F(\text{image}) & F(\text{template}) & F(\text{result}) \\
(r_1, i_1) & (r_2, i_2) & (r_1 r_2 - i_1 i_2, r_1 i_2 + r_2 i_1)
\end{array}
$$

i.e. four real multiplications and two additions.

This is done across the whole image, multiplying matching elements to give the resulting element.

The reverse Fourier transform then needs to be implemented on the result to put it back into the complex spatial domain.

### Technique 14.2  Hartley convolution

USE  The Hartley two-dimensional transform can be used to convolve a template with an image. If both are large (see below for definition of large), this is faster than convolution in the spatial domain.

OPERATION  Pad out the template array and the image array with zeros so that they are of size $(N + n - 1) \times (M + m - 1)$, where the template is $m \times n$ and the image is $M \times N$.

For example, with a $3 \times 3$ to be convolved with a $2 \times 2$ template, pad both of them to $4 \times 4$:

$$
\begin{array}{ccc}
0 & 1 & 2 \\
4 & 5 & 6 \\
8 & 9 & 10
\end{array}
$$

is padded to

$$
\begin{array}{cccc}
0 & 1 & 2 & 0 \\
4 & 5 & 6 & 0 \\
8 & 9 & 10 & 0 \\
0 & 0 & 0 & 0
\end{array}
$$

and

$$
\begin{array}{cc}
1 & 2 \\
7 & 3
\end{array}
$$

is padded to

$$
\begin{array}{cccc}
1 & 2 & 0 & 0 \\
7 & 3 & 0 & 0 \\
0 & 0 & 0 & 0 \\
0 & 0 & 0 & 0
\end{array}
$$

Now perform full two-dimensional Hartley transforms on each array. In the above case this gives

| Image | | | | Template | | | |
|---|---|---|---|---|---|---|---|
| 11.25 | 2.25 | 3.75 | $-5.25$ | 3.25 | 3.25 | 0.75 | 0.75 |
| $-2.25$ | $-3.75$ | $-0.75$ | 2.75 | 3.25 | 1.75 | 0.75 | 2.25 |
| 3.75 | 0.75 | 1.25 | $-1.75$ | $-1.75$ | $-1.75$ | $-1.25$ | $-1.25$ |
| $-9.75$ | $-0.25$ | $-3.25$ | 1.25 | $-1.75$ | $-0.25$ | $-1.25$ | $-2.75$ |

Now 'multiply' them by evaluating

$$
R(u, v) = \frac{NM}{2} [I(u, v)\,T(u, v) + I(u, v)\,T(N - u, M - v) \\
+ I(N - u, M - v)\,T(u, v) \\
- I(N - u, M - v)\,T(N - u, M - v)]
$$

Giving, for the above example

$$
\begin{array}{rrrr}
585 & -33 & 45 & -213 \\
-417 & 75 & -49 & 39 \\
-105 & -11 & -25 & 45 \\
-27 & -59 & 25 & 125
\end{array}
$$

Now do a reverse Hartley on the $R$ array to get the convolved solution

$$
\begin{array}{rrrr}
0 & 1 & 4 & 4 \\
4 & 20 & 33 & 18 \\
36 & 72 & 85 & 38 \\
56 & 87 & 97 & 30
\end{array}
$$

Bracewell (1986) gives a full description of this convolution operation using Hartley transforms.

It can also be shown that if the original template is symmetric (i.e. if it were partitioned into four matrices of equal size, one at each corner, these matrices would all be identical), then the odd terms in the multiplication would all be zero, so that the convolution would simplify to one multiplication per element.

Fourier and Hartley transformations do involve a significant number of multiplications and, generally, unless the templates are large, it is impractical to implement convolution using this method for just one image and one template. However, if there are $I$ images and $T$ templates, requiring $I \times T$ convolutions to compare each image with each template, then working in the frequency domain reduces the expense considerably.

An object identification system used convolution to compare the scene of objects in view with a set of templates of known objects. Objects in five different scenes had to be recognized. The orientation and shape of the objects was known to be constant. But their positions (if any) in each image were unknown.

With five images (each $225 \times 225$) and 10 object templates (each $32 \times 32$), using standard aperiodic convolution there would be approximately 52 million multiplications per template giving a total of 2500 million multiplications.

Alternatively (figures are approximate), using $2N \cdot \log_2 N$ as the number of multiplications for the one-dimensional Hartley transform, and $2M \cdot \log_2 M$ as the number of multiplications for the column transform to the $T$ array gives for the $(225 + 32 - 1) \times (225 + 32 - 1)$ images (image and template)

$$256 \times 2 \times 256 \times \log_2 256 = 1 \text{ million multiplications for the rows}$$
$$256 \times 2 \times 256 \times \log_2 256 = 1 \text{ million multiplications for the columns}$$

i.e. 2 million floating-point multiplications required for the Hartley transform.

Following the same logic

| | |
|---|---|
| Hartley transforms on all the 5 scene images | 10 million |
| Hartley transforms on all 10 templates | 20 million |
| Element by element multiplication | 13 million |
| Hartley transforms on the 50 results | 100 million |
| Total | 143 million |

The machine used had a floating-point processor so that there was negligible time difference between the integer and floating-point multiplication. Consequently this second method was favoured for the work.

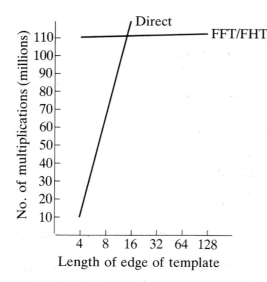

**Figure 14.2** For a 1024 × 1024 image, any convolution with a template greater than 16 × 16 is best done in the frequency domain.

## 14.4 MEASURING CONVOLUTION OPERATIONS

A number of authors quote optimal sizes for consideration of convolution using frequency space as opposed to the direct shift, multiply, and add method. Niblack (1986), in particular, deduces the following ratio:

$$\frac{\text{FFT work}}{\text{direct}} = \frac{10s^2 \cdot \log_2 s + 2ws \cdot \log_2 s + 4s^2}{(s - w + 1)^2 w^2}$$

where $s$ is the edge length of the image and $w$ is the edge length of the template window.

Figure 14.2 illustrates the cost of convolution in frequency space.

Correlation is convolution in another guise. In the Fourier domain it relies on calculating the complex conjugate (changing the sign of all the elements in the imaginary array) of the Fourier image prior to element multiplication.

Optical properties of lenses and mirrors can be expressed in frequency domain terms. This means that frequency domain techniques can be used to describe linear filters of real optical instruments.

Clearly, the frequency domain lends itself to describing periodic functions. Images with any periodicity can often best be analysed in the frequency rather than the spatial domain.

## 14.5 DECONVOLUTION

Deconvolution is the reverse of the convolution process. For convolution we write

$$R = I * T$$

where $R$ is the resulting image, $I$ is the initial image, and $T$ is the template.

Deconvolution determines $I$ (the original image) given $R$ and $T$

$$I = R*^{-1}T$$

where $*^{-1}$ denotes deconvolution.

It can be shown that deconvolution of $R$ by $T$ is equivalent to convolution of $R$ by some 'inverse' of the template $T$, say $T'$. This inverse can be calculated in the spatial domain.

Consider (periodic) convolution as a matrix operation. For example

$$\begin{matrix} 1 & 2 & 3 \\ 4 & 5 & 6 \\ 7 & 8 & 9 \end{matrix} \quad * \quad \begin{matrix} 1 & 1 & 0 \\ 1 & 1 & 0 \\ 0 & 0 & 0 \end{matrix} \quad \begin{matrix} 12 & 16 & 14 \\ 24 & 28 & 26 \\ 18 & 22 & 20 \end{matrix}$$

is equivalent to

$$\begin{matrix} A \end{matrix} \qquad\qquad \begin{matrix} B \end{matrix} \qquad\qquad \begin{matrix} C \end{matrix}$$

$$(1\ 2\ 3\ 4\ 5\ 6\ 7\ 8\ 9) \begin{pmatrix} 1 & 0 & 1 & 0 & 0 & 0 & 1 & 0 & 1 \\ 1 & 1 & 0 & 0 & 0 & 0 & 1 & 1 & 0 \\ 0 & 1 & 1 & 0 & 0 & 0 & 0 & 1 & 1 \\ 1 & 0 & 1 & 1 & 0 & 1 & 0 & 0 & 0 \\ 1 & 1 & 0 & 1 & 1 & 0 & 0 & 0 & 0 \\ 0 & 1 & 1 & 0 & 1 & 1 & 0 & 0 & 0 \\ 0 & 0 & 0 & 1 & 0 & 1 & 1 & 0 & 1 \\ 0 & 0 & 0 & 1 & 1 & 0 & 1 & 1 & 0 \\ 0 & 0 & 0 & 0 & 1 & 1 & 0 & 1 & 1 \end{pmatrix} = (12\ 16\ 14\ 24\ 28\ 26\ 18\ 22\ 20)$$

Each column of $B$ corresponds to the elements of the template shifted to give the correct multiplying patterns. See Gonzalez and Wintz (1977) for details of how these patterns can be determined.

Now we have

$$AB = C$$

But $C$ is known, and $B$ can be guessed at, so, by simple matrix algebra

$$AB = C$$

therefore

$$ABB^{-1} = CB^{-1}$$

giving

$$A = CB^{-1} \qquad \text{(assuming } B^{-1} \text{ exists)}$$

In other words, it is necessary only to find the inverse of the matrix $B$ above, and multiply the vector $C$ by it to obtain the result required.

The inverse of a $9 \times 9$ matrix is relatively easy to calculate. This is not the case for the inverse of a matrix with *each side* being VGA, say, $640 \times 480$ elements, i.e. the matrix will have $640 \times 480 \times 640 \times 480$ elements—approximately $100\,000\,000\,000$.

The practical alternative is to do the deconvolution in frequency space. Since convolution in frequency space is a multiplication of elements, deconvolution is an equivalent dividing of elements.

## 14.6 CONCLUSION

By virtue of this book attempting to cover so many topics, the reader will realize that this summary can only be a taster of the power of image manipulation in the frequency domain. The applications in Chapter 18 hint at other uses—and there are many. As a part of the image processor's tool-kit, some frequency space transformation software is essential.

# 15

## IMAGE COMPRESSION

### 15.1 INTRODUCTION

Compression of images is concerned with storing them in a form that does not take up so much space as the original. Elementary compression can be illustrated by comparing the work of artists with that of computer-aided designers. CAD experts would not normally hold a full bit-map of the work they had produced. For example, it may be that they are interested in specifying a particular widget on a car. If this widget appears many times in the final drawings, they would wish to specify the widget only once and have the system draw it for them each time. Thus they would specify the widget in terms of $(x, y, z)$ coordinates and how these coordinates related to one another. The CAD output would therefore be a file of $(x, y, z)$ coordinates together with some relational detail.

This is not how artists would work. With an electronic paintbrush they might wish to shade an area with a particular ink, gradually increasing the amount of shading by using the paint brush over some part of the area again and again. The file would have to be a full memory map of all the pixels in the original piece of work. It could not simply contain the $(x, y)$ coordinates of areas and their relationships.

In both of the above cases, however, an image is displayed. Clearly, different data structures are best for each type of image for minimum storage requirements. Minimum storage is not a useful end in itself and compressing images to minimum storage levels is itself a time-costly exercise. However, if images are to be held on or transferred between machines, minimum storage reduces hardware costs.

This chapter is about compression of *grey-level* images and considers how it might be used in sending real-time pictures along slow lines.

## 15.2 TYPES AND REQUIREMENTS

Compression systems need to offer the following benefits:

- Speedy operation (both compression and unpacking).
- Significant reduction in required memory.
- No significant loss of quality in the image.
- Format of output suitable for transfer or storage.

Each of these depends on the user and the application.

There are four approaches that may be adopted to compression:

1. Statistical compression—i.e. the coding of an image based on the grey levels of the pixels in the whole image.
2. Spatial compression—i.e. coding the image based on the spatial relationship between pixels of predictably similar types.
3. Quantizing compression—i.e. reducing the resolution or the number of grey levels available.
4. Fractal compression—i.e. coding the image as a set of parameters to fractal generating functions.

In practice, all of these approaches are used. It is often the case that more than one method is implemented on a set of data. This chapter looks at the methods separately. It will become apparent how they may be combined.

A useful academic reference is Netravali and Haskell (1988). They consider a much wider selection of compression and communication methods for images than can be covered in this text.

## 15.3 STATISTICAL COMPRESSION

At the time of writing, the International Standards Organization is considering a standard for sequential colour image data compression. The algorithm used is likely to be one using, among other things, the Huffman coding system. This is a statistical coding system based on the assumption that the histogram of grey levels is not normally flat.

When the histogram of grey levels is flat, the best statistical compression coding system is the normal binary system where each pixel is allocated a binary value between 0 and 15, say. Since each of the values is equally likely to occur, the fact that each pixel is allocated 4 bits for whatever value means that the image is coded easily and sensibly. Thus VGA with $640 \times 480$ and 16 colour levels is coded as 4 bits $\times 640 \times 480 = 150K$ of memory. If, however, we know that of the 16 colour levels, four are used for 60 per cent of the time, four more for a further 30 per cent and the rest for 10 per cent of the time, then we could make the following coding scheme:

Frequently used four colours

$$
\begin{array}{l}
000 \\
001 \\
010 \\
011
\end{array}
$$

Next most frequently used colours

$$
\begin{array}{l}
1000 \\
1001 \\
1010 \\
1011
\end{array}
$$

The rest

$$
\begin{array}{l}
11000 \\
11001 \\
11010 \\
11011 \\
11100 \\
11101 \\
11110 \\
11111
\end{array}
$$

This means that the length of the original (150K) is reduced to

$$[(0.6 \times 3) + (0.3 \times 4) + (0.1 \times 5)] \times 640 \times 480 = (1.8 + 1.2 + 0.5) \times 640 \times 480$$
$$= 3.5 \times 640 \times 480 = 131.25K$$

Note that the 'average' length of pixel value has been reduced from 4 bits to 3.5 bits, despite the fact that some pixels are using 5 bits to hold their values.

It can be shown that with $M$ grey levels, each with probability of $P_0, P_1, \ldots, P_{M-1}$, the number of bits required to code them is at least

$$-\sum_{i=0}^{M-1} p_i \log_2 p_i$$

**Technique 15.1  The Huffman code**
USE  To reduce the space that an image uses on disk or in transit.

OPERATION  Order the grey levels according to their frequency of use (probability of occurrence), most frequent first.

Combine the two *least used* grey levels into one group, combine their frequencies, and reorder the grey levels.

Continue to do this until only two grey levels are left.

Now allocate a 0 to one of these grey-level groups and a 1 to the other, then work back through the groupings so that where two groups have been combined to form a new, larger, group which is currently coded as 'ccc', say, code one of the smaller groups as ccc0 and the other as ccc1.

EXAMPLE  Table 15.1 shows how this method works for a nine-colour system.
From this we obtain

| | | | |
|---|---|---|---|
| 0 | 100000 | 5 | 01 |
| 1 | 10001 | 6 | 000 |
| 2 | 101 | 7 | 1001 |
| 3 | 001 | 8 | 100001 |
| 4 | 11 | | |

**Table 15.1**

|  | Original | | Reordered | | Combining groups | | | | | | | | | | | | |
|---|---|---|---|---|---|---|---|---|---|---|---|---|---|---|---|---|---|
| | Col. | Freq. | Col. | Freq. | Freq. | Col. | Freq. | Col. | Freq. | Col. | Freq. | Col. | Freq. | Col. | Freq. | Col. | Freq. | Col. |
| 63 →00 | 0 | 450 | 5 | 5500 | 5500 | 5 | 5500 | 5 | 5500 | 5 | 5500 | 5 | 6230 | 63 | 7270 | 081724 | 11730 | 635 |
| | 1 | 800 | 4 | 3520 | 3520 | 4 | 3520 | 4 | 3520 | 4 | 3520 | 4 | 5500 | 5 | 6230 | 63 | 7270 | 081724 |
| | 2 | 1620 | 3 | 3340 | 3340 | 3 | 3340 | 3 | 3340 | 3 | 3340 | 3 | 3750 | 08172 | 5500 | 5 | | |
| | 3 | 3340 | 6 | 2890 | 2890 | 6 | 2890 | 6 | 2890 | 6 | 2890 | 6 | 3520 | 4 | | | | |
| | 4 | 3520 | 2 | 1620 | 1620 | 2 | 1620 | 2 | 2130 | 0817 | 3750 | 08172 | | | | | | |
| | 5 | 5500 | 7 | 830 | 830 | 7 | 1300 | 081 | 1620 | 2 | | | | | | | | |
| | 6 | 2890 | 1 | 800 | 800 | 1 | 830 | 7 | | | | | | | | | | |
| | 7 | 830 | 0 | 450 | 500 | 08 | | | | | | | | | | | | |
| | 8 | 50 | 8 | 50 | | | | | | | | | | | | | | |

Resultant coding

```
635 → 0
   63 → 00
      6 → 000
      3 → 001
   5 → 01
081724 → 1
   08172 → 10
      0817 → 100
         081 → 1000
            08 → 10000
               0 → 100000
               8 → 100001
            1 → 10001
         7 → 1001
      2 → 101
   4 → 11
```

193

i.e. the storage has improved from $19\,000 \times 3$ bits $= 57\,000$ bits to $51\,910$ bits. Clearly this is not much of a saving, but when 256 grey levels are used and the histogram is far from level, the savings can be very considerable. For example Gonzales and Wintz quote the 16 grey-level Landsat coding for channel 1 of the satellite as compressing an average of 4 bit code down to 2.75 bits per pixel.

Other compressed codes include B-codes and shift codes, but their average word length is usually greater than the Huffman code.

## 15.4 SPATIAL COMPRESSION

Here we consider the image as a long sequence of integer grey values, $row_1$, $row_2$, $row_3$, and so on. Some of these values are the same as their neighbours

$$
\begin{array}{cccccc}
& & \text{Image} & & & \\
1 & 2 & 1 & 1 & 1 & 1 \\
1 & 3 & 4 & 4 & 4 & 4 \\
1 & 1 & 3 & 3 & 3 & 5 \\
1 & 1 & 1 & 1 & 3 & 3 \\
\end{array}
$$

Giving a sequence

$$1 \quad 2 \quad 1 \quad 1 \quad 1 \quad 1 \quad 1 \quad 3 \quad 4 \quad 4 \quad 4 \quad 4 \quad 1 \quad 1 \quad 3 \quad 3 \quad 3 \quad 5 \quad 1 \quad 1 \quad 1 \quad 1 \quad 3 \quad 3$$

i.e. 24 values.

### Technique 15.2 Run length encoding

USE To reduce the space required by an image, particularly when there are many pixels of the same value located next to each other.

OPERATION The run is encoded by creating pairs of values, the first representing the grey level and the second how many of them are in the run

$$(1, 1) \quad (2, 1) \quad (1, 5) \quad (3, 1) \quad (4, 4) \quad (1, 2) \quad (3, 3) \quad (5, 1) \quad (1, 4) \quad (3, 2)$$

In the above example this would give

$$1 \quad 1 \quad 2 \quad 1 \quad 1 \quad 5 \quad 3 \quad 1 \quad 4 \quad 4 \quad 1 \quad 2 \quad 3 \quad 3 \quad 5 \quad 1 \quad 1 \quad 4 \quad 3 \quad 2$$

i.e. 20 values, a saving of four on the original.

Run length encoding can be combined with the Huffman code at this point since the histogram of run lengths is very unlikely to be flat. Normally it is skewed in favour of short run lengths of 1 or 2, hence the code for the values 1 and 2 can be made very short in terms of bits, while the code for the longer run lengths will be longer. It might be preferable to implement the Huffman code only on the run lengths (i.e. not on the grey levels as well). For example

$$\text{grey level} \,|\, H(\text{run length}) \,|\, \text{grey level} \,|\, H(\text{run length}) \,|\, \text{grey level} \ldots$$

## 15.5 CONTOUR CODING

Contour coding has the effect of reducing the areas of pixels of the same grey level to a set of contours that bound those areas. If the areas of same grey level are large with a simple edge (i.e. not jagged), then the compression rate can be very good.

Consider the following image:

```
1  1  1  1  1  1  1  1  2  2  2  2  2  2  2
1  1  1  1  1  1  1  2  2  2  2  2  2  2  2
1  1  1  1  1  1  2  2  2  2  2  2  2  2  2
1  1  1  1  1  1  1  2  2  2  2  2  2  2  2
1  1  1  1  1  1  1  1  1  1  1  2  2  2  2
```

There is one boundary evident here. An edge detector would give

```
0  0  0  0  0  0  0  0  1  0  0  0  0  0  0
0  0  0  0  0  0  0  1  0  0  0  0  0  0  0
0  0  0  0  0  0  1  0  0  0  0  0  0  0  0
0  0  0  0  0  0  0  1  1  1  1  0  0  0  0
0  0  0  0  0  0  0  0  0  0  0  1  0  0  0
```

The edge starts at $(8, 0)$ and moves to

$$(7,1) \quad (6, 2) \quad (7, 3) \quad (8, 3) \quad (9, 3) \quad (10, 3) \quad (11, 4).$$

In practice, the moves are in one of eight directions

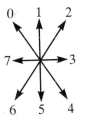

Therefore we could code the line as $(8, 0)$—the starting point—followed by

$$6 \quad 6 \quad 4 \quad 3 \quad 3 \quad 3 \quad 4$$

Each move can be represented by three bits, so the whole compression code would be

$$\text{length of } (8, 0) + (7 \times 3) \text{ bits}$$

With an image of maximum size $16 \times 16$, this would be

$$(4 \times 4) + 21 = 29 \text{ bits}$$

Of course, this does not take into account the actual grey level of the region that the contour is surrounding. In practice, it is best to make all contours circular, so that they return to the originating pixel—if necessary along the path that they have already traversed—and to identify the grey level that they lie on and enclose.

With the original image

```
1  1  1  1  1  1  1  1  2  2  2  2  2  2  2
1  1  1  1  1  1  1  2  2  2  2  2  2  2  2
1  1  1  1  1  1  2  2  2  2  2  2  2  2  2
1  1  1  1  1  1  1  2  2  2  2  2  2  2  2
1  1  1  1  1  1  1  1  1  1  1  2  2  2  2
```

this would mean

### Grey level 1 enclosure

```
1  1  1  1  1  1  1  1  1  1  1  1  1  1  1
1                                         1
1                                         1
1                                         1
1  1  1  1  1  1  1  1  1  1  1  1  1  1  1
```

Note that this is just the whole image, so the contour does not need to be kept.

### Grey level 2 enclosure

```
         1  1  1  1  1  1  1
      1                    1
   1                       1
      1  1  1  1           1
               1  1  1  1
```

Giving the data

| Grey level | Start | Sequence |
|---|---|---|
| 1 | (0,0) | |
| 2 | (0,8) | 3  3  3  3  3  3  5  5  5  5  7  7  7  0  7  7  7  0  2  2 |

Given a 4-bit plane and an image $16 \times 16$, this requires $24 + (20 \times 3)$ bits $= 84$ bits, compared with $16 \times 16 \times 4$ bits $= 1024$ bits, in the original, or $10 \times (4 + 4) = 80$ bits if compressed by run encoding, i.e. a compression to $(84/1024) \times 4 = 0.328$ bits per pixel.

When the contour is not simple, as in the following example, then it becomes necessary to have a rule for searching out the whole contour without missing any part:

```
1  1  2  2  1  1  1  1  2  2  2  2  2  2  2
1  1  1  1  2  1  1  2  2  2  2  2  2  2  2
1  1  1  1  1  2  2  1  1  1  1  1  1  1  1
1  1  1  1  2  1  1  2  2  2  2  2  2  2  2
1  1  1  1  2  2  2  1  1  1  1  2  2  2  2
```

If the outline contour is still the 1-valued background, then the 2 starts at (2, 0) and goes

A decision then has to be made as to which route is taken. A simple rule is to always look to the left first. If we use this, then the continuation is

As this goes back along the row of 2s in row 1, it hits the same point as it has already traversed. Using the 'look left' system, however, it goes the opposite way through this pixel and starts on a new contour

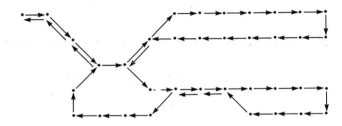

Clearly both of these methods rely on the image having a significant amount of repeated material. As soon as the image becomes complex, the coding becomes less efficient than sending the original image. However, most images do contain a significant amount of repeated material.

An exercise in sending real-time video images over telephone lines involved the use of a 19 200 baud modem and an image consisting of a 3-bit plane 320 × 256 pixels. It was found that because the grey levels were limited to 8 there were a number of repeated sequences, particularly because the image was of a face against a plain background. Using Huffman encoding of run sequences, the system could be sent in real time.

## 15.6 CHANGING THE DOMAIN

There are occasions when it is beneficial to convert the image from the spatial domain into the frequency domain and use this as the basis for compression.

A 256 × 256 8-bit plane image was found to contain no high frequencies. This image was Fourier transformed into real and imaginary planes. It was found, when an optical transform had been applied to the results, that the new values near the centre of the planes were between 10 and 1000, whereas outside of the 40 × 40 square box of pixels at the centre the rest of the values were almost all zeros.

It has to be said that such images are unlikely. Any image with a set of recognizable edges in a variety of positions, or with regions with definite boundaries has to use high frequencies to describe the discontinuous edges.

However, in the above example, it would be sensible to then store the 40 × 40 = 1600 values at the centre of the frequency planes, ignoring the rest. Reconstruction is done by placing the $40 \times 40$ square back into a frequency image with zero being assigned to the positions outside of the centre.

If the square used is too small, then rings may develop around points on the final image as too many of the higher frequencies have been removed. This is called 'ringing'.

The reduction is

original $\quad 256 \times 256 \times 8$ bits $= 516\,288$ bits
new $\qquad 40 \times 40 \times 16$ bits $\times 2$ planes $= 51\,200$ bits

i.e. a compression ration of 10:1.

The operations in the frequency domain are less automatic than some of the other operations. If there is regularity in the image, then the part of the frequency image that represents the regularity needs to be saved as well. This has to be done by inspection software, which decides what is worth keeping and what is worth throwing away.

### Technique 15.3  Compression using the frequency domain
USE  To reduce space required for an image—normally one without too many discrete edges.

OPERATION Convert the image to the frequency domain using Fourier transform or Hartley transform.

Threshold this new image removing all values less than $k$.

If what is left is significantly less than the original image, then, using one of the spatial region techniques described above, store the rest of the values.

If it is not significantly less, increase $k$—remembering that by doing so more information will be lost in the final reconstruction of the original image.

## 15.7  QUANTIZING COMPRESSION

This technique involves reducing the number of grey levels, say from 256 to 16, thus reducing the number of bits required to hold an image. The easiest, though most unsatisfactory, way to do this is to divide all the grey levels by a factor—in the above case the factor is 16. This is unsatisfactory as it takes no account of the spread of grey levels in the image. It may be, for example, that the image is entirely composed of grey levels between 0 and 128. This means that the number of new grey levels representing the image is now only 8 instead of the full 16.

### Technique 15.4  Quantizing compression
USE Reducing space required for an image by allowing the number of grey levels or colours to be restricted.

OPERATION  Let $P$ be the number of pixels in an original image to be compressed to $N$ grey levels.

Create a histogram of the grey levels in the original image.

Identify $N$ ranges in this histogram such that approximately $P/N$ pixels lie in each range.

Identify the median (the grey level with 50 per cent of the pixels in the range on one side of it and 50 per cent on the other) grey level in each range. These will be the $N$ grey levels used to quantize the image.

Now store the $N$ grey levels and allocate to each pixel a group ($0$ to $n-1$) according to which range it lies in.

For example, consider the following image:

```
2 9 6 4 8 2 6 3 8 5 9 3 7
3 8 5 4 7 6 3 8 2 8 4 7 3
3 8 4 7 4 9 2 3 8 2 7 4 9
3 9 4 7 2 7 6 2 1 6 5 3 0
2 0 4 3 8 9 5 4 7 1 2 8 3
```

which is to be compressed to 2 bits per pixel, i.e. $N=4$ grey levels. The histogram is

```
0  **
1  **
2  ********
3  **********
4  ********
5  ****
6  *****
7  ********
8  ********
9  ******
```

65 pixels, down to 4 grey levels = 16.25 in each range. The best ranges are

```
      0  **
13    1  **
      2  ********

20    3  **********
      4  ********

      5  ****
17    6  *****
      7  ********

15    8  ********
      9  ******
```

with median grey levels 2, 3, 6 and 8.

The new image becomes

```
0 3 2 1 3 0 2 1 3 2 3 1 2
1 3 2 1 2 2 1 3 0 3 1 2 1
1 3 1 2 1 3 0 1 3 0 2 1 3
1 3 1 2 0 2 2 0 0 2 2 1 0
0 0 1 1 3 3 2 1 2 0 0 3 0
```

Clearly, a loss of information has gone on but this has been minimized by ensuring that the groupings are as equal as possible. The technique is not dissimilar to the histogram equalization allocation technique that can be found in Chapter 5.

## 15.8 FRACTAL COMPRESSION

Claims have been made that fractal compression can offer up to 10 000:1 compression and with conventional algorithms added in the ratio can be improved to 1 000 000:1 (Beard, 1990). Discussion of the methodology is beyond the scope of this book; however, the principle behind the practice is to use very simple functions which operate in more dimensions than the single-dimensional real plane to *generate* highly complex and totally predictable patterns. These simple functions can be specified by a set of parameters and it is these parameters that are discovered from a real image and can regenerate that image— perhaps with some level of error. Much of this work has been carried out by Barnsley who has developed a video modem, described below. Normal 640 × 480 VGA, it is claimed, can be compressed into 5800 bytes, and fractal graphics workstations are available which operate similarly, from a user's point of view, to a normal workstation, but hold their images as fractal transform codes.

## 15.9 REAL-TIME IMAGE TRANSMISSION

A well-explored method of compressing a sequence of images involves sending differences in successive images without sending the full image. This relies on the fact that most real-time vision systems send many images of the same type before changing the image to a new scene. For example, most television programs will dwell on a scene for at least 5 seconds before moving onto another scene. At 25 frames per second it means that the full first frame is sent and then only differences are transmitted for the next 124 frames. These differences lend themselves to run length encoding or simple vector encoding where the non-zero difference values are identified in terms of their position and value. For example

| Image 1 | Image 2 |
|---|---|
| 1 1 2 2 1 2 2 1 | 1 1 2 2 1 2 2 1 |
| 1 2 2 1 1 2 1 1 | 1 2 2 1 1 2 1 1 |
| 1 1 4 4 4 1 1 1 | 1 1 2 4 4 4 1 1 |
| 2 1 4 4 4 1 1 1 | 2 1 1 4 4 4 1 1 |
| 1 2 4 4 4 2 1 1 | 1 2 1 4 4 4 1 1 |
| 1 1 2 2 2 1 1 1 | 1 1 2 2 2 1 1 1 |

3 bits per pixel, 48 pixels per image = 144 bits per image

Here the block of 4s has moved one pixel to the right in the image. If the first image is sent, then the differences, mod 8, are now

$$0 \quad 0 \quad 0 \quad 0 \quad 0 \quad 0 \quad 0 \quad 0$$
$$0 \quad 0 \quad 0 \quad 0 \quad 0 \quad 0 \quad 0 \quad 0$$
$$0 \quad 0 \quad 2 \quad 0 \quad 0 \quad 5 \quad 0 \quad 0$$
$$0 \quad 0 \quad 3 \quad 0 \quad 0 \quad 5 \quad 0 \quad 0$$
$$0 \quad 0 \quad 3 \quad 0 \quad 0 \quad 6 \quad 0 \quad 0$$
$$0 \quad 0 \quad 0 \quad 0 \quad 0 \quad 0 \quad 0 \quad 0$$

Vector encoded

$$(2, 2) = 2, \ (2, 5) = 5, \ (3, 2) = 3, \ (3, 5) = 5, \ (4, 2) = 3, \ (4, 5) = 6$$

6 vectors, 6 bits per position, 4 bits per difference = 60 bits

Or modified run length with a sequence

number of zeros|difference|number of zeros|difference|. . .

$$18 \mid 2 \mid 2 \mid 5 \mid 4 \mid 3 \mid 2 \mid 5 \mid 4 \mid 3 \mid 2 \mid 6 \mid 10$$

6 bits per 0 count, 4 bits per difference = 66

Difficulties arise when the scene does change because the amount of information for a full new scene to be received in one frame time may be more than the frame transmission time available.

A system receiving the images above can receive 100 bits per 1/25th second. If the images are transmitted at one image or one image difference per 1/25th second, then a change in scenery (requiring 144 bits of information) cannot be sent in the allotted time.

One solution is to transmit ahead of display. That is, the receiver has a series of buffers for images to be displayed. When the differenced images are sent, they are allocated less than the 1/25th of a second in terms of transmission, but are still displayed for 1/25th of a second. The receiver thus has a series of pictures already in memory ready to display. When a full scene is sent, the receiver makes up the full scene over, say 3/25ths of a second while, at the same time, displaying three images it has already got. Providing the scenes do not change too frequently, the system can always work ahead of itself so as to cope with major changes in scene.

Fractal compression has made the video modem a reality. The fractal transform has been implemented on VLSI chips and this converts 30 frame per second video $320 \times 200 \times 8$ bit for normal telephone line operation.

## 15.9.1 Motion

Identifying motion is more of a problem. The image may still have the same constituent parts; they may have just all shifted in one direction. In the worst case with a kind of chequerboard original, shifting might cause the last and next images to be so different at the pixel level that virtually the whole image has to be re-sent, and yet no new information, apart from motion information, is actually necessary.

One technique is called block matching.

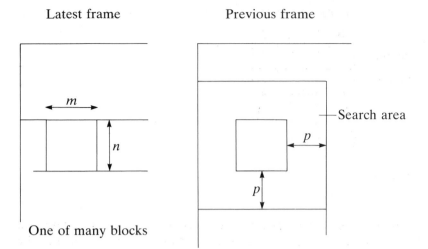

**Figure 15.1** Search area for block matching

**Technique 15.5  Block matching for motion prediction**
USE Saving space by estimating what motion has occurred between past and present images, then only saving the changes.

OPERATION Tile off the latest frame into blocks. Each of these blocks is then compared with blocks of the same size from the previous frame that are near in position to the block on the latest frame.

This has to be done for all blocks in the latest frame. Then the best match (and the corresponding predicted movement vector) is determined. This is called full-search block matching.

Does the block shown in Fig. 15.1 correspond to a block of pixels of the same size anywhere in the search area of the previous frame? ($p$ is typically 7.)

The technique is processor intensive. If the tiling is of size, say, $m \times n$ and the area of search is $p$ pixels up, down, left, and right of the block, then for each block there needs to be $(2p + 1)^2$ comparisons of blocks. If the whole frame is $M \times N$ pixels, then there needs to be $MN/mn$ total block operations.

This is best done by hardware. Motion estimation chips are available that can perform this kind of operation and can be hooked up to other chips in parallel if one chip is not fast enough (see Artieri and Colavin, 1990).

## 15.10  QUADTREES

An image may have large regions of homogeneity (same coloured pixels), and may be rectangular in character, i.e. it might be made of box-shaped regions. A quadtree representation of the region might well offer significant compression if these assumptions are true.

A quadtree is a recursive segmenting of an image into four parts, i.e. the original image

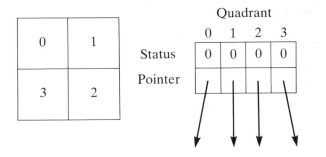

**Figure 15.2** Basic quadtree data structures.

is cut into four equal quarter images, and these, in turn, are cut into four equal images, and so on. Clearly, if the original image is $2^n \times 2^m$ where $n$ and $m$ are integers, then at the bottom of the tree there are $2^{2n}$ (if $n < m$) images of a row or column of pixels. If $n = m$, then there are $2^{2n}$ individual pixels—i.e. the number of pixels in the original image.

Breaking the image down that far is pointless. In addition to the values in all the pixels (held in the original image) there is a need for the tree structure to be held—and this alone requires significant space. The quadtree becomes valuable when many of the quarter images near the root of the tree need not be considered further because the whole quarter image is homogeneous. Figure 15.2 illustrates the principle.

Compression ratios are totally dependent on the structure of the original image.

## 15.11 IMAGE STANDARDS

Many compression standards are currently in use. PC-compatible files have extensions such as .BM, .PIC, .PCX, .PIG, .TIFF, .GIF, and many others. This text cannot give a substantial description of each of these compression standards, most of which are relatively complex.

## 15.12 EXERCISES

**15.1** Compare the compression of the following image using (a) Huffman coding, (b) contour coding, and (c) run length coding. The image has a grey level range of 0–7.

```
1 1 1 1 5 5 5 5 2 2 2 2
1 1 1 5 5 5 5 5 5 2 2 3
1 1 5 5 5 5 5 2 2 3 3 2
1 1 1 1 5 5 5 2 2 2 2 2
1 1 1 1 1 1 5 2 2 2 3 2
1 1 1 1 1 1 1 1 1 1 1 1
```

**15.2** Construct a quadtree for the following:

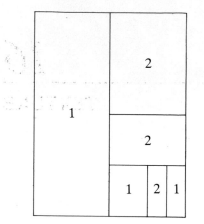

# *16*

# TEXTURE

## 16.1 INTRODUCTION

Texture is about regular patterns of pixels. A useful way of identifying whether a region contains a texture is to ask if the region were to be extended, whether the composition of the new extension region is wholly or partially predictable from the region itself. This means that regions of one plain colour could be said to have a texture, so could regions of measurable randomness (such as a snow storm effect), so could a chessboard or a grained wood surface.

Analysis of texture can be used to segment an image, identify repeating patterns, and in the real world it is useful in the analysis of, for example, paper fibres, weaving patterns, bacterial colonies, road and planet surfaces, and picture interference.

Particular textures may be definable mathematically. Regular randomness can be expressed in terms of fractal texture, while a chessboard may be totally definable in terms of texels (the unit of texture, also sometimes called texons or sub-patterns) and an associated statistical or grammatical set of construction rules.

This chapter looks at a number of ways of identifying and describing textures, measuring them, and predicting them.

Texture problems often cannot be solved simply by basic statistical or spatial operations. For example, how do you distinguish between different textures when their average intensity levels are the same?

What is the texture gradient, and direction, intuitively visible below?

## 16.2 IDENTIFYING TEXTURES

If we use the loose definition of texture above, then identifying a texture in an image is about identifying a predictability in the pattern of pixels. There are two concepts here:

1. Some primitive pattern of one or more pixels exists.
2. This primitive pattern is repeated at partially predictable intervals and directions after a partially predictable transformation.

The first of these means that every texture has a texture element (a texel) associated with it—even if the texel is just one pixel of an approximate grey level. The second means that there has to be a set of rules governing how these texels repeat.

A number of approaches can be used to discover the texel and the rules for repetition. Clearly these two are interrelated in terms of discovery. If only one whole or part of a texel is present, then there may or may not be a texture; if, indeed, there is a texture, it cannot be discovered. As soon as more than one texel is present then it is possible to recognize a pattern.

Some texels repeat at linearly regular intervals (e.g. every 5 inches) in a set of known directions (e.g. north/south and east/west), as is true, for example, on a chessboard or flowery wallpaper. Repetition of a pattern means that if both the distance between repetitions of the pattern (call it wavelength) and the direction of repetition can be obtained, then prediction of continuation of the texture (i.e. the definition of a texture) can be satisfied.

Clearly, terms like wavelength and direction suggest that conversion of the texture pattern into frequency space using Hartley or Fourier transforms would be valuable.

### Technique 16.1  Frequency space analysis of texture
USE To determine whether there is any regular repeating pattern identifiable in an image.

OPERATION Select a rectangular area of texture on which the transformation is to be implemented. This area should contain as many texels as possible and must contain more than one texel. For convenience choose the length of the sides of the rectangle to be a power of 2.

Implement a frequency transform and get a power spectrum (see Chapter 13).

Ignore the low-frequency values and identify directions and wavelengths of high-frequency peaks normal to one another, e.g. wavelength = 5 north/south and wavelength = 7 east/west.

Going back to the original image, grid the rectangle with a grid of direction and size discovered above. Each element of the grid is then an approximation to a texel.

The next approach below describes similar work but in the spatial domain and allows for more descriptive statistics for the texture under consideration. It is a sledge-hammer algorithm in that it assumes no prior knowledge of the kind of texture likely to be involved. This is rare. Textures can be forecast in most applications so that a more refined approach, using the prior knowledge, can be implemented.

The technique creates a set of arrays that describe a texture. The technique will also work particularly well if the texels do not vary in size and repeat at linearly predictable intervals.

**Technique 16.2 Spatial grey-level dependence matrices** (SGLDM) (also called co-occurrence matrices)

USE To classify a texture. To give values to different properties of a texture.

OPERATION This approach computes an intermediate matrix of measures from the digitized image data and then defines features as functions on this intermediate matrix.

Given an image $I(x, y)$ we define different matrices $S_{d, \theta}(i, j)$ where the $d$ and $\theta$ have values as described below.

An entry at position $(i, j)$ $S_{d, \theta}(i, j)$ is the number of times grey level $i$ is oriented with respect to grey level $j$ such that if

$$I(x_1, y_1) = i \quad I(x_2, y_2) = j$$

where $I(x, y)$ is the grey level at position $(x, y)$ of image $I$, then

$$x_1 = x_2 + d \cos \theta, \quad y_1 = y_2 + d \sin \theta$$

Because of the sheer volume of calculations involved, the values of $\theta$ are normally limited to range from 0 to $3\pi/4$ in steps of $\pi/4$.

**Analysis of the matrix** The matrix is a tally, or contingency table. It is possible to do some simple statistics on the table to determine 'expected' tallies assuming that there is no correlation at all. The process is illustrated below for a $2 \times 2$ table.

**Technique 16.3 $2 \times 2$ Contingency table analysis**

USE A simple check for texture patterns.

OPERATION Consider a table for a binary image with grey levels 0 and 1 only. $S_{d, \theta}$ might look like:

| Grey levels | To | |
|---|---|---|
| | 0 | 1 |
| From | | |
| 0 | 12 | 25 |
| 1 | 15 | 40 |

Evaluate the sums

|  | To | | |
|---|---|---|---|
|  | 0 | 1 | Sum |
| From |  |  |  |
| 0 | 12 | 25 | 37 |
| 1 | 15 | 40 | 55 |
| Sum | 27 | 65 | 92 |

The expected values for a random image are for element $(i, j)$

$$\frac{\text{sum of row } i \times \text{sum of column } j}{\text{total sum}}$$

Overall in the above table this gives the expected values to be

|  | To | | |
|---|---|---|---|
|  | 0 | 1 | Sum |
| From |  |  |  |
| 0 | 10.86 | 26.14 | 37 |
| 1 | 16.14 | 38.86 | 55 |
| Sum | 27 | 65 | 92 |

A good approach, now, is to test the hypothesis that the entries are not random, i.e. ask the question: what is the probability that the entries in the contingency table show no correlation?

This can be determined by evaluating the squares of the differences of the observed and expected values, dividing by the expected value to normalize the expression, and then looking up the significance level in chi-squared tables.

$$\frac{(12-10.86)^2}{10.86} + \frac{(25-26.14)^2}{26.14} + \frac{(15-16.14)^2}{16.14} + \frac{(40-38.86)^2}{38.86} = 0.2833$$

(Note that with a binary image like this, the chi-squared test requires Yates' correction to be performed. Normally, with more than two grey levels this correction is not required.)

The number of degrees of freedom is $n + m - 1$ (where the table is of size $n \times m$), in the above case: $2 + 2 - 1 = 3$ degrees of freedom. This suggests that the differences from the expected values are not significant, i.e. no texture has been found.

## 16.3 USING SGLDMs

It is now possible to define a number of functions including measure of texture energy, entropy, correlation, inertia, and local homogeneity. By way of illustration, two of these are shown below.

Homogeneity($d$, $\theta$) (also called energy) is the sum of the squares of all the elements in the $S_{d,\theta}(i,j)$ matrix.

$$\sum_i \sum_j S_{d,\theta}(i,j)^2$$

This is going to enhance large values that appear in the matrix and this energy function can be plotted for different $d$ and $\theta$ to give an indication of the periodicity and direction of the texture.

Contrast($d$, $\theta$) (or inertia) is the sum of $(i-j)^2 S_{d,\theta}(i,j)$. This gives an indication of the grey-level range in the texture region. For example, if all the pixels in the region were the same, $S_{d,\theta}(i,j)$ would only be non-zero when $i=j$, so the inertia would be zero. If they were all different in direction $\theta$, say by one pixel image being light and the next dark, then inertia would be high when $d=1$.

$$\sum_i \sum_j (i-j)^2 S_{d,\theta}(i,j)$$

Comparing these values from different matrices is meaningful only if the sums of the entries in the SGLDMs are equal. Appropriate normalization has to take place if this is not the case.

The following example illustrates each of these properties. Consider the following two images with grey-level range 0–9:

```
4 4 4 6 6 4 4 4 7 7        4 4 4 4 4 4 4 4 4 4
4 4 6 6 4 4 4 4 7 7        4 4 4 4 4 4 4 4 4 4
4 6 6 6 4 4 4 7 7 7        4 4 4 4 4 4 4 4 4 4
6 6 6 4 4 4 7 7 7 4        4 4 4 4 4 4 4 4 4 4
6 6 6 6 4 7 7 4 4 4        4 4 4 4 4 4 4 4 4 4
6 6 4 4 4 7 7 7 4 4        4 4 4 4 4 4 4 4 4 4
6 4 4 4 7 7 7 4 4 7        4 4 4 4 4 4 4 4 4 4
4 4 4 7 7 7 4 4 7 7        4 4 4 4 4 4 4 4 4 4
```

Given $\theta = 0°$, then for $d = 1$ we have

|   | $j$ 0 | 1 | 2 | 3 | 4 | 5 | 6 | 7 | 8 | 9 | | $j$ 0 | 1 | 2 | 3 | 4 | 5 | 6 | 7 | 8 | 9 |
|---|---|---|---|---|---|---|---|---|---|---|---|---|---|---|---|---|---|---|---|---|---|
| 0 | 0 | 0 | 0 | 0 | 0 | 0 | 0 | 0 | 0 | 0 | | 0 | 0 | 0 | 0 | 0 | 0 | 0 | 0 | 0 | 0 |
| 1 | 0 | 0 | 0 | 0 | 0 | 0 | 0 | 0 | 0 | 0 | | 0 | 0 | 0 | 0 | 0 | 0 | 0 | 0 | 0 | 0 |
| 2 | 0 | 0 | 0 | 0 | 0 | 0 | 0 | 0 | 0 | 0 | | 0 | 0 | 0 | 0 | 0 | 0 | 0 | 0 | 0 | 0 |
| 3 | 0 | 0 | 0 | 0 | 0 | 0 | 0 | 0 | 0 | 0 | | 0 | 0 | 0 | 0 | 0 | 0 | 0 | 0 | 0 | 0 |
| 4 | 0 | 0 | 0 | 0 | 23 | 0 | 3 | 10 | 0 | 0 | | 0 | 0 | 0 | 0 | 72 | 0 | 0 | 0 | 0 | 0 |
| $i$ 5 | 0 | 0 | 0 | 0 | 0 | 0 | 0 | 0 | 0 | 0 | | 0 | 0 | 0 | 0 | 0 | 0 | 0 | 0 | 0 | 0 |
| 6 | 0 | 0 | 0 | 0 | 7 | 0 | 10 | 0 | 0 | 0 | | 0 | 0 | 0 | 0 | 0 | 0 | 0 | 0 | 0 | 0 |

| 7 | 0 | 0 | 0 | 0 | 5 | 0 | 14 | 0 | 0 | 0 | | 0 | 0 | 0 | 0 | | 0 | 0 | 0 | 0 | 0 | 0 |
| 8 | 0 | 0 | 0 | 0 | 0 | 0 | 0 | 0 | 0 | 0 | | 0 | 0 | 0 | 0 | | 0 | 0 | 0 | 0 | 0 | 0 |
| 9 | 0 | 0 | 0 | 0 | 0 | 0 | 0 | 0 | 0 | 0 | | 0 | 0 | 0 | 0 | | 0 | 0 | 0 | 0 | 0 | 0 |

energy = 1008                    energy = 5184
contrast = 175                   contrast = 0
(72 entries)                     (72 entries)

And for $d = 2$

$$j$$

|     | 3 | 4 | 5 | 6 | 7 | 8 |
|-----|---|---|---|---|---|---|
| 3   | 0 | 0 | 0 | 0 | 0 | 0 |
| 4   | 0 | 10 | 0 | 5 | 18 | 0 |
| $i$ 5 | 0 | 0 | 0 | 0 | 0 | 0 |
| 6   | 0 | 12 | 0 | 4 | 1 | 0 |
| 7   | 0 | 9 | 0 | 0 | 5 | 0 |
| 8   | 0 | 0 | 0 | 0 | 0 | 0 |

energy = 716
contrast = 312
(64 entries)

The number of matrices can be significantly limited if some identification of the periodicity and direction of the texture can be obtained at an early stage. One method, already discussed, is to produce a power spectrum. An easier method is to consider directional autocorrelations.

### Technique 16.4 Directional autocorrelations to determine periodicity

USE To determine whether there is any repeating pattern in a particular direction without using frequency space.

OPERATION This technique involves taking a series of pixels that are next to each other in some direction in the image (e.g. a horizontal row or a vertical column), and correlating them with themselves after shifting them to the right by one pixel, two pixels, three pixels, and so on.

The correlation coefficient is calculated each shift using

$$r = \frac{\dfrac{\Sigma xy}{n} - \dfrac{\Sigma x \, \Sigma y}{n^2}}{\sigma_x \sigma_y}$$

(Note that if the lags are few and the row is long, then $\sigma_x \sigma_y$ can be ignored.)

These are plotted against lag. Where there is a marked peak in the curve it is reasonable to suggest that a periodicity exists. Depending on the size of the peak, an estimate of how predictable the texture is from that periodic repetition can be made.

Figure 16.1 illustrates the kind of plot that might be expected from this technique.

For example, a row of pixels (i.e. direction 0°) would typically consist of 640 pixels on VGA 16-colour mode. To make the illustration reasonable we shall consider an image 10 pixels wide with a 0–9 grey-level range.

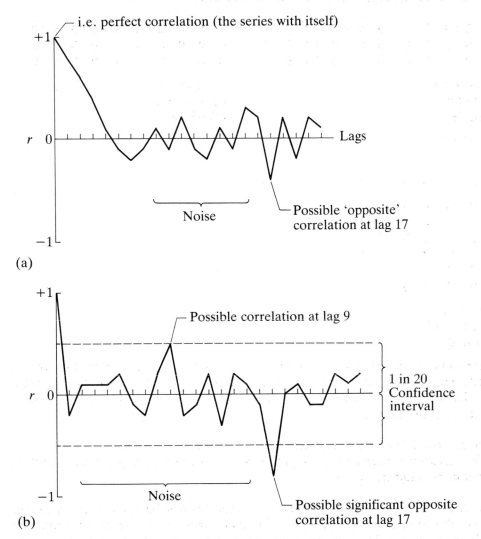

(a)

(b)

**Figure 16.1** Autocorrelation plots. It is better to remove the trend first (by differencing the pixels (i.e. basic edge detection) to give the type of autocorrelation function shown in (b).

| | | | | | | | | | | | Correlation coefficient |
|---|---|---|---|---|---|---|---|---|---|---|---|
| Row values: | 1 | 8 | 3 | 2 | 7 | 6 | 2 | 1 | 9 | 7 | |
| shift 0 | (1 | 8 | 3 | 2 | 7 | 6 | 2 | 1 | 9 | 7) | 1.00 |
| shift 1 | | (1 | 8 | 3 | 2 | 7 | 6 | 2 | 1 | 9)7 | − 0.20 |
| shift 2 | | | (1 | 8 | 3 | 2 | 7 | 6 | 2 | 1)9  7 | − 0.71 |
| shift 3 | | | | (1 | 8 | 3 | 2 | 7 | 6 | 2)1  9  7 | 0.27 |
| shift 4 | | | | | (1 | 8 | 3 | 2 | 7 | 6)2  1  9  7 | 0.53 |
| shift 5 | | | | | | (1 | 8 | 3 | 2 | 7)6  2  1  9  7 | − 0.31 |

The parentheses show reduction in length of sequence comparison. Note that with 640 pixels this reduction would not be significant when looking for short repetitions in textures.

This is important as the calculation of the standard deviations (the denominator of the correlation fraction) of each series, when the series is long and the shifts are short, can be neglected. In that sense this is not a good example.

Shift 2 and shift 4 both show significant coefficients. (It is possible to implement a $t$-test on the size of the coefficients to determine how significant each is. This can be found in any good statistics text.)

The shift 2 correlation coefficient is negative, suggesting that when the original pixels are bright, the shifted pixels are dark, and vice versa. The shift 4 correlation is positive, suggesting a repetition of the sequence.

Given that information it would be reasonable to classify the sequence at 0 degrees as partially repeated every four pixels. To classify further it would be useful to construct the SGLDM for (0°, 4 pixels) and calculate the entropy, contrast, etc.

**Problems** This technique does require the user to identify what texture is required. For example, most scenes contain pixels that are close in value to their neighbour. This falls well within the earlier definition of texture in that the pixels are predictable—given the value of one pixel, a good prediction of the neighbour to that pixel is the same value as the original pixel. A plane surface (all value 128, say) has a totally predictable texture. We might write the texture definition as:

$$V(x + i, y + j) = V(x, y) \qquad \text{where } i, j = -1, 0 \text{ or } 1$$
$$\text{and } V(x, y) \text{ is the pixel value at position } (x, y)$$

A simple chequerboard effect might be written

$$V(x \pm 1, y \pm 1) = V(x, y) \qquad \text{where } V(x, y) \text{ is the pixel value at position } (x, y)$$

But what happens if these two are combined. This is typical of a scene with texture. There is the background texture and then one or more foreground textures. A good model of this is, for example, the sales figures for an ice-cream company that is doing well. The firm will have a steadily rising sales graph (somewhat like a row of pixels that all have highish values and are brighter at one end than the other). Also the sales will go down in the winter and up in the summer about this trend. To predict the next figure *both* (and maybe more) of these factors need to be taken into account.

Coming back to reality, if a chequerboard texture (varying between $-5$ and $+5$) is added to a scene (with values 50–200) it will be lost in the general trend of the image—i.e. there is a high correlation between a pixel and its neighbour so that the correlation coefficient after a few shifts will still be near 1.0. It may well not have flagged the weak chequerboard texture as being present.

One way around this is to consider, instead of the series of pixel values, the differences between each value and its neighbour. This new series then loses the 'trend' from the old series and the autocorrelation plot then identifies the chequerboard effect (see Fig. 16.1).

This is classical forecasting theory (see, for example, Box and Jenkins 1970), but is also the same as performing an elementary edge detection before implementing the texture search.

## 16.4 TEXTURE GRADIENT

Formally this is the direction of maximum rate of change of the projected primitive size.

We assume that a texture is present on a flat surface, a perspective 'photograph' of the surface has been obtained, and we wish to know the rotation and orientation of the surface. This is easy if we know the shape of the texel—see the section on geometric transformations in Chapter 6.

### Technique 16.5  Identification of surface rotation and orientation

USE  When a surface with texture is viewed, it is possible to determine the angle of viewing of that surface. This (sketched) technique illustrates how it may be done.

OPERATION  If the texel shape is not known, a good approach is to identify a regular, linear texture direction. This gives the rotation of the plane.

Look right-angles to it for a perspective transformed texture.

If this is found, an estimate of the 'height' of the camera above the surface can be made, and therefore so can an estimate of the orientation of the plane.

## 16.5  TEXTURE SEGMENTATION

There are many methods for texture segmentation (i.e. identifying regions of the same type of texture), see, for instance, Wilson and Spann (1988) and Ballard and Brown (1982).

Texture images are most easily segmented when there is prior knowledge available about the textures on the image. Without this knowledge it is necessary to identify and classify the different textures. This, in itself, is a substantial task, particularly if it is to be automated.

### Technique 16.6  Automated texture type identification

USE  To classify all the regions in an image by their textures.

OPERATION  Split the image into equal sized rectangles (such as a chequerboard) and using either frequency domain analysis or SGLDM (as above) classify the texture in each rectangle.

Some of these rectangles will contain more than one texture. If the rectangle size is small enough, some will contain only one texture. Look for matching rectangle classifications. Where two rectangles match, then identify this as a texture type. Where one rectangle matches no other rectangle, discard the classification.

Clearly the size of the rectangles is critical. They must be large enough for the texture to be recognized, and small enough to contain only one texture. Without any prior knowledge this is very difficult.

Now to do the segmenting.

### Technique 16.7  Automated texture segmentation

USE  To classify all the regions in an image by their texture.

OPERATION  Combine rectangles which lie next to each other and have the same classification of texture into regions.

For the discarded rectangles, subdivide them into quarters and test each quarter to see if it is a known texture. (This test requires less area than the original identification.)

If the quarter rectangle has the texture of one of its neighbouring regions, add it to the region.

If the quarter rectangle texture is still unidentified, either perform the quartering again or make a new region with this 'unidentified' texture.

If the quarter rectangle texture is the same as the texture of a region not neighbouring it, then start a new region with this quarter rectangle.

One interesting approach to segmentation is proposed by Tuceryan *et al.* (1988). Here a texture of single dots (like that shown at the beginning of this chapter) is put into a polygon framework called Voronoi polygons. Once this is done the lines can then be used as edges, and these small regions combined to larger ones.

## 16.6 EXERCISES

**16.1** If the autocorrelation technique is used on an image of parallel lines set at 45° to the $x$-axis, how can the orientation of 45° be identified?

**16.2** Construct the SGLDMs for the non-constant image in Section 16.2 for 45° and 1 pixel, and 135° and 1 pixel.

**16.3** Evaluate energy and contrast from the SGLDM in Exercise 16.2 and comment on your results.

# OTHER TOPICS

## 17.1 INTRODUCTION

Inevitably a book like this cannot cover much more than some of the frequently used techniques in computer vision. It could be left like that, but there are a number of related topics that usefully form a final look at algorithms and approaches to problems.

This chapter briefly looks at three related topics. The techniques presented for each topic are simple and illustrative, and only marginally reflect the complexity of the real-life algorithms employed. Each topic is currently, and will be for the foreseeable future, a subject for serious research and development. They attract grants from many quarters, and each has a number of application areas where they can be effective.

## 17.2 TOMOGRAPHY AND IMAGE RECONSTRUCTION

Much research and development has been given over to the production of devices that can present a visual model of what is not visible to the eye because of some non-removable obstruction. In particular, a lot of medical work cannot be done without accurate knowledge as to the three-dimensional presentation of individual organs inside the body. The 'brain scanner' has been much acclaimed in this respect. It is able to present to a doctor a series of two-dimensional 'slices' of the brain which, if enough slices are taken, allows the creation of a full internal and external three-dimensional model of the brain.

Equally, ultrasonic scanning devices are used in medicine for foetal inspection, the image requiring reconstruction prior to display.

On a different tack, one island in the Atlantic has a water-table that varies according to season and weather within the season. Since water is scarce and normally collected by pumping it to the surface from wells, the water authorities need to know the position of the water-table to make the best judgements as to which wells it is best to use on any particular day. A model of the water-table is created by constructing it from a set of electrical resistance measurements taken from around the island.

This section is concerned with the collection of data from sensors placed around a solid object and then the construction of a useful model of the reality inside the object. The general term covering this kind of work is computerized tomography, a tomograph being a slice across a body.

### 17.2.1 Overview of image collection methods

The techniques for the collection of data from solid bodies broadly involve either the measurement of reflection of some transmitted signal, or the measurement of absorption of some transmitted signal. Radar and ultrasound are examples of measurement of reflective power, while X-ray and magnetic resonance (MR) imaging are examples of absorption measurement. Applied potential tomography (i.e. measuring resistance across a body and creating a tomograph—a model of a slice through the body) can be seen as comprising both reflective and absorption measurements.

In most cases the sensor or sensors measure a one-dimensional projection (along a line) of a two-dimensional image (a 'slice' from a body)—see Fig. 17.1(a). This is not always the case. Recent developments include the provision of 'fan beam' collection where the transmitter does not transmit a single 'ray' but many, non-parallel, rays.

### 17.2.2 Image reconstruction from absorption measurements

It is clear that resolution of the final model is dependent on the number and position of the measurements taken from the initial image. Each measurement is taken at a known $(x, y)$ coordinate (we can ignore the $z$ coordinate by assuming that all the measurements are being taken across a flat surface), with the detector pointing in the direction of the emitter at angle $\theta$, say, with respect to some baseline (see Fig. 17.1b). It may be that the emitter is set to emit only parallel rays and that both emitter and collector can be moved parallel to each other thereby covering the whole body at one angle. With subsequent rotational movement the body can be analysed in a similar way at a second angle.

Each detected measurement is termed a raysum and represents the amount of energy from the emitter that has not been absorbed (attenuated) by the body *and* has therefore reached the sensor. In the case of a reflective system the collected energy represents the sum of all the reflections of the emitted energy that coincide at the sensor. The non-straight ray of energy is a feature of ultrasonics and applied potential tomography, but bending can be ignored with X-ray tomography.

**Technique 17.1 Reconstruction using the summation method (back projection)**
Having collected a set of measurements from parallel movements of emitter and sensor (say 255 measurements across the body − 127 to + 127), and subsequent rotation of the apparatus (say 45 rotational readings), the results look like Table 17.1 (tables of this type are called sinograms).

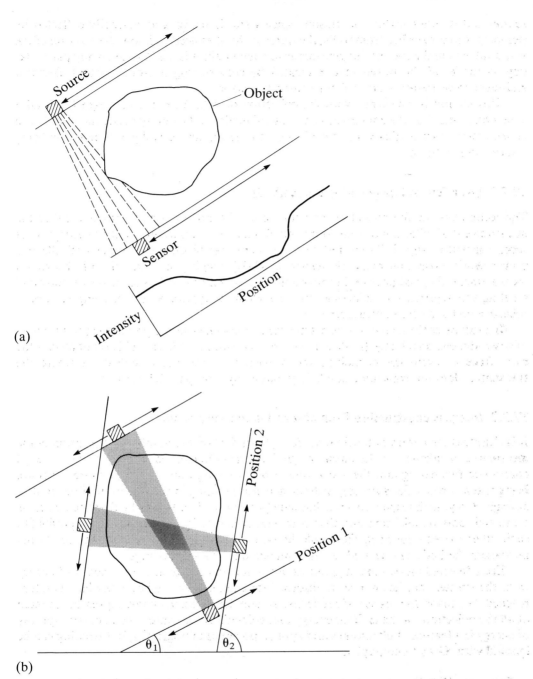

(a)

(b)

**Figure 17.1** Source/sensor measurement. In (b), only two of the many angled positions are shown.

**Table 17.1**

| $\theta$ (degrees) | $R$ | | | | | | | | | | |
|---|---|---|---|---|---|---|---|---|---|---|---|
| | $-127$ | $-126$ | $-125$ | $-124$ | $-123$ | $-122$ | $-121$ ... | 0 | 1 | 2 ... | $+127$ |
| 0 | 20 | 20 | 20 | 18 | 18 | 17 | 17 | 11 | 8 | 7 | 20 |
| 4 | 20 | 20 | 20 | 17 | 17 | 17 | 17 | 11 | 7 | 7 | 20 |
| 8 | 20 | 20 | 20 | 18 | 18 | 17 | 17 | 10 | 6 | 7 | 20 |
| 12 | 20 | 20 | 19 | 17 | 17 | 16 | 15 | 10 | 6 | 6 | 20 |
| 16 | 20 | 20 | 19 | 19 | 17 | 15 | 15 | 9 | 6 | 6 | 20 |
| 20 | 20 | 20 | 19 | 18 | 18 | 17 | 17 | 10 | 5 | 6 | 20 |
| . | . | . | . | . | . | . | . | . | | | . |
| 180 | 20 | 20 | 20 | 18 | 18 | 17 | 16 | 11 | 8 | 7 | 20 |

Now set up a floating-point array, initialized to zero. Allocate coordinates to the array such that the position of the emitter and the sensor would describe a circle bounded by the array (see Fig. 17.2). This is going to hold a scaled version of the restored image. For each reading determine which pixels in the circle inside the floating-point array lie on the path of the ray. Calculate the attenuation matrix from the sinogram in Table 17.1. This is the maximum sensed value when the object is not present less the reading when the object is present (which is likely to be 20 minus the reading in the above example). Share the attenuation equally between these pixels by dividing the attenuation by the number of pixels on the ray and adding this value to each pixel. This means that each pixel represents the cumulation of a number of readings, that number being dependent on how many times the pixel lay on a ray. Consequently, so as not to weight the centre pixel highly because it lies on a ray more often than an outer pixel, it is

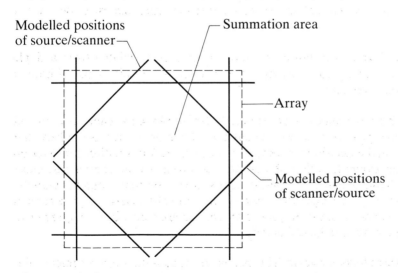

**Figure 17.2** Setting up the back projection.

necessary to hold a second array with the number of times any pixel has been added to, so that at the end the average attenuation of any pixel can be calculated.

The above technique leads to an image that has been blurred by convolution with a value spreading template. Significant improvements can be achieved by removing this convolution. The deconvolution that does the removal can be done at the end of the summation process using techniques described in Chapter 14, or better, as the data is collected (see Ballard and Brown, 1982, for further discussion of this).

## 17.3 MOVING IMAGES

Much of the work of computer vision depends on the improvement of a single image by applying a sequence of algorithms to the image data. When either the camera or part of a scene moves, however, the information that is required often involves a comparison of images so as to deduce information about what has moved with respect to what, and how far away are the moving objects, and, if the camera is moving, how far is it safe to travel without hitting an object. Thus range and movement algorithms are often closely linked. This section looks at some of the geometry of movement (see also Section 3.10), and the kind of equipment required for moving vehicles.

### 17.3.1 Environments

There are a number of environments in which movement takes place from the point of view of computer vision. Each environment has different problems from the practitioner's point of view.

**Single static camera** Movement in scene is detected by analysis of a sequence of images. If either the real size or distance of the object is known, then the other can be calculated. Speed can be calculated if a sequence of images is available and either the size or distance of the object is known.

**Multiple static cameras** Size and distance of the object can be calculated from a single image taken simultaneously by each camera. Speed cannot be calculated without a sequence of images taken over time.

**Moving camera(s)—with human control** For instance, infrared binocular cameras mounted on a military tank. Image processing is used to enhance the images but it is unlikely that software is required to make decisions, except to present more information for decision making. Another similar example is that of air-traffic controllers who, themselves, make the decisions about the flying height of aircraft, but the software presents, together with the radar image, details of the flying height and speed to the controller. Assuming the camera moves a known distance over time, the size, speed and distance of any objects appearing in more than one captured image can be estimated.

**Moving camera(s)—without human control** This has been called autonomous vehicle navigation. The software has to make decisions about where to drive the vehicle given the terrain, the objects in the way, and the capabilities of the vehicle. The operation of a space probe requires this kind of technology. A swift reaction time to avoid a meteorite shower, for example, is required, and this cannot be got from flight control if the signal takes a matter of hours to reach the probe.

The most difficult moving problems are encountered when the vehicle is moving and the objects it is encountering are also moving, all in different directions. This is well illustrated by the fact that it is often most difficult for a walking human to explain the reasoning behind taking a particular route through a crowded concourse.

### 17.3.2 Selection of equipment

Selecting the most appropriate sensory equipment for image acquisition on a moving vehicle depends on a number of factors:

1. Relative velocity of the object with respect to the camera. Clearly, if the camera is travelling 'quickly' with respect to its surroundings, or one object is travelling 'quickly' with respect to the camera, it is necessary to employ an image-acquisition system that can see, analyse, interpret, and direct in a correspondingly short space of time. Overestimating any possible collision velocity leads to unnecessary expenditure on processing power; underestimating velocity, on the other hand, may lead to a collision.
2. With a moving vehicle it is necessary to predict information about the environment with known margins of error and a level of accuracy such that early steering decisions can be made about the safest path. The earlier steering decisions are made the more they will be dampened by time. A late change in direction can cause subsequent large fluctuations in steering.
3. Any analysis of movement requires an algorithm that determines correspondences between points in different images in a time sequence. That is, for example, the tree in the first image taken by a camera from a moving vehicle has to be identified in the second image, third image, etc., in order to estimate its distance. This is relatively easy if the tree is the only visible item on the landscape, but if the vehicle is travelling through a forest, then identifying the correct correspondences is more difficult. Indeed, the software used to find correspondences for an autonomous road vehicle (looking for lines, cat's eyes, car lights, pedestrians, etc.) is likely to be of little use on a tank in rough terrain where none of the above are likely to be a problem. Correspondence identification requires that an interest point in one image be searched for in the next image if it is predicted that it should be there. The next section deals with the correspondence problem.
4. Search areas need to be small as searches are expensive in real time. Consequently, intelligent iterative algorithms are used to determine the most appropriate areas to search for objects based on previous pictures. A number of approaches can be used to restrict the range.

#### Technique 17.2 Restricting the range-of-search
USE When there is motion in a scene and two images can be analysed with a short time difference between them, this technique restricts the search area for an object that appeared in the first image and may have moved by the second image. If the search area can be restricted, a much speedier analysis can be done.

OPERATION The following heuristics are due to Prager (1979).

1. *Maximum velocity.* If previous observations have identified a maximum velocity of any one point in the two-dimensional space, then, knowing that velocity ($v$) and the change in time ($dt$) we can draw a circle around the old image of radius $v \cdot dt$ which is likely to include the new point in the new image.

2. *Small velocity change.* Given the inertia of a point on a body, it is unlikely that the direction of motion since the last observation has changed significantly, providing the observations are close enough in time.

3. *Common motion.* Spatially coherent/ordered points are likely to be in the same order after a short time. So having found the direction of motion of one point in an array of points, corresponding positions for the other points can be guessed and checked.

4. *Consistent match.* Rarely do two points occlude one another. Always look for as many as before unless the prediction is that some will have left the scene.

5. *Known motion.* If the camera is moving, then normally the data on camera movement is known to the system. Using this data improves any prediction made of the position of objects in a new image.

Given the above criteria, it is possible to estimate the minimum power of the machine that is able to collect, process and deliver decisions from the camera.

Depth images are clearly very useful. Since these deliver a distance in each position on the image, a sequence of these images over time delivers the speed, direction, change of speed, and change of direction of any object where a correspondence can be found. It is frequently easier to discover the correspondences by using a light intensity; if this can be coupled to the range data, the information provided by the system will be of much higher quality.

**Camera movement** It may be that the vehicle can only move in certain directions. For example, a car is limited to directed forward or reverse movement; it cannot move sideways. This means that, for navigation purposes, it is unnecessary to sense in any direction apart from a cone forwards and a cone backwards. Alternatively, a robot cleaner may rotate on its own axis and therefore can move in any direction from a given spot and prior orientation.

**Terrain** Ruggedness, power requirements, size, and weight are factors that need to be taken into account, particularly if the vehicle is to be airborne. Predicted collisions are less important if the device is rugged with respect to the collision, e.g. a cleaning robot hitting a wall is no disaster, indeed it might be planned and a tactile sensor might be the only range sensor present; however, if an aircraft under autopilot control hits a tree, the consequences are more complex.

When the moving camera is able to take many pictures, using the range of search restriction heuristics it is often possible to plot the two-dimensional motion, on the image, of the points in real space that have been identified by the interest point operator. The two-dimensional movement of these points is called optical flow.

### 17.3.3  Optical flow

These points, assuming motion of either the camera or of the world, have distance and direction. The flow path equation of a point moving with a constant velocity reveals information about its distance from the camera.

> **Technique 17.3  Finding distance using movement**
> USE  If the speed of the object coming towards the camera (or the speed of the camera moving towards the object) is known, then the distance of the object can be calculated using optical flow.
>
> OPERATION
> $$\frac{\text{length of flow in image}}{\text{speed of flow in image}} = \frac{\text{distance of object from image plane}}{\text{speed of object towards image}}$$
>
> or classically
>
> $$\frac{D(t)}{\mathrm{d}D/\mathrm{d}t(t)} = \frac{z(t)}{\mathrm{d}z/\mathrm{d}t(t)}$$
>
> EXAMPLE
>
> | | | |
> |---|---|---|
> | length of flow from focus of expansion 2-D image | = 2 cm | $D(t)$ |
> | *current* (instantaneous) velocity of 2-D flow | = 0.2 cm/s | $\mathrm{d}D/\mathrm{d}t$ |
> | speed of movement of vehicle towards object | = 3 km/h | $\mathrm{d}z/\mathrm{d}t$ |
>
> $$z(t) = \frac{\mathrm{d}z}{\mathrm{d}t}\frac{D(t)}{\mathrm{d}D/\mathrm{d}t} = \frac{3}{3600}\frac{2}{0.2} = 8.3 \text{ m distant.}$$

### 17.3.4  Epipolar-plane image analysis

What orientation do we give to a camera on a moving vehicle? As has already been shown, analysis of the images is more difficult if the camera is pointing in the direction of the vehicle. Interest points are not moving in a straight line but form a set of parabola when plotted against time. There are occasions when it is better to set the camera orthogonal to the vehicle direction. Clearly, this is going to be of little use in guiding the vehicle but is much more useful in feature discovery.

Using picture storage technology it is quite possible to build a three-dimensional block of two-dimensional images taken from this orientation and then slice a line through the block, horizontally, to give what is called a spatio-temporal surface. Analysis of this surface, as if it were a proper two-dimensional image, can give a lot of information.

If the angles of the lines are measured on this surface, ranges are easily calculated from geometry (Baker and Bolles, 1988). Edge detection and Hough straight line transforms can identify every object in the field of view *without resorting to complex correspondence-finding algorithms*. Finally, the hardware need not store whole images in order to then slice them. It is better to store one horizontal scan line got from the same position in a sequence of images directly into each line of the frame store. Using a 50 Hz frame capture rate VGA,

480 lines are captured in about 9 seconds, thus every 9 seconds there is an opportunity to process detailed movement information.

See Baker and Bolles (1988) for further discussion on epipolar plane analysis. Also see Chapter 15 on compression techniques, which covers the compression of images that include motion.

## 17.4 STEREOSCOPIC IMAGE PROCESSING

### 17.4.1 Introduction

Range image capture has been discussed in Chapter 3. Range images come with their own problems of interpretation, and any attempt to determine ranges from intensity images also poses some problems. One particular problem with stereoscopic images is the correspondence problem, which is described below.

### 17.4.2 The correspondence problem

The correspondence problem is illustrated in Fig. 17.3. Two images, either collected by a moving camera at different times or taken simultaneously from two cameras spaced a known distance and angle apart, are passed through some interest point routine. This routine delivers $n_1$ interest points from the first image and $n_2$ interest points from the second image.

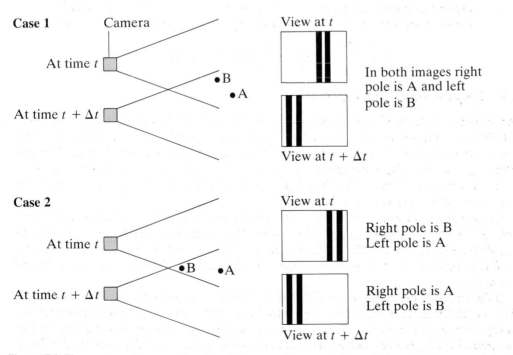

**Figure 17.3** The correspondence problem: how do you match up a pole in one image with the same pole in the next image?

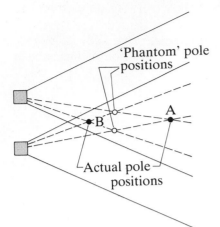

**Figure 17.4** The correspondence problem—phantom creation, the results of using the wrong correspondence in case 2 in Fig. 17.3.

If $n_1 = n_2 = 0$, the problem is trivial in that no objects or movement can be sensed. If $n_1 = n_2 = 1$, on the face of it again the problem is trivial. We may assume (possibly erroneously) that the object in one image is the same as the object in the other image. Given the range of search restriction heuristics above this may be a very good assumption or a poor assumption. Either way it is possible to determine, by simple geometry, where the object is in space with respect to the camera positions, providing the two camera shots were not taken from the same spot.

The difficulty of correspondence occurs when $n_1$ or $n_2 > 1$. Now more information is required to determine which of the interest points in one image correspond with which in the other. Only when this is known can any meaningful calculation of distances be made.

If the objects in the image are mistaken by the system, then Fig. 17.4 illustrates how 'phantom' objects are created with phantom positions. Worse than this, of course, is the fact that the positions of the real objects are not known. If the device holding the cameras is an autonomous vehicle, this could bring about a collision.

If the image is two-dimensional and the relative position of the interest points are not changing (as, for example, with two views of the earth taken with a short time difference from a satellite), then the techniques used in Chapter 3 can be employed to determine correspondences. If relative positions are not constant in two dimensions, then it is necessary to treat the points as individual points, calculate possible distance from all sensible correspondences, and then predict new positions and check whether they are right or not.

> A single camera system was used by an autonomous vehicle to create a three-dimensional map of a room. As the vehicle moved about the room it discovered 'corners' of furniture and other objects. Correspondences were identified by the camera taking two images, spaced a short distance apart; all possible 'corner' three-dimensional coordinates were calculated and a third image taken from another position checked which of the predicted coordinates actually existed.

# 17.5 EXERCISES

**17.1** Consider the following epipolar plane:

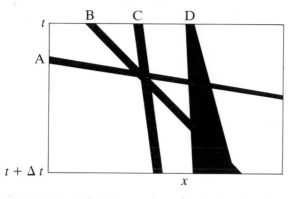

What do you deduce from lines A and B, and C and D? Which direction is the vehicle travelling? Is there any danger of a collision?

**17.2** Given the following data:

| | | |
|---|---|---|
| length of flow from focus of expansion 2-D image | = 3 cm | $D(t)$ |
| *current* (instantaneous) velocity of 2-D flow | = 0.6 cm/s | $dD/dt$ |
| speed of movement of vehicle towards object | = 5 km/h | $dz/dt$ |

How far away is the object?

**17.3** Raysums were taken across a number of shapes that correspond to binary images of letters of the alphabet. Each row below represents a column sum and a row sum from one letter. Determine which letters have the following sums:

| Column sums (maximum possible = 7) | | | | | | Row sums (maximum possible = 5) | | | | | | |
|---|---|---|---|---|---|---|---|---|---|---|---|---|
| 7 | 2 | 2 | 2 | 7 | corresponds with | 2 | 2 | 5 | 5 | 2 | 2 | 2 |
| 7 | 1 | 1 | 1 | 1 | | 1 | 1 | 1 | 1 | 1 | 1 | 5 |
| 7 | 3 | 3 | 3 | 2 | | 5 | 1 | 1 | 4 | 1 | 1 | 5 |
| 5 | 2 | 2 | 2 | 5 | | 1 | 2 | 2 | 5 | 2 | 2 | 2 |

**17.4** Calculate the horizontal, vertical, and all possible diagonal raysums from the following image. Back-project them and compare the original with the result.

| | | | | | | | | |
|---|---|---|---|---|---|---|---|---|
| 1 | 2 | 1 | 1 | 3 | 2 | 2 | 2 | 1 |
| 2 | 3 | 3 | 4 | 7 | 7 | 8 | 8 | 1 |
| 1 | 2 | 2 | 5 | 8 | 8 | 9 | 8 | 1 |
| 1 | 2 | 1 | 5 | 7 | 6 | 8 | 8 | 1 |
| 1 | 1 | 1 | 4 | 8 | 5 | 7 | 9 | 3 |
| 1 | 1 | 2 | 1 | 5 | 1 | 4 | 8 | 7 |
| 1 | 1 | 2 | 2 | 1 | 1 | 2 | 9 | 9 |

# 18

## APPLICATIONS

### 18.1 INTRODUCTION

Computer vision is not always the best solution to a problem. There are many occasions when the problem is so complex that a human solution is significantly better. The human solution to driving a normal road vehicle, for example, is currently much more efficient, practical, and safer than a computer vision solution. A better-than-human solution may be to use rail vehicles or to reorganize road vehicles so that they follow predictable progress rules; however, if the problem is to drive a vehicle as if a human were doing it on ordinary roads through ordinary traffic, then a computer vision solution is not ideal.

Human solutions, however, tend to be slow and inaccurate, and suffer from a lack of rigour and poor perceptions. Nevertheless, the human approach is less structured than the machine approach and many computer vision problems require a much higher level of intellect than the machine can offer. The human vision system can automatically describe in detail a texture, a gradient, an edge, a two-dimensional representation of a three-dimensional shape; it can differentiate between images of different persons, autographs, and colours; it can estimate routes and speeds and avoidance policy; it can identify faulty components and diagnose cancer from an X-ray. A piece of software that could do all this would sell well—but certainly it is some years off before such software will be on the market.

It is not possible to give much more than a flavour of the kind of applications to which computer vision has been put in the last few years. A hopeful sign is that it is now being increasingly used on smaller projects, some of which have funding limited to under £3000. This chapter aims to illustrate both small and large projects and generate applications in the mind of the reader. The author has been connected with a number of these projects in some way and the commentary on these is from direct experience.

226

At the end of this chapter is one substantial application (the optical recognition of Chinese characters) described in a greater level of detail. Within the description of this application are references to the earlier text where some of the techniques are described.

## 18.2 SOME APPLICATION SKETCHES

### 18.2.1 Micro-optics

There are two principal types of electron microscope. In the transmission electron microscope (TEM) a beam of high-velocity electrons is focused onto a thin slice of the specimen under examination. The beam passes through the specimen, and as it does its intensity is modulated. The beam then hits a fluorescent screen and the operator can view the output directly or take a photograph of the screen. It is quite possible to hook this system up to an image grabber—the easiest way being to mount a camera to view the screen. A less indirect capture method is to replace the fluorescent screen with a CCD array, which can be excited directly by the electrons.

The scanning electron microscope (SEM) delivers a very fine beam onto a very small spot on the specimen. This beam slowly scans across the specimen and electrons that are reflected from the specimen are captured by a detector. The system may be hooked directly up to a display or, more often, hooked up to frame store, so that the image is captured in the store before being delivered to the operator's display.

These images can be stored on disk or processed. Processing a sequence of images is discussed in Chapter 5. Recursive averaging (Technique 5.9) is found to be particularly useful as the images are largely stationary but prone to noise; recursive averaging removes the noise by combining many of the previous images into one.

Electron microscopy does not always deliver equal 'luminosity' in terms of electron power or of capture equipment. Thus images may be shaded, not due to a modulation by the sample, but instead because the image was not 'lit' properly with electrons or the capture equipment had certain non-linear characteristics.

Thus it is usually necessary to subtract or divide the captured image from/by a reference image—i.e. one without the sample in position. This is background subtraction, discussed in Chapter 5.

Finally, in order to set up the focus, it is possible to use Fourier transform of an image without a sample (which should give a white noise picture) and then look at the circles produced. Larger circles imply better focus and the more circular (as opposed to elliptic) a circle is, the less the astigmatism (different magnifications in different planes)—see Chapter 13.

Further discussion on this can be found in Shave (1989).

### 18.2.2 Medical imaging

This area of work is so vast that it is impossible to give it due coverage in a small section in one book. Instead the section looks at two specific X-ray applications in which the author has been involved, recognizing that the reader will be able to find many more applications by searching through the literature (particularly the *IEEE Transactions on Medical Imaging*).

A lot of work has been put into the area of improving the readability of an X-ray. The process of image processing in X-ray enhancement requires a goal, just as it does for quality control or highway mapping. The goal is more difficult to determine than in these other two cases because an X-ray is often a means for diagnosis rather than a means to identify a shape that was not otherwise visible. The image-processing goal—to provide a better image for diagnosis purposes—is like asking for a machine to produce a large-scale map so that you can identify a feature on the land. If the feature is a road, then you may be lucky; but if the feature is a colour of a field of grain, then the modelling of land area by a road map is precisely what is not required, in that the useful information is lost.

The goal needs to be narrow so that the image processing can do a useful job of work.

**Chest X-rays** An X-ray of the chest gives a very clear rib structure, a less clear lung structure, and a vague heart structure. If the task is to identify the extent of damage of the rib structure, then apart from some edge detection and edge enhancement of the original, it may be that very little needs to be done.

If the task is to view the lungs, then the rib structure needs to be removed and the lungs enhanced. Various authors have commented on this kind of work and regional histogram equalization has proved useful.

If the task is to view the heart, then more work is necessary—again using regional histogram equalization and false colour presentation—to improve the image.

In most—possibly all—documented cases, image processing has not changed the diagnosis of the problem but it is claimed that doctors have been able to diagnose quicker from the processed image than from the original.

See particularly Sherrier and Johnson (1987), and Murley (1989).

**Carcinoma in mammary glands** Some work at Staffordshire Polytechnic has concentrated on the identification of carcinoma in mammary gland X-rays. These X-rays are often taken with a side view of the breast and the goal was to identify clearly very small cancerous growths. The original images contain a significant amount of blood vessel and other material visible in the breast, and it is most difficult, for the untrained eye, to see a cancer cell group, or for the trained eye to tell all the cancer cell groups if there are many. A simple enhancement technique made the cell groupings very clear.

### 18.2.3 Identification of ratio of intact to broken animal cells

Microscope images of animal cells were captured. These cells were normally surrounded by space and were either intact or 'exploded'. After the images were enhanced, by implementing high- and low-pass filters and then thresholding to black and white, two algorithms were implemented on each image. The first attempted to find automatically the 'top' of any cell on the image. The second attempted to trace a route around the found cell. If the route arrived back at the beginning, then the cell was counted as intact, otherwise the cell was counted as broken. See the work by Lester *et al.* (1978) and Wright (1990).

### 18.2.4 Road tracking

High-definition satellite or high-flying aeroplane images may give a good picture of the ground, its roads, buildings, and geographical features. However, they are not particularly useful for navigation without annotation to indicate the name or number of the roadways. An ideal application of computer vision is the automatic creation of maps from such photographs.

This is a difficult operation. There are a number of algorithms that use edge detection, surface detection, same spectral signature, and knowledge such as 'when there is a sudden stop to the road expect a junction or a bridge'. The problem is split into two parts: road finding and road following.

Road finding aims to identify automatically a point on any road. This is not so easy. Roads may look like rivers, canals, pipelines, or hedges. The spectral signature of a road is required.

Road following aims to take the point on the road and follow it until it comes to the end of the image, identifying, *en route*, where other roads have branched off the road being followed. A number of algorithms can have their results combined to give a good estimate of road position and generate something like a map. Edge following and same spectral signatures are favourites. McKeown and Denlinger (1988) describe a combination of these methods and quote a speed of between 7 and 14 pixels of road followed per second of CPU time on a VAX 11/785.

## 18.2.5 Quality control

One goal of a quality-control computer vision system is to stop the production of some product if the production system starts producing products that are not frequently enough of a sufficient standard. The example, already quoted, of the biscuit manufacturer who wished to count the number of whole biscuits being cooked is a classic one. Vision systems are usually programmed to be product specific—i.e. they would not normally be movable from quality control of matches to quality control of paint surfaces on cars.

The product is usually fed to the system in a known way. The system is set up with lighting and focus standardized. A still 'photo' is analysed regularly by the system rather than, say, 25 frames per second, though the capture equipment may continue to collect frames at that rate with many being discarded. The analysis rate may be clocked by the vision system or may be clocked externally by, for example, a light beam being broken.

The resolution of the system is the minimum required in order that processing is as short as possible.

> A carpet-tack manufacturer wished to control the quality of the carpet tacks being produced. Each tack, as it was produced, was fed down a chute. The chute caused it to be either point up or point down. *En route*, the tack interrupted a light beam. A frame of $30 \times 50$ pixels, 1 bit per pixel, was captured by a permanently resident mono video camera.
>
> The processor then compared the image captured with two binary images already in memory, one representing the tack with the point downwards and the other with the point upwards. The processor counted the number of different pixels for both templates. If the smallest number of differences was greater than a given value, then the tack was rejected by the vision system causing it to be directed to a reject bin, using a small electromagnet.

## 18.2.6 Surface inspection

Viewing the paint on the surface of a car body, for example, requires a system with cameras arranged so as to give a full view of the car, or else a system with a camera on a robot arm. A defect in paintwork is likely to be identifiable as a change in contrast over a small or large area. If the paintwork is shiny smooth, then the smallest contrast change needs to be identified; if the paintwork is more 'noisy', then the defect is not only a function of the change in contrast but also the size of area concerned.

Here one method used is to capture the image and do a convolution with a template. The choice of template is critical. Coulthard (1989) illustrates the use of a $7 \times 7$ template to search for surface defects that are between 1 and 5 pixels in diameter. The template he uses

$$
\begin{matrix}
-1 & 0 & 0 & 0 & 0 & 0 & -1 \\
0 & 0 & 0 & 0 & 0 & 0 & 0 \\
0 & 0 & 0 & 0 & 0 & 0 & 0 \\
0 & 0 & 0 & 4 & 0 & 0 & 0 \\
0 & 0 & 0 & 0 & 0 & 0 & 0 \\
0 & 0 & 0 & 0 & 0 & 0 & 0 \\
-1 & 0 & 0 & 0 & 0 & 0 & -0
\end{matrix}
$$

is a kind of expanded Laplacian operator with the advantage that, despite its size, it is quickly calculated (four negation operations, one double shift, and five additions). A 'trend' in the colour is ignored by the system, but an area of different contrast is picked up.

## 18.3 OPTICAL RECOGNITION OF CHINESE CHARACTERS

This is a résumé of the work described by Suchenwirth *et al.* (1987).

### 18.3.1 Problems

Compared with other writing systems, Chinese characters pose a number of specific problems for optical character recognition. These may be summarized as follows:

1. A very large set of characters ranging from 7000 to 50 000 depending on the dictionary used. This means that taking any set to work with, it is likely that occasionally a character is discovered that is not in the set.
2. The characters may be very complex. Some characters consist of 36 or more strokes. Characters may split up into six components, each of which may be complex. This leads to a minimum resolution for acceptable quality printed character of $24 \times 24$ dots. Clearly, the resolution for the capture of a character must then be better than that, preferably $50 \times 50$.
3. The occurrence frequencies of the characters are very unevenly distributed. One character occurs in more than 4 per cent of text, while many other characters have a frequency of less than one in a million.

### 18.3.2 Image capture

Scanners are preferred partly because an A4 page can be read in one go, whereas a camera could only cope with a small part of the page (about the size of a postage stamp) because of the problems with resolution. Scanners are also preferred because they read the text in a closed environment, i.e. the ambient lighting does not add problems that appear when dealing with camera input.

### 18.3.3 Preprocessing

Occasionally it was found useful to remove the high spatial frequencies on horizontal edges. This was done by passing a simple averaging filter over the image, namely

$$\begin{pmatrix} 0 & 0 & 0 \\ 0 & 0.5 & 0.5 \\ 0 & 0 & 0 \end{pmatrix}$$

i.e. averaging each pixel with its neighbour on the right only.

### 18.3.4 Segmentation

Segmentation into lines of characters could be done in real time as the scanner operated. If it is known that the text is accurately printed, then it is possible to estimate the position of each character in the text, given the position of the first few characters.

    Thus a grey-scale image is inspected, say a window at the top of the text sheet. The ends of the characters are marked, as are the spaces between the lines. These are extrapolated to the rest of the text. Using this method the threshold has to be put in by inspection; however, a more sophisticated technique, described by Suchenwirth *et al.*, can be used, which avoids the grey-scale inspection.

    There are problems in taking the pure white space between dark blobs to represent spaces between the characters. Some characters have a space *within* themselves. Characters are normally of different widths, and in some cases the gap within the character is wider than the gap between characters. Clearly, this is a problem.

### 18.3.5 Scaling

Text typically contains headlines that are larger than the normal text. Thus it is often necessary to handle each character individually, scaling as appropriate. As in English, it is not always useful simply to scale the printed character width and height separately. For example an 'o' may be distorted to an ellipse if the working area is not square.

    Scaling means averaging of the pixel intensities, or interpolating them. This has to be done before any further processing.

### 18.3.6 Edge enhancement

A low-pass filter and a high-pass filter are combined to enhance the edges in the image. These are

$$L = \begin{pmatrix} 0 & 0.2 & 0 \\ 0.2 & 0.2 & 0.2 \\ 0 & 0.2 & 0 \end{pmatrix}$$

for the low-pass filter and a high-pass filter defined as the difference between the original and the low-pass filter. For example, if the image is

$$\begin{array}{ccc} 1 & 1 & 2 \\ 1 & 2 & 2 \\ 2 & 2 & 2 \end{array}$$

the high-pass filter is

$$H = \begin{pmatrix} 1.0 & 0.8 & 2.0 \\ 0.8 & 1.8 & 1.8 \\ 2.0 & 1.8 & 2.0 \end{pmatrix}$$

These are combined as follows

$$\text{final filter} = aL + (1 - a)H$$

and thresholding is then applied.

### 18.3.7 Thresholding

Having captured the character, it is now thresholded. The value of the threshold can be determined by inspection. Alternatively, Otsu's (1979) global threshold can be used (see Technique 5.5).

### 18.3.8 Feature extraction

- Blackness—i.e. the number of pixels set to black.
- Stroke width—from a morphological method.
- Projection profiles—see Chapter 17 on tomography and Chapter 12 on pattern recognition.
- Transitions—in a scan of the image, the number of changes from black to white.

### 18.3.9 Feature algorithms

Template matching is performed using correlation, but instead of squaring the $(I - T)$ part, the absolute value is used. The 'pattern distance' is then the number of pixels where there was not a match.

A grid is passed over the character so that features can be found within each square. This delivers a number of values and a number of vectors for each character.

Stroke density may be calculated using an algorithm similar to the SGLDM algorithms in Chapter 16 on texture.

### 18.3.10 Combining features

Groups of features form a pattern vector which may be plotted (see Chapter 12 on pattern recognition), and a decision vector identified.

Euclidean distance and similarity functions are used to determine the nearness of a character to a particular cluster.

### 18.3.11 Structure analysis

Thinning is used (see Chapter 8 on morphology) to give the basic skeleton of a character. This can be analysed by using a method that follows the stroke (similar to the contouring method outlined in Chapter 7 on segmentation). This also enables interest points to be found—say, by looking for maxima of curvature in the skeleton.

### 18.3.12 Plausibility

When a character has been identified, checks are made that the character is likely to be there. This may be a grammatical check, or simply a check on the frequency of occurrence of the character. For example, if the character may be one of two—in other words the classifier gave a near-equal weighting to each of two possible labellings—then the frequency of occurrence might be used to choose the most likely labelling.

### 18.3.13 Conclusion

The whole exercise was clearly very time consuming. Recognition rates, using the tests above, were of the order of 98 per cent, with some combinations scoring better than others.

## 18.4 FINALLY

Even the smallest image-processing problem requires considerable effort. The tool-kit of software, some of which is described in this book, is unlikely to be sufficient except for the simplest enhancing applications. To do substantial recognition for which software has not yet been written almost certainly means writing some software at some point. It is unlikely that the modules in the tool-kit will fit together appropriately (and operate fast enough) without the practitioner getting his or her hands dirty.

Perhaps that is what is so interesting about image processing and computer vision. It reopens the creative element of algorithm design and coding, which is slowly closing in other areas of software engineering where software design can become simply a process of combining off-the-shelf products.

# GLOSSARY

**Analogue-to-digital (A/D) conversion** In the context of computer vision, the process of changing an image signal—typically a single wire with a varying voltage on it—to a set of patterns of binary digits, one pattern for each pixel in the image.

**Aspect ratio** The ratio of the width of an image to its height. It is typically used to refer to the ratio of the width of a display compared to its height.

**Autocorrelation** The correlation of a series with itself, shifted right or left by a number of places. This can be useful in finding repeated patterns in textures, for example.

**Bandpass filter** A type of filter that allows a band of frequencies between two set frequencies to pass through, but stops any frequencies outside of that band.

**Camera** A device for capturing an image and presenting it in electronic form.

**Capture card** An electronic printed circuit board with components that hook up to the output from a camera and produce a digital pattern that is either sent to the main memory of the computer or held on memory chips on the card.

**Capture software** A suite of programs that control the camera and capture card, allowing the user to collect an image from the camera and put it in an appropriate form inside the memory or on a disk unit.

**CGA** Colour Graphics Adaptor. An early standard for PC graphics giving $640 \times 200$ in monochrome or $320 \times 200$ in four colours. Unsatisfactory for image-processing applications.

**Compression** A means of reducing the storage for an image so that it can be held in a smaller disk space or transmitted from station to station at a faster rate.

**Contour** The pixels that are of the same colour or grey level that lie on the edge of a region of the same colour or grey level.

**Contrast** The spread of grey levels in an image. With a small range the contrast is low, with a large range the contrast is high. A suitable measure of contrast is therefore the standard deviation of the image grey levels.

**Convolution** This consists of the element-by-element multiplication of a template with corresponding elements in an image, summing of the results, and placing the sum in a position (representing the position of the template) in a new array.

**Co-occurrence matrix** See spatial grey level dependence matrix.

234

**Co-processor** A second processor unit or chip inside a computer which, typically, enhances the execution speed. This might be done by the co-processor dealing with all the floating-point calculations (such as the Intel 8087), for example.

**Correlation** The numerical comparison of one image with another. It can be shown that under certain circumstances this is equivalent to convolution.

**Crack edge** The (absolute) numerical differences between grey levels or colour values held in adjacent pixels.

**Dithering** The plotting of a picture on a device that has insufficient grey levels per pixel to show the logical image and insufficient pixels to allow patterning to occur. The process involves plotting the nearest grey level and then propagating the error onto the surrounding pixels.

**DMA** Direct memory access. In computer vision terms, a method of sending a whole image into the main memory of a machine without every pixel value having to be passed through the main processor. This allows the processor to do other work while the transfer is taking place and facilitates a very fast transfer of data.

**Domain** The coordinates in which the system is operating.

**Edge** The pixels that have been discovered by some algorithm to lie between two significantly different regions.

**EGA** Enhanced Graphics Adaptor. Offers CGA plus $640 \times 350$ with 16 colours from 64 available.

**Flood fill** An algorithm that, given a pixel position which lies inside a closed contour, finds the position of all the other pixels in the contour and alters their grey level.

**Fourier transform** A transform that takes a complex plane (real and imaginary numbers) in the spatial domain and converts it to a complex plane in the frequency domain.

**Frequency domain** A set of axes that instead of representing distances such as horizontal and vertical on the $(x, y)$ axes, represent different frequencies: low frequencies on the left, high on the right. Normally the origin of the frequency domain is shown in the centre of the output, and when the frequency space is two-dimensional (as in the power spectrum, for example) the point $(u, v)$ in the space represents the strength of frequency $u$ in the $x$-direction present with the strength of frequency $v$ in the $y$-direction.

**Grey level** A value in a pixel that represents the darkness of the pixel. Normally zero is the darkest value and $2^n$ is the lightest value where $n$ is an integer, typically a multiple of 4.

**Hartley transform** A transform that takes a real plane in the spatial domain and converts it to a real plane in the frequency domain.

**Histogram equalization** An algorithm that reallocates the grey levels in a logical image, without altering their order, so that the new grey levels span, as equally as possible, the full range of grey levels available.

**Hough Transform** A coordinate change that enables shapes of known dimensions to be found in an image.

**Image** A two-dimensional array of pixels (if it is inside the memory of a computer) or a real view that may or may not be digitized. Formally, it may also be described as a two-dimensional light intensity function, or colour function denoted by $f(x, y)$, where $x$ and $y$ denote spatial coordinates.

**Interest point** A pixel identified by an algorithm as a classifying marker for an object in an image.

**Line labelling** An algorithm that allocates one or more labels to edges that have been discovered in an image as part way to classifying objects in an image.

**Negation** Taking the negative of an image, i.e. converting the high-valued grey levels to low-valued grey levels and vice versa. This can be extrapolated to the colour domain by negating the colour levels in an RGB image.

**Noise** Undesirable errors in pixel values in an image, typically caused by electrical interference when the image was captured.

**Normalization** The subtraction from a set of values of the lowest in the set, followed by division of the values by the range of the set.

**Object** A real thing that can be seen partially or wholly in an image.

**Occlusion** The partial or complete hiding of one object by another because one is in the way of the line of sight of the other.

**OCR** Optical character recognition. Algorithms that analyse an image and allocate probabilities to each of a set of characters, indicating which character the image represents.

**Octree** A data structure, similar to a quadtree, except it operates in three dimensions.

**Patterning** The use of an array of pixels which have only a few different grey levels to give the effect of a larger range of grey levels with larger pixels.

**Pixel** A picture element. It is normally considered to be the smallest addressable part of an image. It can be logical or physical—i.e. it can be the memory allocated to holding an element of an image or it can be the spot on the screen that can display one of a range of grey levels or colours.

**Plane** The memory that holds a screen image. A plane is normaly given a size, e.g. an 8-bit plane describes the memory as allocating 8 bits to each pixel and, therefore, $2^8 = 256$ different grey levels or colours are available on the screen at any one time. These are typically selected from a lookup table, which may contain as many as 16 000 000 colours.

**Quadtree** A data structure that allows two-dimensional images to be held in a format that is compressed and, without unpacking, can be combined with other quadtrees to give the impression of logical and arithmetic operations being performed on the image.

**Quantization** The allocation of grey levels to classes such that the number of initial grey levels is greater than the number of classes. Typically, if the number of grey levels in an image is 256 and the display only shows at maximum 16 grey levels, then a simple quantizing function is to divide the grey levels by 16 and truncate the result.

**Quantizing error** The rounding of an analogue signal into a digital integer value means that some small amount of data is always lost when performing digital image processing. If the number of bits in the bit-plane is large enough, this error becomes negligible.

**Region** An area in an image.

**Region growing** The removal of edges so that regions merge.

**Resolution** This may refer to the screen size, i.e. the number of horizontal and vertical pixels, or to the number of bits that are used to represent each pixel, giving the number of grey levels or colour levels available.

**RGB** A colour system that specifies a colour as an addition of an amount of red, green, and blue.

**Segment** A region in an image that has been identified using some algorithm.

**Segmentation** The splitting of an image into areas or regions according to some algorithm.

**Signal-to-noise ratio** The ratio of good data to noise. This might be measured in terms of number of correct pixels to number of noise (wrong-valued) pixels.

**Spatial grey level dependence matrix** A matrix holding the frequencies of pairs of pixel grey levels occurring a known distance and angle away from each other.

**Template** An array of values, normally used to perform a set of arithmetic operations on part of an image before being stepped across the image to perform the same operations again and again.

**Texel** The smallest element of texture which, when it repeats in a certain way, makes up that texture.

**Texture** A region in an image contains texture if the contents of the region is partially or wholly predictable from the rest of the region.

**Thresholding** A quantizing of old grey levels into new grey levels (normally fewer, maybe just two) so as to increase the contrast between selected grey levels.

**Tomography** The creation and study of slices across a body. Various methods are used for studying the human body, including X-ray and applied potential tomography. Classical plant tomography involves the slicing of the plant, very thinly, and creating a microscope slide of the slice.

**Transformation** The changing of grey levels in pixels either as a result of a statistical operation or a geometric operation. The geometric transformations are normally considered to be translation, scaling, rotation, skewing, and reflection.

**VGA** Video Graphics Array. A PC standard that is a minimum standard for useful image processing. It offers CGA and EGA backwards compatibility among its total of 19 modes, including the one used throughout this book that gives 16 colours from 262 144 on the screen and a resolution of $640 \times 480$ pixels. Developments include Super VGA which seems to be settled as $800 \times 600$ with 16 colours.

**Video lookup table** A table that associates the 'logical' colour numbers, which are the numbers held in the memory elements that correspond to the colour on the screen, with the 'actual' colours that the machine is able to display. There is normally a limit on the number of logical colours that can be present on one screen, but the number of actual colours is usually much larger.

**Window** A part of an image.

# BIBLIOGRAPHY

Artieri, A. and O. Colavin (1990) A real-time motion estimation circuit, *Advanced Imaging*, **5**(2), February.

Baker, H. H. and R. C. Bolles (1988) Generalizing epipolar-plane image analysis on the spatiotemporal surface, *Proceedings of the Computer Vision and Pattern Recognition Conference*, University of Michigan.

Ballard, D. H. and C. M. Brown (1982) *Computer Vision*, Prentice Hall, Englewood Cliffs, NJ.

Banic, J., S. Sizgoric and R. O'Neill (1987) Airborne scanning lidar bathymeter measures water depth, *Laser Focus/Electro-Optics*, 48–52, February.

Beard, N. (1990) Compression ratios reach five figures, *Image Processing, Capture, Management and Analysis*, March, pp. 7–8.

Besl, P. J. (1989) Active optical range imaging sensors, in *Advances in Machine Vision: Architecture and Applications*, ed J. Sanz, Springer-Verlag, Berlin.

Besl, P. J. and R. C. Jain (1985) Three-dimensional object recognition, *Computing Surveys*, **17**(1), 75–145, March.

Besl, P. J. and R. C. Jain (1986) Invariant surface characteristics for 3D object recognition in range images, *Computer Vision, Graphics and Image Processing*, **33**(1), 33–80, January.

Box, G. E. P. and G. M. Jenkins (1970) *Time Series Analysis: Forecasting and Control*, Holden-Day, San Francisco, Ca.

Boyle, R. D. and R. C. Thomas (1988) *Computer Vision: A First Course*, Blackwell Scientific, Oxford.

Bracewell, R. N. (1984) The fast Hartley transform, *Proceedings of the IEEE*, **72**(8), 1010–18, August.

Bracewell, R. N. (1986) *The Hartley Transform*, Oxford University Press, New York.

Bracewell, R. N., O. Buneman, H. Hao and J. Villasenor (1986) Fast two-dimensional Hartley transform, *Proceedings of the IEEE*, **74**(9), 1282–1283, September.

Burger, P. and D. Gillies (1989) *Interactive Computer Graphics: Functional, Procedural and Device-level Methods*, Addison-Wesley, Reading, Mass.

Carlotto, M. J. (1988) Pattern classification using relative constraints, *Proceedings of the Computer Vision and Pattern Recognition Conference*, University of Michigan.

Chien, C. H., Y. B. Sim and J. K. Aggarwal (1988) Generation of volume surface octree from range data, *Proceedings of the Computer Vision and Pattern Recognition Conference*, University of Michigan.

Clowes, M. B. (1971) On seeing things, *Artificial Intelligence*, **2**(1), 79–116, Spring.

Coulthard, M. (1989) Scratching the surface, *Image Processing, Capture Management and Analysis*, 40–42, Winter.

DaPonte, J. and M. D. Fox (1988) Enhancement of chest radiographs with gradient operators, *IEEE Transactions on Medical Imaging*, **7**(2), 207–8, June.

Dougherty, E. R. and C. R. Giardina (1986) *Matrix Structured Image Processing*, Prentice Hall, Englewood Cliffs, NJ.

Ettinger, G. J. (1988) Large hierarchical object recognition using libraries of parameterized model sub-parts, *Proceedings of the Computer Vision and Pattern Recognition Conference*, University of Michigan.

Fairhurst, M. C. (1988) *Computer Vision for Robotic Systems: An Introduction*, Prentice Hall, Cambridge, Mass.

Floyd, R. W. and L. Steinberg (1976) An adaptive algorithm for spatial grey scale, *Proceedings of the Society for Information Display*, **17**(2), 75–77.

Foglein, J., K. Paler, J. Illingworth and J. Kittler (1984) Local ordered grey levels as a guide to corner detection, *Pattern Recognition*, **17**(5), 535–543.

Foley, J. D. and A. Van Dam (1984) *Fundamentals of Interactive Computer Graphics*, Addison-Wesley, Reading, Mass.

Freeman, H. (1988) *Machine Vision: Algorithms, Architectures and Systems*, Academic Press, New York.

Gonzalez, R. C. and P. Wintz (1977) *Digital Image Processing*, Addison-Wesley, Reading, Mass.

Haralick, R. M., S. R. Sternberg and X. Zhuang (1987) Image analysis using mathematical morphology, *IEEE Transactions on Pattern Analysis and Machine Intelligence*, **9**(4), 532–550.

Hartley, R. V. L. (1942) A more symmetrical Fourier analysis applied to transmission problems, *Proceedings of the Institute of Radio Engineers*, **30**, 144–50, March.

Hou, H. S. (1987) The fast Hartley algorithm, *IEEE Transactions on Computers*, **C36**(2), 147–156.

Huffman, D. A. (1971) Impossible objects as nonsense sentences, in *Machine Intelligence 6*, ed. B. Meltzer, Edinburgh University Press, 295–323.

Jackson, P. (1989) On the cards, *PC World Focus*, **4**, 31–34, June.

Jarvis, J. F., C. N. Judice and W. H. Ninke (1976) A survey of techniques for the display of continuous tone pictures on bilevel displays, *Computer Graphics and Image Processing*, **5**, 13–40.

Jensen, J. R. (1986) *Introductory Digital Image Processing: A Remote Sensing Perspective*, Prentice Hall, Englewood Cliffs, NJ.

Kamager-Parsi, B. and R. D. Eastman (1988) Calibration of a stereo system with small relative angles, *Proceedings of the Computer Vision and Pattern Recognition Conference*, University of Michigan.

Kennedy, D. N. and A. C. Nelson (1987) Three-dimensional display from cross-sectional tomographic images: an application to magnetic resonance imaging, *IEEE Transactions on Medical Imaging*, **6**(2), 134–140, June.

Lamdan, Y., J. T. Schwartz and H. J. Wolfson (1988) Object recognition by affine invariant matching, *Proceedings of the Computer Vision and Pattern Recognition Conference*, University of Michigan.

Lester, J. M., H. A. Williams, B. A. Weintraub and J. F. Brenner (1978) Two graph searching techniques for boundary finding in white blood cell images, *Computers in Biology and Medicine*, **8**(4), 293–308.

Lilly, P., J. Jenkins and P. Bourdillon (1989) Automatic contour definition on left ventriculograms by image evidence and a multiple template-based model, *IEEE Transactions on Medical Imaging*, **8**(2), 173–185, June.

Limb, J. O. (1969) Design of dither waveforms for quantized visual signals, *Bell Systems Technical Journal*, **48**(7), 2555–2582.

Lipson, J. D. (1981) *Elements of Algebra and Algebraic Computing*, Addison-Wesley, Reading, Mass.

Liu, Y., T. S. Huang and O. D. Faugeras (1988) Determination of camera location from 2D to 3D line and point correspondences, *Proceedings of the Computer Vision and Pattern Recognition Conference*, University of Michigan.

Matheron, G. (1975) *Random Sets and Integral Geometry*, John Wiley, New York.

McKeown, D. M. and J. L. Denlinger (1988) Cooperative methods for road tracking in aerial imagery, *Proceedings of the Computer Vision and Pattern Recognition Conference*, University of Michigan.

Michael, D. and A. Nelson (1989) HANDEX: a model-based system for automatic segmentation of bones from digital hand radiographs, *IEEE Transactions on Medical Imaging*, **8**(1), 64–9, March.

Murley, J. (1989) Recent developments in image enhancement and analysis of digital radiographs, unpublished M.Sc. Dissertation, Staffordshire Polytechnic.

Nalwa, V. S. (1988) Line-drawing interpretation: a mathematical framework, *International Journal of Computer Vision*, **2**(2), 103–124, September.

Netravali, A. N. and B. G. Haskell (1988) *Digital Pictures: Representation and Compression*, Plenum Press, New York.

Niblack, W. (1986) *An Introduction to Digital Image Processing*, 2nd edn, Prentice Hall, Englewood Cliffs, NJ.

Niblack, W. and D. Damian (1988) Experiments and evaluations of rule based methods in image analysis, *Proceedings of the Computer Vision and Pattern Recognition Conference*, University of Michigan.

Otsu, N. (1979) A threshold selection method from grey-level histogram, *IEEE Transactions Systems, Man and Cybernetics*, **9**(1), 62–66, January.

Paik, C. H. and M. D. Fox (1988) Fast Hartley transforms for image processing, *IEEE Transactions on Medical Imaging*, **7**(2), 149–153, June.

Peli, E., R. A. Augliere and G. T. Timberlake (1987) Feature-based registration of retinal images, *IEEE Transactions on Medical Imaging*, **6**(3), 272–8, September.

Prager, J. M. (1979) Segmentation of static and dynamic scenes, COINS Technical Report 79(7), Computer and Information Science, University of Massachusetts.

Redfern, A. (1989) Beyond the VGA, *Personal Computer World*, 184–8, July.

Rioux, M. (1984) Laser range finder based upon synchronised scanners, *Applied Optics*, **23**(21), 3837–44.

Shave, J. (1989) Small but sharp, *Image Processing, Capture, Management Analysis*, 27–8, Winter.

Shirai, Y. (1987) *Three-dimensional Computer Vision*, Springer-Verlag, Berlin.

Sherrier, R. H. and G. A. Johnson (1987) Regionally adaptive histogram equalisation of the chest, *IEEE Transactions on Medical Imaging*, **6**(1), 1–7, March.

Suchenwirth, R. J. Guo, I. Hartmann, G. Hincha, M. Krause and Z. Zhang, (1989) Optical recognition of Chinese characters, in *Advances in Control Systems and Signal Processing*, Vol. 8, ed. I. Hartmann. Friedr. Vieweg & Sohn, Verlagsgesellschaft mbh, Brausweig.

Tou, J. T. and R. C. Gonzalez (1974) *Pattern Recognition Principles*, Addison-Wesley, Reading, Mass.

Tuceryan, M., A. K. Jain and Y. Lee (1988) Texture segmentation using Voronoi polygons, *Proceedings of the Computer Vision and Pattern Recognition Conference*, University of Michigan.

Ulichney, R. (1987) *Digital Halftoning*, MIT Press, Cambridge, Mass.

Wahl, F. M. (1987) *Digital Image Signal Processing*, Artec House, Boston, Mass.

Waltz, D. I. (1975) Generating semantic descriptions from drawings of scenes with windows, Ph.D. Dissertation, AI Lab, MIT, 1972.

Wechsler, H. and J. Sklansky (1977) Finding the rib cage in chest radiographs, *Pattern Recognition*, **9**(1), 21–30, January.

Wezel R. van. (1987) *Video Handbook*, 2nd edn, Heinemann, London.

Wilson, R. and M. Spann (1988) *Image Segmentation and Uncertainty*, Research Studies Press Ltd, England.

Wilton, R. (1987) *Programmers' guide to PC and PS/2 Video Systems*, Microsoft Press, Redmond, Wash.

Winston, P. H. (1972) The MIT robot, in *Machine Intelligence 7*, 431–463, Edinburgh University Press, Edinburgh.

Winston, P. H. (1975) *The Psychology of Computer Vision*, McGraw-Hill, New York.

Wright, J. C. (1990) Automatic methods for the identification of intact animal cells, M.Sc. Dissertation, Staffordshire Polytechnic.

# INDEX